**WITHDRAWN
UTSA LIBRARIES**

AUTOBIOGRAPHICAL SKETCHES

AND

RECOLLECTIONS

AUTOBIOGRAPHICAL SKETCHES

AND

RECOLLECTIONS,

DURING

A THIRTY-FIVE YEARS' RESIDENCE IN

NEW ORLEANS.

BY

THEODORE CLAPP.

 BOOKS FOR LIBRARIES PRESS
FREEPORT, NEW YORK

First Published 1857
Reprinted 1972

INTERNATIONAL STANDARD BOOK NUMBER:
0-8369-6763-1

LIBRARY OF CONGRESS CATALOG CARD NUMBER:
77-38346

PRINTED IN THE UNITED STATES OF AMERICA
BY
NEW WORLD BOOK MANUFACTURING CO., INC.
HALLANDALE, FLORIDA 33009

TO

The Members of the Church of The Messiah

IN NEW ORLEANS, LOUISIANA,

THESE PAGES

ARE AFFECTIONATELY DEDICATED,

BY

THEIR LATE PASTOR,
AND EVER-INDEBTED FRIEND,

THE AUTHOR.

PREFACE.

THOSE who peruse this volume will see that my life, in many respects, has been uncommonly eventful. Nearly thirty-five years have been spent in New Orleans. It has been my lot to pass through twenty most fatal and wide-spreading epidemics, including the yellow fever and cholera. Besides, during many of those summers which were reported to have been healthy by the medical authorities, I have witnessed a great deal of suffering and mortality among unacclimated strangers.

It may be a mere fancy, but it has always struck me as a fact, that in Louisiana nature itself is, in many elements, less steady and uniform than in the higher latitudes of our country. Not unfrequently the alternations of health and sickness, joy and sorrow, commercial prosperity and misfortune, sweep over the Crescent City with the suddenness and fury of those autumnal hurricanes which occasionally visit it, by which in a few moments of time the strongest edifices are levelled with the dust, the majestic live oaks and cypresses prostrated, and the vessels along the levee overwhelmed in the flood.

It has been my duty one day to officiate as a

clergyman, when a lovely daughter, shining in all the charms and freshness of life's green spring, stood before the bridal altar, and took upon herself the beautiful vows of wedlock; the very next, and in the same room, by the side of her coffin, I have been called to preside over that melancholy scene which is the termination of all earthly prospects. Standing in the pulpit one Sabbath, my attention was arrested by the interesting form of a young gentleman before me, in the plenitude of health, and listening with apparent attention to my words. The Tuesday morning following it became my duty to accompany his corpse to the Cemetery, and to write a letter announcing the sad event to the surviving relatives in a distant land.

Transitions from life to death equally sudden have been common occurrences in my experience. The New Orleans epidemics often prostrate hundreds of friends and neighbors in a day, and like the flash from the tempest-bearing cloud in a starless night, disclose to survivors the perilous rocks upon which the bark of life may be dashed to atoms in an instant. As to mortality, the bloodiest battles of modern times can scarcely compare with the ravages of yellow fever. In 1853, more lives were destroyed than the British army lost on the field of Waterloo. A volume, however ably written, could not worthily portray the wretchedness caused by a single epidemic — its long annals of bereavement, of widowhood, of orphanage; its unutterable griefs, solitude, and destitution; its heart-rending spectacles of thousands who fell without a relative or friend near to close their eyes and perform the last sad offices for their remains.

Amid such melancholy scenes a merciful Father has allowed me to live more than a third of the present century. The inhabitants of New Orleans have treated me with a noble and unfaltering generosity. I have been familiar in the confidence of families of every name and denomination, not excepting the Creoles of the Roman Catholic church. I have had access to all grades of character and condition, in hours of sorrow, misfortune, gloom, and despair; and when the faces of friends grew dim around their dying beds, and the outward world was receding forever from their view, it has been my privilege to point their spiritual eyes to that Redeemer who has conquered death and all our enemies, who can enable us with joy and composure to drink the last bitter cup of mortal grief, and beyond the dark and dying struggle has promised at last to introduce the race of man to the progressions of an eternity, constantly increasing in the freshness, extent, beauty, and plenitude of its divine, unimaginable charms.

During the period just referred to, my leading views concerning Christianity have attracted a considerable share of public attention. By many persons they have been much commended; by some they have been severely denounced, as tending to give countenance to errors hostile to the dearest principles of morality and religion. Both of these classes have, in some respects, misunderstood and misrepresented my real sentiments. This, in addition to the facts mentioned in the preceding paragraphs, makes me anxious to place on record a short narrative of my teachings, doings, and sufferings, from the commencement to the close of my ministerial career in New Orleans.

To accomplish such an object it is necessary to enumerate some of the antecedents of my earlier days in the successive scenes of a New England home, school, college, and theological training. It may be said further, that I have been repeatedly urged within the last few years to write my life by several clergymen of different sects, on the ground that such a work would afford something of novelty, interest, and instruction for readers of every character, however diversified by religious faith and predilections. Such, in general, are the reasons which have induced me to prepare this volume for the public. I pray that the offering may go forth under the auspices of Him who is ready to help all sincere laborers in the field of philanthropy; that it may not be entirely useless nor unedifying to the Christian community in general; and especially that it may be read with satisfaction by the numerous friends, north, south, east, and west, with whom I have the happiness to be personally acquainted.

The reader of these pages will be pleased to bear in mind that the author has not attempted to exhibit the *identical* words of the various conversations herein recorded, but those which he believes are essentially harmonious with what was actually spoken.   T. C.

LOUISVILLE, March, 1857.

CONTENTS.

CHAPTER I.

                                        PAGE

My early History. 7

CHAPTER II.

College and Theological Studies. . . . 17

CHAPTER III.

Andover. 32
License. 43
Ordination. 43
Settlement in Lexington, Kentucky. . . . 43
Anecdotes in Relation to the First Visit of the Rev. Sylvester Larned to the Valley of the Mississippi. . . . 43
Peculiar Style of his Preaching. 47

CHAPTER IV.

First Trip down the Mississippi.	62
Walnut Hills.	62
General Appearance of the Coast.	64
Character of Stephen Poydras, Esq., the Philanthropist.	66
Arrival at New Orleans.	69

CHAPTER V.

My First Sermon in New Orleans.	83
Extemporaneous Preaching.	83
Pecuniary Condition of the Church at Mr. Larned's Death.	93
Generous Offer made by Judah Touro, Esq.,	94
His peculiar Character,	95
Admission to the Presbytery of Mississippi.	95
Its Results.	100
Marriage.	113

CHAPTER VI.

General Remarks upon the Epidemics which have prevailed in New Orleans.	115
Asiatic Cholera in the Fall of 1832 and the Summer of 1833.	117

CHAPTER VII.

Change in my Theological Opinions and Style of Preaching. 153
Liberal Course pursued by the Congregation, with Respect
  to these Modifications. 173
Generous Manner in which I was treated by my Presbyterian
  and other Trinitarian Brethren in the Ministry. . 175

CHAPTER VIII.

Epidemics of 1837 and 1853. 185
Remarks on the Popular Views as to the Insalubrity of New
  Orleans. 187
The Causes of Yellow Fever, and its Remedies. . . 203
Its Bearings on the Morals of the Crescent City. . 209

CHAPTER IX.

The State of Religion in New Orleans Thirty-five Years
  ago. 222
The Roman Catholic Church of Louisiana. . . 223
Its auspicious Influence on the Welfare of its Votaries, social,
  moral, and spiritual. 235
The Peculiar Difficulties which Christianity encounters in
  New Orleans at the Present Day. . . . 246

CHAPTER X.

Symptoms often accompanying the last Stages of the Yellow Fever, &c. 255

CHAPTER XI.

On the Connection between my Religious Teachings and the Prevailing Character of the Peculiar Experiences through which I have passed in New Orleans. . . 265

CHAPTER XII.

Dangerous Illness. 284
Convalescence. 286
Journey to Europe. 296

CHAPTER XIII.

Incidents of Travel in Europe. 313
Reflections which a superficial View of the Old World awakened in my Mind. 321

CHAPTER XIV.

Some further Particulars with Regard to my Interview with Mr. Carlyle. 345
Erroneous Impressions prevalent among the wise Men of Europe concerning the United States. . . . 356
The Alps. 366

CHAPTER XV.

Interior of France. 373
The Monotonous Aspect of its Scenery. . . . 379
Manner of keeping the Sabbath on the Continent of Europe. 380

CHAPTER XVI.

Conclusion. 385

1*

AUTOBIOGRAPHY

OF

REV. THEODORE CLAPP.

CHAPTER I.

MY EARLY HISTORY.

I WAS born in Easthampton, Hampshire county, Massachusetts, on the 29th of March, 1792. The place of my nativity is in the far-famed valley of the Connecticut River, and is remarkable for the beauty of its landscape; scarcely exceeded by that of Boston and its vicinity, as seen from the State House. The house in which I lived was adjacent to the church and parish school. From my earliest time I can remember that both these institutions were zealously, if not successfully, employed in developing the higher faculties of my nature. Parental example and instruction did all in their power to promote my intellectual and moral culture.

What was the result of all these combined advantages? Did they make the morning of my life calm, bright, and beautiful? Parents and teachers watched over and labored for my advancement with the utmost assiduity. More kind-hearted, sincere, and conscientious persons never lived. They, perhaps, achieved all that was possible, considering the principles upon which my education was conducted. This was intended primarily to instil into my mind the distinguishing doctrines of Calvinism. In the nursery, the school room, and the pulpit I was taught " that all mankind, (infants as well as adults,) by the fall of Adam, lost communion with God, are under his wrath and curse, and so made liable to all the miseries of the present life, to death itself, and to the pains of hell forever." The first instance of death which I witnessed was that of a little brother. Standing on the vestibule of life, in the smiles and beauty of his innocent age, he was cut down by the illness of a few hours, —

> "Like some fair flower the early spring supplies,
> That gayly blooms, and e'en in blooming dies."

He had been my constant companion. I loved him as my own soul. It was impossible to realize that I should hear his voice and enjoy his company no more on earth. In the paroxysms of my grief I said to a weeping mother, " Will our dear Loring never, never awake again ? " She replied, at first, only with louder and deeper sobs. It was near the sunset of a lovely afternoon, at the close of spring. From a window by which the corpse lay was a prospect of gardens, shrubbery, orchards in bloom, green meadows, lofty mountains, and the distant glories of an unclouded sun, on the verge of the horizon. Pointing to the magnificent scenery, she said, with an expression of despair, indelibly impressed on my memory, "Your brother will never open his eyes again to look on me nor you — he will speak to us no more — no more listen to the voice of father, mother, brother, or sister — no more join in your plays — no more see the sun rise, nor hear the birds sing."

Her words filled my heart with unutterable feelings of desolateness and sorrow. Not a syllable was said with respect to that better world beyond the mysterious grave, where surviving relatives and friends may hope to meet the loved and lost, and take them again to their everlasting embrace, on the beautiful shores of a land immortal. For though she firmly believed in heaven, her creed made the question an awful, heart-rending uncertainty — whether she was destined at last to embrace all her children there —

> "There ever bask in uncreated rays,
> No more to sigh or shed the bitter tear,
> While circling time moves round in an eternal sphere.

Next morning the funeral was solemnized. The officiating clergyman, in the course of his remarks, observed, that in every instance death was caused by man's disobedience to the divine command, and should be considered in the case of children, who died before they were capable of actual transgression, as a just punishment for that hereditary guilt and depravity transmitted from our first parents to all their posterity. "The sinfulness of an infant," said he, "that is not old enough to do a wrong act itself, consists in the guilt of Adam's first sin, the want of original righteousness, and the corruption of his whole nature." "We might hope," he added, "that the benefits of the atonement would be extended to the millions who go to the grave in the period of infancy; but God, in perfect consistency with infinite justice and holiness, might have left all mankind, without an exception, to perish forever in that state of sin and misery, which flowed inevitably from the first act of transgression committed in paradise."

Such were the ideas which the original teachings of beloved parents and venerable ministers impressed on my mind. All the subsequent instructions that were given me on this momentous theme, by my superiors in age and wisdom, were of an import equally gloomy and preposterous. No inconsiderable part of all the preaching to which I listened in my youth went to show, that mortality, weakness, pain, the countless forms of disease, sick rooms, death beds, graveyards, hospitals, the shroud, coffin, and tomb were the necessary, inevitable consequences of the first sin. I was even taught that an incensed Creator manifests his wrath in the volcano, earthquake, flood, storm, thunder and lightning; the excesses of heat and cold; sterility of soil; bleak, rocky wastes; briers, thorns, and thistles; poisonous plants and reptiles, and all other objects in nature that are the sources of pain and fear to our misguided and unhappy race.

These melancholy views of human life were most cordially and fully received, without even a suspicion that they could be fallacious. For they were infused into, what appeared to my unformed judgment, the embodiments of the most sacred, sublime truths — into prayers, public and private, sermons, conversation, books, the interpretations of Scripture, and all the religious literature around me. They had been handed down, I was told, by nearly all the wise and good of former generations. I could not doubt their reality. True, they were so repulsive that I kept them out of sight as much as possible; but, in spite of my efforts, they would obtrude themselves upon my mind often enough to darken and imbitter, to a serious extent, each passing day. They hung a cloud upon the serene and bright morning — the unutterable beauties of early dawn — the various and ever-renewed wonders of heaven above and earth beneath, which were given to kindle and nourish in the soul even of childhood a deep, joyous sense of the constant presence of that great Father, in the plenitude of whose infinite life, light, truth, love, wisdom, power, and beneficence, we shall move and have our existence forever.

I am almost afraid to utter my real sentiments, lest it might expose me to the charge of being uncharitable to those who differ from me in theological opinions. I fully believe that if all children living could be enabled to see God as he really is, — unveiled and unperverted by the false lights in which his character is too often presented, — could they, from the beginning, be led up to a correct perception of the true nature and principles of his government, as revealed by Jesus, they would almost spontaneously resist temptations to sin and folly, and cleave with an unfaltering trust to the infinite One, as the

little infant does to the bosom of its fond mother.
They would not dream that a real evil could, by any
possibility, be inflicted upon the objects of his love
and care.

Indeed, children should be early initiated into the
certainty of suffering a just punishment for all the
wrong which they may commit; but, at the same
time, they should be carefully taught the doctrine,
that punishment is only one of the innumerable forms
under which boundless Love has been pleased to
make a revelation of his will and character; that it
is one of the strongest proofs of his infinite, everlasting, and immutable purpose to bring back all sinners, finally, to the paths of peace and holiness.
Make a child believe that our heavenly Father can
hurt him, or allow him, by any evil whatever, to be
seriously and forever injured, and from that moment
he becomes incapable, even, of that highest love for
the Supreme, which, as our Saviour teaches, constitutes the essence and glory of evangelical faith.

In New England, generally, at the period I am
referring to, the first impression which children,
almost without an exception, received of God, was
that of a Being from whom they had less to hope,
and more to fear, than from all the wicked men
and demons in the universe. This impression was
strengthened by the uniform tenor of pulpit teachings. Hence religion was set before them, not with
the bright aspect and radiant smile of a good angel,
but looking like a fiend, with maniac eye, dishevelled
hair, wrinkled brow, pallid and emaciated countenance — her expression that of unrelenting severity

— her hands armed with whips and scorpions, to drive us from every beautiful scene of nature into rugged and desolate paths, beset with briers and thorns, and bordered by impenetrable gloom. How can children admire the character ascribed to the great Parent, in the general strain of pulpit ministrations. It is a character "that they should not love if they could."

When will the veil of darkness and deformity be removed from the face of the most glorious object of contemplation in the universe ? When will religion be presented to children with more to cheer, animate, and encourage, and less to awe, depress, and break down their naturally buoyant and joyous spirits ? It is high time that those accents were heard in every nursery, school, and temple of worship, which fell so gently and eloquently from the lips of Jesus eighteen hundred years ago.

More than we can imagine do children every where need the ministries of a true, hopeful, and cheering Christianity, which shall bind them to God's throne by the ties of a supreme, absorbing love ; draw out their hearts in unreserved confidence in the Most High, and forbid even the possibility of a fear or suspicion, that they can fail of reaching, ultimately, the regions of immortal and boundless good. The young would almost spontaneously choose the morally pure and beautiful, were they brought up with the certainty upon their minds of enjoying a future life, free from sin, pain, sorrow, sickness, and death, with the other attendant evils of mortality, in the presence and society of all whom they loved on earth.

It is said that the American savage, when transported to England or France, sees nothing in the splendid creations of art, and the luxuries of the highest civilization, half so dear to his soul, as the smoky wigwam, the widely-extended prairies, and interminable forests of his native land. This attachment to the scenes of early life is a universal characteristic of humanity, yet it is possessed in very different degrees. The barbarian has more of it, I believe, than many persons who come into existence amid the richest blessings which education and refinement can impart. When I call up before me the spot where I drew my first breath; the beautiful valleys, rivers, hills, ponds, plains, and grand mountain scenery; the old school house, with its thousand associations; the humble church; its bell, ringing the solemn call for worship; its choir, raising the voices of praise; and above all, that sacred retreat, that nursery of my youth, where a mother's warm heart and a father's wisdom put forth all their energies to guide me in the pleasant paths of knowledge and honor; the whole, indeed, to-day presents to my mind a picture of surpassing loveliness. But it is a loveliness which, during the season of my boyhood, I could neither understand nor appreciate. Not until a later period could I realize the many charms of that humble home in which my childhood was passed.

Farther back than memory reaches, I learned to spell and read. When my nature panted for freedom, I was shut up in a parish school, most of the day, during two thirds of the year. The one to which I was sent was kept in a small, uncomfortable building, with narrow windows, unventilated, insupportably warm in summer, and cold in winter. In such a dungeon, subjected to a routine of irksome tasks, unrelieved by maps, charts, diagrams, globes, and other aids in the acquisition of knowledge, and which make it a pastime to the young, I was placed, for the best part of twelve years, to be instructed in the rudiments merely of reading, writing, arithmetic, and grammar. Sunday was the only holiday in the week. At sundown each Saturday night, all secular labors were brought to a solemn pause. Till the sunset of the next day, we were never allowed to leave the house, except to enter the church. In prayers, sermons, conversation, and books, heaven was represented to us under the symbol of an everlasting Sabbath day. What an ingenious expedient to make religion appear beautiful to the young, loving, and innocent mind! These, and other things which I have no space to enumerate, produced, as I suppose, a singular anomaly in my personal experience. The actual amount of happiness which has fallen to my lot, was less in childhood than it is to-day. I was not so happy at ten as at twenty. Increase of years, and wider experiences, have not contracted, but enlarged, the sphere of my enjoyments. I have learned to look upon the world, with all its imperfections, in the light presented by the poet: —

> "Cease, then, nor order imperfection name;
> Our greatest bliss depends on what we blame;

Know thy own point; this kind, this due degree
Of blindness, weakness, Heaven bestows on thee.
Submit; in this or any other sphere,
Secure to be as blest as thou canst bear;
Safe in the hand of one disposing Power,
Or in the natal or the mortal hour.
All nature is but art, unknown to thee;
All chance, direction which thou canst not see:
All discord, harmony not understood;
All partial evil, universal good."

CHAPTER II.

COLLEGE, AND THEOLOGICAL STUDIES.

ON the anniversary of my birthday, March 29, 1810, I commenced learning the Latin grammar, under the tuition of a clergyman distinguished for his classical attainments and skill in teaching. Previous to that time, I was acquainted with no language but my vernacular tongue. By the end of September of the same year, besides minor selections, I had perused, translated, and parsed the entire works of Virgil, Cicero's orations against Catiline, Sallust, and the Commentaries of Cæsar, among the Latin classics, together with the Greek Grammar, the Greek New Testament, and the "Græca Minora," which at that time was much used in fitting students for college. My preceptor, who had been a professor of ancient languages in one of the best universities of New England, was pleased to say that I was sufficiently acquainted with the writings above mentioned to become a teacher of them in any academy or school of the land. He thought my case presented a remarkable instance of rapid proficiency, and that no person of the same age ever made more extensive acquirements in so short a space of time. He said, one day, after examining me critically in Latin and Greek, "Few men ever possessed an intellect more ardent and powerful than yours. By habits of persevering and systematic exertion, you

2 *

may become entitled to a distinguished rank among scholars, and be qualified to defend Christianity against the specious errors now openly and ably taught by some of the leading clergymen and literati of Boston and Cambridge. We require a class of ministers to meet the present exigency, who, in addition to true godliness and profound theological attainments, will be able to gratify their hearers with the fascinations of a graceful delivery and an elegant style." From that day, I began to entertain, at times, serious thoughts of devoting myself to the clerical profession.

I look back upon the summer of 1810 as one of the happiest parts of my early life. The window of my study looked out upon a rich natural landscape — fields in verdure, gardens, orchards, running water, animals grazing, and other objects suitable to such a scene. Especially before breakfast and late in the afternoon, I used to look away from my books, to hold communion with the various forms of nature; to enjoy, in sweet repose, the sense of beauty. Memory has kept that prospect before my mind ever since. To the present day, I delight in its contemplation.

"For my gayer hours,
It has a voice of gladness, and a smile,
And eloquence of beauty, and it glides
Into my darker musings, with a mild
And healing sympathy, that steals away
Their sharpness, ere I am aware."

Those meadows, those fairly-rounded hills, meandering streams, waving woods, white cottages, and fine buildings, have always been mine, and have actually contributed as much to my real enjoyment as if, to use the parlance of law, they had been conveyed to me in fee simple.

All the essential interests of mankind centre in the soul. The poorest man, as well as the rich, owns as much of the outward world as images to his view the grandeur, loveliness, and perfections of God; as enables him to comprehend the Maker of all; to imbibe the inspirations of his Spirit, to attain those noble thoughts and holy affections, which are the only source of all the real blessings that lie within the compass of time, or within the boundless range of future and eternal developments. Virtue, heaven, immortality, exist not, and never will exist for us, but as they exist in the perceptions, feelings, thoughts of our minds. He is the richest and wisest person who sees most of God in the outward, physical universe, in the pages of sacred writ, and in the wonders of his own nature. Offices, stocks, monopolies, mercantile gains, sugar and cotton estates, lands, freighted ships, and rich mines, can do nothing of themselves to awaken those sentiments, without which every human soul is dark, debased, impoverished, and miserable.

I cannot remember the time when I did not prize opportunities of study more than any other temporal blessing, simply because nothing else within my reach afforded equal pleasure. It was my ruling passion. To most youth there is not a more abhorred exercise than that of committing to memory, before the understanding can perceive their use and application, the grammatical forms, rules, and principles of a dead language. But I never could be cloyed with this kind of labor. Strange as it may appear, in seasons of relaxation, spontaneously, without an effort, my mind used to run over the declensions of the nouns and the conjugations of the verbs in the Latin and Greek grammars, with as true a pleasure as the poet or musician feels in the prosecution of his favorite studies. I was so pleased with the story of Virgil's Æneid, the naturalness and beauty of its scenes, and characters, and sentiments, that I went through it with an accelerating interest which rendered me almost insensible to the toil of mastering language. Occasionally, boys will make their appearance on the stage having the same mental idiosyncrasies. It is the natural result of an eternal law. Hence it is certain that the ancient classics will never sink into oblivion. Let those who have a taste for their beauties be gratified. I suppose there are persons whose peculiar powers and sensibilities of mind qualify them to be more useful, as well as happy, in learning and displaying to the world the wonders of Greek and Roman literature, than they could be in any other department of human activity. Those works of genius which the most cultivated nations of the earth have concurred in admiring as models, for so many centuries, can never be lost. They must have been framed by the standard of nature : —

> " Unerring nature, still divinely bright,
> One clear, unchanged, and universal light,
> Life, force, and beauty must to all impart,
> At once the source, and end, and test of art."

In September, 1811, one year and a half from the time my preparatory studies commenced, I was admitted into the junior class of Yale College, Connecticut. One of the gentlemen who examined me remarked that I had compressed into the short space of eighteen months acquisitions which no young man, however vigorous his intellect, should attempt to accomplish in less time than four years. The fact is, that I had studied hard, from fourteen to sixteen hours a day, without any efficient out-door exercise. This last want I endeavored to supply by taking very little food. I lived chiefly on bread and water. Milk I was very fond of, but it operated as a narcotic. The carrying out of this programme, which I might have foreseen, produced disastrous consequences. It reduced me to a skeleton, and brought on a complication of alarming ailments. I was induced to call in a physician. He prescribed abstinence from study, seclusion, and a course of medicine. In one hour from the time he left my room, I determined, without permission of the faculty, to take a journey for my health. Throwing the pill box and vial out of the window, at 9 o'clock P. M. the same day, I was a passenger in the mail stage running from New Haven to Albany. Here I wrote to my father, and the president of the college, to explain the reasons of an elopement which, in their sight, must have seemed mysterious, if not criminal. In a few days, kind answers were returned to my letters; I was excused, and encouraged to travel on, if it made my health any better.

Every week I felt stronger as I advanced, and

never stopped, except a few days at a time, till I reached my home at Easthampton, in the autumn of 1812. For seven months, I had wandered, sometimes on horseback, sometimes on foot, sometimes in a stage coach, wagon, or buggy, through all the western and central portions of New York, from Albany to Buffalo. Travel, hunting, fishing, rough fare, sleeping on the floors of log cabins, fatigue, wet, cold, a constant change of scenery, and a succession of stirring adventures among those who were then considered by many as *border ruffians*, completely metamorphosed my physical condition, and, without a particle of medicine, placed me again in the full enjoyment of life and health. I have mentioned this item of my experience as illustrative of the chief causes of debility, consumption, and premature death, among the students of our colleges and universities. Had I followed the advice of my physician, I could not have lived through my junior term. To be sure, I graduated one year later in consequence of this excursion; but it was the means of my adopting a system of exercise quite as essential to growth of mind as reading and meditation. During the two last years of my collegiate course, and the three devoted to the study of theology, I never failed, in all sorts of weather, to walk at least five miles every day, besides spending an hour in sawing wood, working in a garden, or some other labor equally active and invigorating. Proper diet, exercise, sleep, and cleanliness, are the immutable conditions, not only of physical, but also of spiritual health.

A chronological account of my life's progress is not required by the purpose of the present work. If attempted, it could not be done by my plain, prosy pen with sufficient spirit and beauty to interest my readers. The object before me is to trace a slight outline of those events and incidents only which reflecting persons can look at with pleasure, and I hope with profit, unconnected by the relations of time, or cause and effect. The celebrated Walter Scott once observed, that in an ordinary ride in a stage coach, he never found a man so dull, if a free conversation were opened, as not to utter thoughts to him original and instructive, which he would have been very sorry not to have heard. Were it possible, this record should represent experiences, the perusal of which would not be less edifying to great and distinguished minds than the conversation of illiterate, plain, but sincere and honest people in general.

It is a commonplace remark, that the events which determine the course of one's life are controlled by some unseen and irresistible power. I shall now advert to an item of my personal history that may serve as a commentary on the following words of Scripture: "O Lord, I know that the way of man is not in himself; it is not in man that walketh to direct his steps." The last year of my residence in New Haven, I was much in the society of a classmate by the name of Hopkins. The strongest attachment grew up between us; we were never apart when disengaged from our studies; we received the nicknames of Damon and Pythias, the story of whose friendship will never die, so long as Grecian literature is read and admired. Our class graduated September, 1814. It was agreed that, after spending a few weeks at our respective homes, we should meet and journey in company to Litchfield, Connecticut, to attend a course of lectures in the most respectable and systematic law school then existing in the United States. In determining to pursue the legal profession, we were guided chiefly by the belief that its principles were more congenial to our mental tastes and characters, than either those of medicine or divinity.

Young Hopkins lived about ten miles north of Easthampton, on the banks of the Connecticut. He wrote that he should pass my father's house in the stage on a certain Wednesday. I was ready to take my seat with him at the time specified; but when the coach arrived, my friend was not among the passengers. The conclusion was, that some trivial circumstance had induced him to put off starting for a day or two. I waited patiently through the week, without seeing him, or hearing from him; I then learned that he had been detained at home by serious illness. Immediately I went to visit him. He received me with much emotion, saying, "My work on earth is finished, and in a few hours I shall take my departure to

> 'That undiscovered country from whose bourn
> No traveller returns.'"

He was perfectly calm and undismayed at the prospect of death, about which he conversed with much pathos and eloquence. When I bade him the last farewell, with my hand clasped in his, he said to me, " O that it were in your power to view this world as it now appears to me, from the borders of the grave. Were I to recover, and enter upon life again, with my present thoughts and feelings, instead of going to Litchfield, I should repair to Andover, or Princeton, and become qualified for the ministry. The memory of disinterestedness, of self-sacrificing labors for our fellow-beings, and the hope of a glorious immortality through Christ, are the only sources of peace and support in a dying hour."

These words sank so deeply on my heart, that I could hardly think of any thing else for months after his death. They produced a total revolution in my views and plans for life. I could not realize that he had been removed from my presence and society. It seemed as if he was still alive, and regarding me with a sympathy purer and deeper than ever. The unshaken belief that he was a constant witness of my doings, was an irresistible motive, prompting me to make every endeavor to lead such a life as would give him the greatest joy, till permitted by a merciful Saviour to meet again on the shores of a happy immortality. The project of devoting myself to the practice of law was abandoned, and in a few weeks I commenced the study of theology.

It might be argued that I acted with entire freedom in choosing a vocation which this beloved friend, in his last moments, urged me to embrace. But choice is in every instance an effect. This effect is always produced by some motive acting on the will. To say that I could have made an opposite choice with perfect ease, is the same thing as to assert that I have power to resist the strongest motives which can be presented to my mind. In that case, I may trample under foot the most powerful inducements offered by the Creator himself to persuade me to obedience, and, in spite of his almighty will, tread the downward path to ruin. It is self-evident, then, that the events and circumstances which led me to adopt a profession for life, came from God, and exerted an influence upon my will, which, at the time, was as much beyond human control as the winds, weather, tides, or seasons. A true philosophy resolves all the differences, both physical and moral, which exist among men, into " the will and arbitration wise of the Supreme." " I know, O Lord, it is not in man who walketh to direct his steps."

I will relate another anecdote bearing upon the same point. In the summer of 1821, I spent a few weeks at a celebrated watering place in Kentucky. At that resort I met a large number of intelligent and fashionable people from the principal cities of the west and south, and a few from New Orleans. Their time was passed in scenes of pleasure, gayety, and excess, which I had never witnessed in the staid regions of New England. When Sabbath came, a discussion took place at the breakfast table, with regard to the best manner of spending the morning. "We cannot," some said, "desecrate the day by dancing, cards, and frolic. This would be a trespass on the laws of civility as well as the church." The company finally concluded, if possible, to have preaching; and the ball room was selected as the only place sufficiently large to afford suitable accommodations. It so happened that I was the only clergyman present. I had no written sermon with me, nor any kind of manuscript which would answer as a substitute. There was no time for premeditation, nor did I believe it to be in my power to deliver an extemporaneous discourse.

It was with some difficulty that a Bible was found. The master of the hotel acknowledged that there was none in his possession. Not a person there could furnish a copy of the Scriptures, except myself, and that was in the Hebrew and Greek languages. To escape from a disagreeable dilemma, it occurred to me that I might insist upon the impropriety of using the word of God in an unknown dialect. This was done. The argument seemed plausible, and for a moment held forth a prospect of deliverance. At this juncture the landlady recollected that a missionary, travelling through those parts a few weeks before, had left some books at the house. Among them might be the one which the occasion called for. When the servants were interrogated on the subject, one of them said that the books had been stowed away in the garret. A search was made. A Bible was found and laid upon the table at that end of the ball room appropriated to musical performances. The room was soon filled with a silent and attentive audience. There were none in the company willing to sing. After a short prayer, I sat down in the greatest agitation and uncertainty.

All at once the thought struck me that I would read the first Psalm, and make some remarks on it —

"Blessed is the man that walketh not in the counsel of the ungodly," &c. A few days before I had read, with great attention and delight, Dr. Paley's chapter on happiness, in his Moral Philosophy. Its leading ideas were fresh in my mind. With their help, and that of the Psalm, I was enabled to discuss, very imperfectly, the question, How shall happiness be found? I spoke forty minutes by the clock, and though the thoughts of the address were trite, superficial, and commonplace, it was one of the most effective discourses which I ever pronounced, simply because it suited the place, the hearers, and the occasion.

This address was the primary cause of my settlement in New Orleans. There happened to be in the audience two gentlemen of that city travelling for health, who were trustees of the Rev. Mr. Larned's church, my illustrious predecessor. He had fallen in the epidemic of the preceding year. They were gratified with my extemporaneous effort, but were total strangers to me, and I never saw their faces till I became personally acquainted with them the next winter, on my first visit to Louisiana. As soon as they returned home, and at their suggestion, a letter was written to me at Louisville, by which I was invited to succeed Mr. Larned as pastor of the Presbyterian Church in New Orleans. I declined the first invitation, and also the second, because I was determined to spend my days in Massachusetts. Waiting at the falls of the Ohio for the commencement of steamboat navigation, which was obstructed by ice and low water, I received a third invitation. In it the trustees proposed my returning to Boston by the way of New Orleans, pausing to preach a few Sabbaths for them, long enough to form a partial acquaintance with the congregation and the place. This proposition I was constrained to accept.

I went on the excursion to the springs just referred to, with much hesitation and reluctance. It was done merely to please some intimate friends, whose urgent solicitations overcame my will. The first week of my sojourn in New Orleans, I assured the trustees that nothing could induce me to stay there longer than three months. At the expiration of this time I made every effort in my power to get out of the city forever. But God is stronger than man, and he was pleased to confine me there thirty-five years.

A power as omnipotent as that which makes the sun rise, or rivers descend, shaped the whole course of my professional existence and career in New Orleans. One item subtracted, or changed as to the circumstances above specified, would have modified my destiny, and colored my days with different hues for life. If it be asked what cause makes the fortunes of one man so different from those of another, the only scriptural and philosophical answer is, the *will of God*. In defiance of my strongest wishes, I was compelled to settle in Louisiana. I did not covet the allotment. Twenty-five years ago, if any man had prophesied that I should one day become a Unitarian, the reply to his prediction would have been, " Is thy servant a dog, that he should do this thing ? " Then I should have thought it as likely that I might, at some future time, turn pirate, or highwayman, as to become an advocate of liberal Christianity. Either contingency would have appeared to me equally shocking and improbable. To-day, next to that of God's existence, the strongest conviction of my understanding is a belief in the doctrine of the final holiness and happiness of all mankind. And the most inscrutable phenomenon within my observation is that of an intelligent, good man who really doubts this great central, sublime truth of the gospel. I would also remark that the causes which brought about this revolution in my theology are as much beyond human volition as the motion of the planets. Profoundly do I admire these words of the Holy Spirit: "It is not in man that walketh to direct his steps." Cowper was an Orthodox, Calvinistic poet, the genuineness of whose piety is universally admitted. Hear his words:—

> "God gives to every man
> The fortune, temper, understanding, taste,
> That lift him into life, and let him fall
> Just in the niche he was ordained to fill."

In another place he writes as follows: —

> "Happy the man who sees a God employed
> In all the good and ill that checker life,
> Resolving all events, with their effects
> And manifold results, into the will
> And arbitration wise of the Supreme.
> Did not his eye rule all things, and intend
> The least of our concerns, (since from the least
> The greatest oft originate,) could chance
> Find place in his dominion, or dispose
> One lawless particle to thwart his plan,
> Then God might be surprised, and unforeseen
> Contingencies might alarm him and disturb
> The smooth and equal course of his affairs."

Yet every man is perfectly free and accountable, and deserving of punishment when he does wrong. Every man has his own way — so he feels and believes — so he actually has. It is equally certain that God has his way in every thing. If he has not, then there is something in the universe superior to his almighty will. In this case, it may be inquired, Is not every man *directed* by God? Is he not *unavoidably compelled* to do as he does? Was it not *impossible* for him to do otherwise? These questions cannot be fathomed by philosophy, or theological science. If man were not free in a certain sense, he could not be blameworthy nor punishable. Still all concede that if he were not a creature of circumstances and influences beyond himself, it would be impossible for God " to work in *him to will and to do of his good pleasure*," and finally conduct him to everlasting life. The same Power that overcomes the infidelity of *one* human heart, can overcome that of *all*, if it be his sovereign pleasure.

CHAPTER III.

ANDOVER. — LICENSE. — ORDINATION. — SETTLEMENT IN LEXINGTON, KENTUCKY. — ANECDOTES IN RELATION TO THE FIRST VISIT OF THE REV. SYLVESTER LARNED TO THE VALLEY OF THE MISSISSIPPI. — PECULIAR STYLE OF HIS PREACHING.

WHEN I was a student in the Theological Seminary at Andover, Massachusetts, it was my good fortune to occupy, for some months, a dormitory in the private residence of the celebrated Dr. Woods, at that time professor of dogmatic theology in this far-famed institution. I was allowed by the doctor occasionally to sit with him in his own private study to learn my daily lessons. Only one condition was imposed — that I should never interrupt him by asking questions when engaged in writing. He treated me with uniform kindness, and apparently with great confidence. I regarded it as a most enviable privilege to spend so many of my hours in the presence of such an eminent saint and theologian. One morning, when we were both absorbed in our studies, a stranger intruded himself into our presence, to solicit advice in regard to some church difficulties that had occurred not long before in a town some miles distant. On the announcement of his errand, I instantly rose to leave the room; but the professor told me that I had better stay and go on with my labors, else I might not be prepared for the next recitation. After the gentleman had made a full statement of his case, Dr. Woods gave substantially the following decision. I do not pretend to give his precise words.

" Your friend has indeed grossly violated the laws of holiness; but his misconduct is not generally known. It has come to the knowledge, you say, of but very few persons, who are all friendly to him and the church, and are anxious that the scandal should spread no farther.

"Moreover, he is a man of great popularity and consideration in the place of his residence. He is very rich, and liberal in his contributions to religious and charitable societies. By bringing his case publicly before the church for discipline, you may do an irreparable injury, not only to the man himself, but also to his amiable, unoffending family. In my judgment, no good could possibly accrue from such a measure. You had better pass it by with a private admonition, and continue to use his elevated position and extensive influence in building up the Redeemer's cause in your peaceful and flourishing parish."

After this case was disposed of, a second was presented for deliberation. A member of the same church had been heard to avow repeatedly his disbelief in the doctrine of the Trinity. He was in the habit of talking against it among his acquaintances. True, his moral character was unexceptionable; nay, it was excellent — rich in every virtue that could serve to make one a light, charm, ornament, and blessing in society. "But," said the doctor, "no matter how good or benevolent he is; disbelieving the Trinity, he denies the faith once delivered to the saints, and is not fit to be the member of a Christian church. He should be arraigned for heresy, and if he continue contumaciously in error, let him be excommunicated."

The deacon then bade us farewell. During the above consultation, my lesson for the morning was totally unheeded. Two thoughts had for the first time entered my mind. *First*, a rich member of the church, honorable in the eyes of the world, may be dissolute with impunity. *Secondly*, it is not so heinous an offence to break the seventh commandment, as to affirm that there are not three persons in the Godhead. Previous to this day, I had supposed that those *within* were always not only superior in goodness to any persons *outside* of the church, but were also invariably actuated by the principles of unsullied honor, unswerving truth, and impartial justice to all men, without regard to the distinctions of wealth, rank, fashion, or office. It was painful to give up my long-cherished and implicit faith in the spotless purity of ministers and professors of religion.

Dr. Woods not only permitted, but urged me to apply to him, whenever I needed assistance in solving difficult problems relating to theology, or the interpretation of Scripture. A sermon had been preached in the chapel, in support of the doctrine of plenary inspiration, as it is called, or that the original Bible was dictated by the infallible Spirit of God — a standard of faith and practice in which there was not a single error — nothing deficient and nothing superfluous. The assertion was, that not only all its thoughts came directly from Heaven, but even its words; that man had no more share, strictly speaking, in producing the sacred Scriptures, than in creating seas, stars, or planets. Human hands, indeed, inscribed the words on parchment, but they were directed by a supernatural, resistless influence, so that it was not in their power to record a syllable but what was in accordance with the will of God.

A suspicion that this view of the subject was untrue I had never before entertained for a moment. It had been inculcated in my hearing from the nursery up, by all those whom I listened to as oracles, as teachers of indisputable authority. But the sermon just referred to had the effect to set me thinking and doubting on the subject. Two difficulties struck my mind. Was it possible that the disgusting impurities and horrid imprecations recorded in some parts of the Old Testament (for examples, see Psalm cix., and twenty-third chapter of Ezekiel) should have emanated from a being of infinite love and holiness? Further, it was admitted on all sides, that the original manuscripts of the Bible are not in existence. Every copy now in the world came from uninspired hands. Into our version, then, or any other version extant, corruptions may have crept, though its authors were ever so upright and careful.

With hope and confidence, I applied to the doctor to relieve me from these painful misgivings. I said to myself, It is indeed a glorious privilege to be the member of an institution which can guide the anxious, inquiring student through the intricacies of error, and help him up the mountain of divine truth, "laborious, indeed, at the first ascent, but else so smooth, so green, so full of goodly prospects and melodious sounds on every side, that the harp of Orpheus was not more charming." I thought that if I could look at revealed religion aright, it would appear to me only beautiful, grand, and harmonious. The first objection was met by the remark, that "because God is infinite, we are not competent to sit in judgment on the morality of his doings. Parts of revelation may seem to contravene man's ideas of refinement, honor, and rectitude. But God's *thoughts are not as our thoughts, nor his ways as our ways.* What to the infinite One is fit, proper, and benevolent, may appear to short-sighted, sinful mortals deformed, monstrous, unjust, and even malevolent. It is enough for us to know that God is boundless purity; therefore, in the blessed volume which he has mercifully vouchsafed to indite for our salvation, and which is a transcript of himself, there cannot be any thing corrupt or unholy. As it came from God, every item of it must be *Godlike*, from the first verse of Genesis to the last of the Apocalypse."

Such was the reasoning put forth to quiet my doubts as to plenary inspiration; to reconcile the discrepant, to explain the absurd, and throw a haze of moral beauty over passages inexpressibly abhorrent to my natural, unperverted taste and reason. Notwithstanding my youth and inexperience, I then felt, with all the force of intuition, that if God's sovereignty were divorced from what we are compelled, by the very constitution of our nature, to regard as pure and righteous, then all the dearest interests of mankind, for time and eternity, would be afloat upon a boundless sea of doubt and peril; and the way would be prepared for baptizing the foulest despotism by the name of almighty and infinite goodness.

The second objection was answered by advancing a fallacy. "True," said the great man, "all the Bibles now in the world are but transcripts of an original which vanished from the face of the earth centuries ago. But from the infinite wisdom of God, it follows that he would not suffer a book composed by himself to fail of accomplishing the end for which it was given. It is reasonable, then, to believe that the transcribers of the sacred volume, in every age and place, have been the subjects of a divine influence, qualifying them to set forth God's word in the various languages spoken by man, according to its primeval import and genuineness."

The above instances are fair samples of the sophistical arguments employed to defend the peculiar dogmas then taught at Andover. My desires to find the truth were most sincere and intense; but instead of being gratified, they were doomed to constant disappointment. Reading and studying the prescribed books and theses only served to thicken my darkness and multiply my perplexities. The professor said to me one day, that my chief difficulties undoubtedly arose from the fact that I had not been thoroughly drilled in the principles of *implicit faith*.

He defined implicit faith to be "*a trusting to the word or authority of another, without doubting or reserve, or without examining into the truth of the thing itself.*" "The doctrine of the Trinity," he remarked, "is inexplicable to human reason, and fruitless attempts to solve the mystery may unsettle one's faith, and plunge him into infidelity."

But was it not my mission at Andover to investigate truth, independent of human authority, creeds, and formulas? "No," said Dr. Woods, "your proper business here is to learn to read the Bible aright, and to receive its plain, undisputed assertions with an unquestioning credence, as the oracles of God. It is within the legitimate province of reason to inquire, *first*, whether the Bible is divinely inspired; and *secondly*, what does it actually teach? Further than this you cannot go. Reason is not competent to decide upon the philosophy of Scripture. We receive the teachings of God, however strange or incomprehensible they may appear to us, simply because we know that he cannot utter an untruth."

These memorable sayings furnished a clew enabling me to escape from the labyrinth in which I had been long wandering. From that day to the present, the object of all my researches has been to ascertain whether God has actually spoken to the children of men in the Bible, and what is the real import of the communications therein addressed to us. I have stood firmly upon this platform for the last forty years. I love the original Scriptures; have read them by day, and meditated thereon by night.

The study of the Bible, according to the most

approved rules of exegesis, has led me to repudiate the theological views which were embraced at the Andover Seminary when I lived there. They have also been repudiated virtually by the great body of the New England churches. A milder and more rational faith prevails among the descendants of the Puritans, than that of their stern, rugged forefathers. Genuine Calvinism has died in the Northern States, by a necessary and almost imperceptible decay. Professor Stuart, of Andover, did more, in his time, to bring about this revolution than Harvard University and all the Unitarian writings combined.

The opinion is quite common in the Southern and Middle States, that evangelical religion of late has suffered an alarming degeneracy among the people of New England in general. These lugubrious views are chiefly confined to clergymen of different denominations — clergymen, too, most sincere, pious, good, and charitable. They see that some of the long-established creeds and forms of our venerable ancestors are fading away. Opinions which they held sacred and essential are now not only controverted, but denied and trampled under foot, by Unitarian and other kindred sects. Multitudes look upon this deviation from the ways of our predecessors as the prolific parent of intemperance, libertinism, profanity, desecration of the Lord's day, and other abominations. This is not to be wondered at. The contemporaries of our Saviour were perfectly honest in charging him with the most odious offences — irreverence towards God, dangerous heresies, intoxication, breaking the Sabbath, consorting with gluttons and wine bibbers, and preaching doctrines which tended to latitudinarianism, and the subversion of all wholesome laws, both human and divine.

I would say to all those clergymen who cherish gloomy forebodings about the fate of revealed religion, that if you are sincere in the belief that the Bible came from God, you cannot consistently entertain any apprehensions in regard to its accomplishing the ends for which it has been given to the world. If a man, when gazing upon the sun in its sublimity, as it is sinking below the horizon, should say to you, "I am afraid we shall never see the sun again — that it has set to rise no more;" would you not regard him as partially deranged — at least as laboring under some strange hallucination? How much more absurd to be afraid lest man's folly and delusions shall blot out the uncreated sun of righteousness, that illumines the moral universe with an eternal radiance! It is the promise of Jesus that the gates of hell shall never overthrow the religion of the New Testament. It will survive all the vicissitudes to which human society is liable, and demonstrate its legitimate claims to that lofty character which it assumes, as being not only the glorious, but the *everlasting* gospel of the blessed God. What a low estimate must that man form of Christianity who supposes that it can be reasoned, legislated, frowned, laughed, or ridiculed out of the world!

Church history tells us of the rise, decline, and disappearance of many denominations that, in their day, undoubtedly, were necessary and useful, and represented the highest religious development of which their respective votaries were capable. Could the admirers of those ancient forms come back from that unseen world, where pride, bigotry, and contention will never be known, they would be able to trace scarcely a resemblance between the ecclesiasticism of the present times and that mode of worship and teaching to which their prayers, their writings, their fortunes, and their lives had been devoted in vain. But still, praised be God, revealed religion has lost none of its original powers. And though all the various sects that flourish in our day were swept into oblivion, along with the accumulated rubbish carried down by the resistless surge of time, Christianity would live on in undecaying bloom and beauty. Archbishop Whately says, "Christ did not ordain an immutable outward style for administering his religion, but left the machinery of its forms and rules free, that, by a spontaneous unfolding, they might accommodate themselves to the ever-varying wants, taste, and progress of humanity. A system wanting this freedom and flexibleness would carry strong proof in itself that it did not emanate from God. Different ages require different modes of worship and communion."

Geologists have proved that our globe, from the beginning, has been constantly going through a succession of changes, while the principles by which it is governed have always remained the same. So it is with the church of Christ. In essence, it is the same yesterday, and to-day, and forever. Yet it is continually manifesting itself in new and higher forms of glory. The church evinces nowadays her love for man in practical reforms never before attempted. Think of what is doing among us for the reformation of juvenile offenders; for the improvement of discharged convicts; for the training of the blind, the deaf, and the dumb. Think of those splendid palaces, reared for the accommodation of the insane and idiotic; think of the numerous institutions for the relief of widows and orphans; for the benefit of seamen; for the promotion of temperance; for the suppression of war; to ameliorate the condition of prison houses; and to exalt the state of the dependent, industrial classes generally. Then we have tract societies; missionary enterprises; the gratuitous distribution of Bibles and other books; Sunday schools, free libraries, lyceums, &c.; by which powerful instrumentalities the truths, hopes, and motives of the gospel are so wielded as not only to secure the salvation of the young and inexperienced, but also, in many cases, to arrest and reclaim hardened and inveterate offenders. To assert that, under such a multiplicity of divine means, — such a rich, unprecedented array of appeals and agencies, — our people are not advancing in religion and morality, is just as absurd as to deny that the happiest system of agriculture is adapted to increase the products of our fields, or to deny that the best appliances of education tend to promote the diffusion and increase of knowledge. No creeds, no forms, are essential to practical Christianity, but simply a life of pure, humble, and systematic beneficence. The recognition of this principle, coeval with Jesus Christ, is a characteristic of the present age, and a cheering proof that we have renounced fables for truth — "have left the *good old times* far behind, never to see them again but in the retrospect of things gone by." It is ushering in a brighter era, when Christianity will bear, in rich abundance, fairer flowers and more delicious fruit than the world has ever yet tasted.

To me the principles of the gospel are unassailable and incomparable. They give us rules, hopes, and consolations infinitely beyond the reach of human philosophy. Take away this last and only prop amidst the wreck of all earthly hopes and possessions, and to what shall the departing spirit cling for salvation, as it looks into the grave? It has no Jesus to lean on; it must sink in remediless agony and despair. Human reason admires the truths of the Christian revelation; human experience affords them her loud and uniform testimony, and they find a congenial response in the affections of every noble heart. What are these truths? I would answer, in general, the paternity of God; the brotherhood of man; that true religion consists in piety, purity, and disinterestedness, and an existence of immortal blessedness for all mankind beyond the grave.

In October, 1817, license to preach the gospel was given me, by an association of Congregational ministers in my native county. A few weeks previous, I had made an engagement to spend a year, in the capacity of chaplain and teacher, to a private family, in the neighborhood of Lexington, Kentucky. When I reached the place of my destination, the Rev. Mr.

Larned, my predecessor in the First Presbyterian Church, New Orleans, was expected to arrive there daily. His fame had preceded him as an eminent pulpit orator. On a Saturday afternoon, advertisements were posted along the streets and public places, that he would preach in a certain pulpit the next morning, at the usual hour of holding services. Long before the appointed time, the house was completely filled, and multitudes sought in vain for an admission. When he arose, and pronounced the text, — " He is the propitiation for our sins," — I thought that with such a subject, however ably discussed, it would be entirely beyond his power to answer the excited expectations of the audience. But he had scarcely uttered half a dozen sentences, before all fears of his failing vanished from my mind. I was rapt, elevated, and carried away, in common with others, by the charms of his singular and overpowering eloquence. I will present a brief sketch of this remarkable sermon.

He began by saying, that " all acknowledged because all felt their need of a Saviour. Your lot, my hearers, is cast in pleasant places, and you have a goodly heritage; your city is in the midst of regions on which Nature lavishes her richest gifts. You have all the comforts and elegances which wealth, art, and refinement can bestow. Still the capacious desires of your immortal minds are not satisfied, because they crave that higher and better good which an outward world can neither give nor destroy. Jesus came to point our eyes to the only and narrow way that leadeth unto life. Your earthly possessions must perish. You may be great and powerful; magnificent in talents, designs, and achievements; admired, honored, and caressed by your contemporaries. Can such advantages save you? —

> 'The boast of heraldry, the pomp of power,
> And all that beauty, all that wealth e'er gave,
> Await alike the inevitable hour;
> The paths of glory lead but to the grave.'

"When we reflect what human life is, however fortunate; when we consider the ordinances and appointments, — the sudden alternations of health and sickness, joy and sorrow; these indescribable scenes of endurance, privation, and bereavement; these painful sunderings of the ties of affinity, friendship, and affection that sadden our present existence, — how obvious is it that the cross of Jesus is our only hope! For this makes it certain that the works of creation, the events of life, and the destinies of a coming world, are but the unfoldings of a Father's infinite wisdom; that whatever befalls us between the cradle and the tomb, though so strange, inscrutable, and trying, is working to issues great and glorious beyond the reach of thought and imagination. Jesus came to assure us that the Power which brought man into existence is eternal, boundless, uncreated, and immutable love — a love that taketh care for all; not one is neglected; that watcheth over all; that provideth for all; for infancy, childhood, mature years, decrepit age; for want, for weakness, for joy, and for sorrow, in every scene of this or another life; so that all forms of sin and evil shall finally redound to the glory of God, and aid in accomplishing the unsearchable wonders of redeeming mercy revealed in the gospel. The teachings of Christ enable us to say all is good, all is well, all is right, and shall be forever. Faith in Jesus, then, is an inheritance, a refuge, and a rest for the soul, from which the fates and fortunes of a mortal lot cannot shake it.

"The gospel has abolished death, and brought to light that spirit-land where the mysteries of earth will be explained — the land of brightness and beatitude, — the land of an immeasurable progress in wisdom and glory — where, instead of trials, there will be only triumphs; instead of darkness, the effulgence of an unveiled eternity; instead of the bitter tears of sorrow, the beamings of an ever-increasing joy beyond the possibility of sin and temptation. 'Thanks be unto God for his unspeakable gift.' What is death to a true Christian? It is the hour of release from the burdens of mortality; the hour of reunion with the absent loved ones, who have gone before us; the hour when our inherent, irrepressible longings after fairer forms of beauty, and more ecstatic degrees of bliss than earth affords, will verge to their rich, everlasting consummation. When I look on that cross, illuminated by the radiance of God's own divinity, I exclaim, How inexpressibly precious is the light it sheds on our dark world, opening a way for all mankind through the gloomy shadows of sin and sorrow, and through the dark gates of the tomb, to the enjoyment of an inheritance incorruptible, undefiled, and unfading!"

I do not pretend to state the exact words of the orator on this occasion, but the leading ideas of the address, which were indelibly impressed on my memory. He did not even allude to the doctrine of Christ's death being a substituted punishment, a vicarious sacrifice to appease the divine wrath, in order to make the salvation of mankind possible. Passing by all the unintelligible points of controversial theology touching the atonement, he presented to view a beautiful and striking picture, which needed only to be looked at to win admiration — a picture of man's frail, eventful life from the cradle to the grave. The whole audience saw that the portrait was true to nature; and every one present, in spite of his creed, was made to feel that without the hopes of the gospel he had no outward prop to lean upon, no satisfying source of inward reliance, no adequate object for his ever-expanding loves, and no asylum to betake himself to in trouble, want, peril, sickness, or the final hour. He did not dogmatize about Jesus Christ, but produced in the hearers a profound conviction, that without a Saviour they were living in a fatherless and forsaken condition, poor, benighted, trembling orphans, upon a bleak and boundless waste, destitute, deserted, forlorn, and forsaken. The effect was wonderful. Tears were shed by those who had never before wept at the thought of all that is glorious and all that is tremendous in the prospects of immortality. Many of those seated in the pews at the beginning of the sermon found themselves standing up at its close. They performed the act of rising unconsciously.

Yet the entire delivery of that powerful discourse did not occupy more than thirty minutes. I had the honor of sitting in the pew of one of the most distinguished orators of Kentucky then living, whose son is now vice president of the United States. He remarked, on coming out of church, "That was a burst of natural eloquence infinitely superior to any thing I ever heard before, either in the pulpit, forum, legislative hall, or popular assembly."

No doubt Mr. Larned's sermons were indebted for much of their impressiveness to the striking superiority of his personal charms and accomplishments. A head of the most perfect outline; the fire of genius flashing from large, prominent blue eyes; the fine features kindled up with intelligence; a symmetrical and Apollo-like form; a deep-toned, musical, penetrating voice, whose whisper could be heard through the largest audience; and a general mien unembarrassed, easy, and natural, at once graceful and dignified, — conspired to bestow on him a combination of natural advantages for speaking impressively which very few of our race have ever possessed. A distinguished statesman, who for many years was a member of Congress, and familiar with the first of American orators, remarked that " until he had seen Mr. Larned he had never beheld in the human form a perfect union of the sublime and beautiful. His statue, if chiselled by the hand of a Powers, would be pronounced, by all competent judges, to deserve a place among the finest models in the galleries of either ancient or modern sculpture."

Again, his eloquence was characterized by the easy, simple, unstudied manner in which he delivered his thoughts. There were no marks of art and labor either in what he said or in his mode of saying it. He did not appear before an audience in the air of an erudite, authoritative, pompous divine, a formal, *ex cathedra* sermonizer, but as an earnest, affectionate, loving friend, pouring forth the rich, glowing, unpremeditated effusions of his heart with the fulness and rapidity of a torrent, and with the apparent artlessness and simplicity of a child. His language was indeed rich and singularly appropriate. He was full of metaphors, lively images, and pleasing allusions; but they flowed from him without effort, and he seemed to speak as he did, in obedience to an irresistible impulse, because he could not help it. Every one knows that simplicity is the crowning ornament of the most effective eloquence. It is that dress of nature without which all beauties are imperfect, and fail of making a full and complete impression.

The sermons of Mr. Larned were free from the parade and dry technicalities of theological science. He never manufactured a discourse out of general and speculative propositions. He never couched the truths of Jesus in abstract metaphysical terms. Any child could comprehend his subject, words, arguments, and illustrations. It is universally admitted that no trait of good writing or speaking is more important than perspicuity. Of what avail the erudition and reasoning of the preacher, unless he be clearly understood? No ornaments can give lustre and beauty to a sermon when its language is ambiguous and its arguments are obscure.

Mr. Larned had studied the volumes of the human heart and human life more attentively than the sombre tomes of school divinity. Hence, though so young, he was enabled, in the happiest manner, to accommodate instructions to the different ages, conditions, and characters of the diversified classes composing a large, promiscuous audience. Each of those who listened to him heard something that seemed particularly addressed to himself — exactly suited to his trials, temptations, wants, sins, or sorrows. Those sermons are not only most interesting, — most powerfully occupy the imagination, — but also the most useful, which advance what touches a person's habitual conduct and cherished principles in every-day life. They discover a sinner to himself in a light in which he never saw his character before, and which awakens within him the strongest desires to be delivered from bondage, and raised to a new and better state. The object of every sermon should be to persuade men to become good; not to discuss some abstruse theory; to make a display of ingenuity and acquirements; nor to put forth startling novelties, but to make the hearers better, to give them clearer views, and more profound impressions of divine, eternal truths.

Although the subject of these remarks was endowed with the strongest sensibilities of soul and loftiest powers of expression, he never allowed the impetuosity of his feelings to transport him beyond proper limits. The ardor of his genius never diverted his attention from the point of discussion, nor betrayed him into any improprieties of look, manner, or expression. His friends never had occasion to remark, after leaving the church, that their pastor in the unconscious fervor of the moment, had uttered some imprudences, which an enemy or stranger might turn to his personal disadvantage, or to the detriment of the glorious cause which he espoused. This close attention to argument and propriety of words, this self-command, this supremacy of reason, this undeviating attention to the decorums of time, place, and character, amidst the loftiest strains of eloquence, was one of the most captivating and persuasive charms of his pulpit exercises.

The manner of speaking, whose most prominent traits have just been specified, is, in the strictest sense of the phrase, a gift of nature. One could no more acquire it by art and study than he could raise the dead, or arrest the planets in their course. He on whom it has been conferred speaks with the same ease with which he walks the ground or breathes the air.

> "Some beauties yet no precepts can declare,
> For there's a happiness as well as care.
> *Preaching* resembles poetry; in each
> Are nameless graces which no methods teach,
> And which a master hand alone can reach."

A perfectly correct, graceful, impassioned orator is a phenomenon which the world seldom sees, since so many extraordinary natural talents must concur in his formation. But most public speakers might be instructive and interesting, if they would only follow nature, speak in public as they do in private, and only when they have proper materials for a discourse, and have previously considered and digested the subject.

We read that "the righteous perisheth and is forgotten." Why? Because moral greatness is too plain, quiet, and unostentatious to become the theme and wonder, the gaze and admiration, of those who live only for the evanescent possessions and pleasures of time and sense. The exploits of the soldier, though degraded as to moral character, may be blazoned all over the civilized world, and go down on a wave of glory to future times. The pens of learned historians, the tuneful measures of the poet, the eloquence of orators, the finest creations of the pencil and the chisel, have often been employed to perpetuate the name and achievements of bad men, — oppressors and robbers, — whose lives appear only hateful and infamous in the sight of the Christian and philanthropist. But after all, clergymen have no just cause to be dissatisfied with their peculiar condition and allotments. If a minister of the gospel be sincere and faithful, no matter how poor, opposed, persecuted, or despised he may be, yet he is, in reality, among the happiest of our race. His lot is preëminently glorious. Amidst the severest trials he breathes the atmosphere of an immortal world. The "soul's calm sunshine," nobleness of heart, large attainments of wisdom, conscious peace and virtue pure, open to him the sources of perennial, sacred, and constantly increasing bliss. A clergyman who has no taste for his profession must lead a life of degradation and wretchedness. Of all men living, a hypocrite in the pulpit is, perhaps, the most mean, odious, and unhappy.

I remember my intercourse with Mr. Larned with peculiar satisfaction. I was personally and intimately acquainted with him. We were classmates at the university for one quarter. Our rooms were adjacent, and I saw him every day under all the various phases which a collegiate life presents. There was a correspondence between us during his residence in New Orleans. The last letter which I received from him was written but a few days previous to his death. These circumstances, with a deep sense of the wonderful superiority of his native genius, make me anxious, if possible, by this brief notice, to rescue his name from absolute oblivion.

No man was ever more agreeable in the social circle. Though he was a great talker, yet no one ever felt in his company that he talked to gratify pride or pedantry, or for vain show of any kind. He would often charm the listeners who hung on his words, and even move them to tears, when he seemed quite as unconscious of the power he was exercising, as a child engaged in thoughtless prattle with surrounding playmates. It was often said that he was as affable and social among the vulgar, illiterate, and profane, as when conversing with more congenial spirits. Yet his conversation was always unexceptionable in a moral point of view. A gentleman, travelling with him on a steamboat, observed that he conversed often with the crew, the deck passengers, and even with certain persons who were known to be professed gamblers. Some present thought this freedom was very improper in a clergyman. He excused himself by saying that all men are equal in the sight of God; that he felt bound to be civil and kind to every person within his reach, irrespective of character; that the most humble and ignorant individual on board might communicate to him, if an opportunity were offered, some fact or item of experience which would suggest useful thoughts for the discourse which he expected to preach the next morning. It was a noble observation, and the practice that it implied doubtless contributed materially to increase his knowledge of human nature, and the uncommon skill which he displayed in touching the sensibilities of those whom he addressed. How often are the piety and learning of clergymen absolutely inefficient from their want of a thorough knowledge of men, and a more extensive acquaintance with the world!

Whilst in New Orleans, Mr. L. was in the habit of receiving visitors as guests at the breakfast or dinner table. This was done to save time. In this manner he formed an acquaintance with a large circle of gentlemen, both Americans and Creoles, belonging to other denominations. On one occasion the Catholic clergy of New Orleans, in a body, partook of his hospitalities. It is thought by many that his outdoor influence did more good than all his labors in the pulpit. Although his susceptible and finely attempered constitution was so social in its tendencies, — although he was so youthful, buoyant in spirits, full of the sallies of wit, humor, and anecdote, — yet he always maintained inviolate the dignity and proprieties of the clerical vocation. No one ever accused him of saying or doing any thing unbecoming the character of a clergyman.

When Mr. Larned was only eighteen years of age, he had occasion to journey from Pittsfield, Massachusetts, his native town, to Albany, New York, in the stage. On the way, a lively conversation was kept up among the passengers, on a great variety of topics. At the hotel where they stopped for the night, an English traveller of the highest intelligence, inquiring the name and profession of Mr. L., observed, " Among the persons of all countries whom I have seen, that young man shines most in conversation, and possesses the greatest powers of eloquence." Such was the impression which he universally made on educated men of every name and nation, who came within the reach of his fascinating powers.

One of the attendant physicians of the Charity Hospital, who was living when I first went to New Orleans, told me that during the awful epidemic of 1820, Mr. Larned almost daily visited that institution, up to the very week of his death. He passed much of his time in the abodes of sorrow, want, and bereavement. In him the widow and orphan, the sick and forsaken, the destitute stranger and seaman, the tenant of the hospital, and the criminal chained down in his dungeon under sentence of death, found a warm-hearted, efficient friend. In the epidemic of which he was a victim, August 31, 1820, he called on the church treasurer one morning for pecuniary assistance, saying that his means were exhausted, and nothing appeared to him more inconsistent than to pray for the sick and dying, without furnishing them with the supplies which their physical wants demanded. To a physician who urged him to flee from the destructive pestilence, he said, "I may lose my life by staying here this summer, but I cannot leave without violating my most imperative convictions of duty. Death does not seem so great an evil as that of deserting my post to escape the yellow fever." Was there ever a more beautiful offering laid on the altar of benevolence, religion, or patriotism?

When I reflect upon the charms of the character but faintly sketched in the above remarks, its unsullied honor, unswerving truth, and unflinching faithfulness, its noble, self-sacrificing, disinterested, and magnanimous spirit, I feel how unfounded and unjust is the sneering, disparaging insinuation of the sceptic, that there is no reality in virtue ; that it is but a pleasing fiction, a poetic dream. I thank Heaven that the light of heroism and religion has shone more or less brightly on all the preceding generations of men. It is my happiness to believe that goodness exists in every latitude and longitude; that every where throughout the wide field of humanity, the roses of virtue bloom; that in every community are those who are good because they love goodness; good in the inmost recesses of their hearts, good in their most retired and secluded hours, when no eye but that of the Omniscient beholds them. Yes, there are hearts in the worst neighborhoods on the banks of the Mississippi, and among the ruffians (to use the parlance of the day) on our border settlements, whose sympathies are warm, generous, and noble. In every class of my fellow-beings, for the last forty years, I have met persons enamoured of the charms of moral excellence. I have found those who, though poor and illiterate, born and reared beyond the sphere of church influences, manifested in their daily deportment the forgiving spirit of the gospel, (the sublimest form of holiness;) who, amid scorn, insult, injuries, and misrepresentation, expressed neither in the countenance, nor by words, nor by actions, the principles of scorn, hatred, or retaliation. I have seen mothers grow more kind, gentle, subdued, and forbearing, in proportion to the unfaithfulness, the cruel neglect, and unthankfulness with which they were treated by the members of their own households, partners and children. Every day have I been struck with the proofs, not of man's native corruption, but of his original rectitude and glory. God made human nature. If it does not work out the results which he intended, must he not look upon mankind with feelings of sorrow and disappointment?

Tuesday succeeding the Sabbath on which Mr. Larned delivered the discourse which has been already described, I rode with him from Lexington to Frankfort, the capital of the state. After our arrival, he was invited to preach the same evening, at seven o'clock, before the legislature of Kentucky. In this body were several gentlemen whose names had been famous throughout the Union, and who had been representatives and senators in Congress.

The news of his successful effort at Lexington had reached the place before him, and raised high expectations. When Mr. Larned arose to read the hymn, a person who sat near me said, "If that *boy* can utter any thing about religion to enchain the attention of this thoughtless, ungodly crowd, I shall confess indeed that he is a prodigy of eloquence."

When Mr. Larned announced his subject, it seemed to me most unsuited to the place, hearers, and occasion. These words were his text: "*He that believeth on the Son of God hath the witness in himself.*" The topic discussed was, the evidences of Christianity — a topic presenting a vast, boundless field of thought. How could he even enter upon it, I said to myself, in the short space of a single sermon? After I went to my room, I made the following memoranda in my note book, giving not so much the exact words of the discourse as its leading thoughts. "Not one person in a hundred thousand," said the orator, "has the mind and means, books and leisure, requisite to investigate the truth of the Bible upon logical principles. But there is one way by which all, however weak and unlettered, may arrive at satisfying convictions on this subject, without examining the external proofs, documents, and objections appertaining to the divinity of the Scriptures.

"Is there one in this audience who has doubts as to the heavenly origin of Christianity? Act upon the platform of the text, and your unbelief will gradually and imperceptibly give way, as the bright and balmy effulgence of morn dispels the mist and darkness of night. When you rise from your bed tomorrow morning, read a few verses of the Sermon on the Mount, or some devotional part of the Old Testament; then, kneeling down, offer to Heaven a sincere prayer that you may be guided through the trials, duties, and perils of the day by the spirit and principles of what you have just read in his word. Go forth, and act as nearly as you can in conformity with your matin orisons. Do this with all your soul every day forward, and before the expiration of the present year you will have imbibed unconsciously the elements of a true religious faith. You will feel the divinity of the Bible, though you may not be able to argue the question with the sceptic. ' With the heart man believeth unto salvation.' Praying sincerely, and acting accordingly, will cause your soul to be warmed with the beams of a Creator's love.

"You will then ' have the witness in your own bosoms,' that revealed religion is a celestial, refreshing stream from the inexhaustible Fountain of life. In this way, you may acquire a faith of a more adamantine firmness, a more intimate and unwavering conviction, than any variety or amount of reading, study, and scholastic attainments could inspire, unaccompanied by prayer and a good life. There is no royal road to heaven. The king and his subjects, the noble and ignoble, the wise and the ignorant, the master and the slave, can commune with God, and feel his inspiration, only as they lead prayerful, humble, just, pure, and conscientious lives. As to the unspeakably important subject of personal religion, the decisive question is not, What are your thoughts, researches, philosophy, or creeds? but, What are your lives? Only those who do the will of God can have true faith in him. This evening, you have, perhaps, youth, bloom, friends, opulence, power, and all that a worldly taste most covets. But reflect, I beseech you, how soon these shadows must vanish. When the days of darkness shall arrive, when affliction and bereavement shall sink down like an incubus upon your hearts, when the stern realities of life shall have scattered your visionary hopes, — and that time must soon come, — you will be the victims of unrelieved gloom, misgiving, and despair, unless sustained and soothed by an unfaltering trust in that almighty, infinite, eternal, and unchanging love, revealed in the person, mission, teachings, miracles, death, and resurrection of the Son of God."

These thoughts were recommended by all the charms of a natural, easy, graceful, dignified, and solemn manner, pronounced with tones and variations of voice clear, full, and melodious as the strains of the richest music.

This sermon was but twenty-five minutes in length. It is impossible to describe the effect it produced. It was a universal observation, "We never heard any thing like that from the pulpit before." The remark was strictly applicable to my own feelings. Indeed, Mr. Larned gave me new ideas about the best mode of preaching. I learned from him the utter worthlessness of mere doctrinal, controversial sermons. He delivered two addresses on topics concerning which there is the greatest diversity of opinion in the Christian world; yet in these sermons he did not so much as allude to any of the popular dogmas of the day. One could not have divined, from any thing which he said, to what particular sect he belonged. His appeals embraced only truths that are undisputed and indisputable — truths that strike a chord which God has strung in every human heart.

I have been a traveller in the old world. It left upon my soul an impression of mighty things, which will forever remain in my mind — the ineffaceable images of grandeur. I have crossed the Alps, and looked down upon those lovely vales that derive an increased beauty from the stupendous objects around them. I have seen the glories of Europe — its cities, palaces, castles, cathedrals, gardens, and galleries of art. But none of these objects do I remember with as deep emotions of wonder, admiration, and delight, as the preëminent genius, and the noble, disinterested conduct, of that young, fearless missionary, who laid down his life to add another church to the temples of the living God in New Orleans.

Mr. Larned entered Williams College, in his native state, when only fourteen years of age. He studied theology at the seminaries of Andover and Princeton, and commenced his professional life in the spring of 1817, being about twenty years of age. He died on the 31st of August, 1820, — a victim of the yellow fever, — in the morning of life, and to human view, just entering upon a brilliant and useful career.

CHAPTER IV.

FIRST TRIP DOWN THE MISSISSIPPI. — WALNUT HILLS. — GENERAL APPEARANCE OF THE COAST. — CHARACTER OF STEPHEN POYDRAS, ESQ., THE PHILANTHROPIST. — ARRIVAL AT NEW ORLEANS.

In the winter of 1821, I left Louisville for New Orleans, to preach a few weeks, as I have before mentioned, in the pulpit of the First Presbyterian Church, which had been vacated by the death of Mr. Larned. The waters were high, and the steamboat on which I embarked moved with great speed. In less than a week I was wafted beyond regions where the ice and snow still held dominion, into the temperature, verdure, fragrance, and beauty of spring. The effect of such a sudden transition was enchanting. On the borders of the river we saw but one small town, (New Madrid,) between the mouth of the Ohio and Warrenton, in the State of Mississippi. Just before reaching this place we were cheered with the green tops of the Walnut Hills, where Vicksburg now stands. They were then beautiful and rich eminences, covered with an abundance of those trees whose name they bear. It was not till some years afterwards that the first house was erected on these bluffs. To-day it is the site of a large commercial city, from which vast quantities of cotton are shipped; whose broad streets, handsome public buildings, and numerous churches, show that its inhabitants are intelligent, refined, opulent, and liberal.

In the rear of this city, the country is rich and beautiful, the hills crowned with neat houses, the valleys and plains presenting a landscape of almost continuous and highly-cultivated plantations. In New England, many persons think that this part of the south has a population almost semi-barbarous — characterized by lawlessness, profanity, desecration of the Sabbath, gambling, intemperance, and deeds of sanguinary violence. This impression arose from the setting up of a few isolated instances of disorder and bloodshed, which found their way into the newspapers, and sent a thrill of horror throughout the Union. I have travelled extensively in the State of Mississippi, and can testify that, all things considered, — the lateness of its admission into the confederacy, the various disadvantages and hinderances in the progress of a frontier settled by an aggregation of adventurers from all quarters of the civilized world, — it is not inferior even to Massachusetts or Connecticut in the manifestations of moral excellence, truth, honor, justice; a patriotism willing to die for the land it loves; a philanthropy that is ready to pour out its treasures and its life for the common weal.

Here we began to discover the magnolia grandiflora, an ever-verdant laurel, with its thick, soft, dark foliage and fragrant flowers, which do not put forth at once, but bloom in succession for a long time. It was delightful, after having passed through an unbroken, inundated wilderness for nearly eight hundred miles, to come suddenly into the climate of the palmetto or fan palm, the China tree and catalpa, the wild honeysuckle and jessamine. Here, in the month of March, the wild wood displays such a variety of flowers of every scent and hue, that the gale is charged with fragrance, as if wafting odors from " Araby the Blest." On our left hand was an almost uninterrupted line of bluffs, between two and three hundred miles, commencing at Walnut Hills and terminating at Baton Rouge; either bounding the river, or receding far enough from the shore to afford bottom lands, which have long since been converted into luxuriant, widely-extended cotton plantations. They have an endless variety of figure, and are crowned with beech, hickory, and holly trees. Even to this day, the traveller beholds no dwellings on these finely rounded eminences, because, in the apparently salubrious breezes of summer, by which they are fanned, there lurks a malaria much more noxious to health and life than that which hangs over the low, swampy lands at their bases.

On the right hand shore was the same forbidding scenery that had filled our entire horizon for several days — impervious, tangled, sunken, interminable forests; the crape, the funereal drapery of long moss, completely covering the branches, and sometimes the whole trunks of the trees; boundless ranges of cypress, live oak, and malaria — the favorite haunts of alligators, moccason snakes, mosquitoes, and other nameless, most abhorred species of animated nature. I said to myself, If there are *"fauces orci"* — an entrance to the lower world — in our country, it must be somewhere in these dismal, marshy tracts, more hateful than the fabled Styx of Grecian mythology. Now, after a lapse of thirty-five years,—in ascending or descending the river, — you see on the same shore, every two or three miles, a splendid plantation, with the usual appurtenances. When a stranger inquires the use and object of a cluster of little buildings — neat white cottages lying about the principal house — he is told that they are the habitations of the laborers. There the negroes live in separate families. Each of them has as good a dwelling, furniture, table, and other physical accommodations, as the great body of laborers in the free states. True, they are not as elevated in the scale of intelligence and enterprise; if they were, they would not be slaves. It is not in the power of man to meliorate their condition so long as their intellectual and moral development remains unchanged.

A little below the city of Natchez, on the western shore, commences that artificial mound of earth called "the levee," of considerable elevation, and extending down to the neighborhood of the Balize. Were it not for these mounds, the rich, beautiful, and productive strip of soil, called "the coast," would be annually inundated and incapable of cultivation. The word *coast* is used to designate the land bordering the Mississippi River, for two or three hundred miles above its mouth. At Point Coupé, the coast commences wearing the aspect of a country which has long been beautified by the plastic hand of skilful agriculture. Here, too, you begin to see extensive orange groves, intermingled with the wide-spreading and verdant branches of that venerable tree, the live oak — the monarch of southern forests. Here, too, you see that magnificent plant, which the French call "peet," with its foliage perfectly green during the winter, and the extremities of its leaves terminating with thorny points.

In this village, our attention was directed to the mansion of Stephen Poydras, Esq., a gentleman who was alike distinguished for his wealth, personal excellence, and public charities. Good people, I said to myself, must live all over the world; for they are found here in the midst of an old settlement of French Catholics and slaveholders, where a Protestant minister was never seen, and where the Catechism of the Westminster Assembly of divines was never taught. With this gentleman I became intimately acquainted. A more pious, upright, self-denying, humble, generous man never lived. He was every whit as good as the late Amos Lawrence, of Boston, and quite as charitable. But has the name of Poydras been blazoned through our land? Did any one ever pronounce his eulogy in Faneuil Hall, or in any of the New England pulpits?

O, no; he was a Frenchman and a slaveholder. "Can any good thing come out of Nazareth?" Yet, in every respect, Poydras was not inferior to the greatest of those philanthropists whose lives have shed such an undying lustre upon the land of the Puritans. He endowed an orphan asylum in New Orleans, which will bear down his name forever. It is called after him. It was the only institution of the kind in the city in 1821. In the dreadful epidemic of the succeeding year, it took in hundreds of destitute orphans, that might otherwise have perished. He gave the proceeds of a very handsome property, amounting, I believe, to twenty thousand dollars per annum, to be distributed in marriage portions to a number of poor girls in the parish of Point Coupé and the adjoining parishes. He gave, in particular, a rich endowment to the school of the district where he lived, besides various other magnificent charities, which I have not space to mention. Let the really great have their names written on pillars more durable than brass, —

> "Higher than pyramids, that rise
> With royal pride to brave the skies;
> Nor years, though numberless the train,
> Nor flight of seasons, wasting rain,
> Nor winds, that loud in tempests break,
> Shall e'er their firm foundations shake."

All the material glories of earth will one day vanish "like the baseless fabric of a vision." The elements will waste even the marble of our tombs, and our worldly achievements be lost in everlasting forgetfulness; but those beneficent deeds by which we kindle smiles on the face of helpless orphanage, decrepit age, or indigent manhood, — by which we impart wisdom to the erring, give light, encouragement, and consolation to those who are sinking beneath the allotments of a mysterious Providence, — will *never* die. Instinct with the spirit of a divine life, they will cross the theatre of time, and the gulf of death, and grow more beautiful through the countless ages of an unending existence.

Below Point Coupé, the banks on both sides of the river are uniform. The levee is continuous. The cultivation of cotton, rice, and sugar cane is regular and universal. The breadth of the cultivated lands is generally two miles — a perfectly uniform strip, conforming to the shape of the river, and every where bounding the deep forests of the Mississippi swamp with a precise line. For two hundred miles, plantation touches plantation. I have seen in no part of the United States, not excepting the Connecticut River, a more rich and highly cultivated tract of the same extent. It far exceeds that on the banks of the Delaware. Noble private residences, massive sugar houses, neat villas, and numerous negro quarters succeed each other in such a way that the whole distance has the appearance of one uninterrupted village. The mansion houses are spacious and airy, some of them costly and splendid, situated in the midst of orange groves and pretty gardens, in which abound the delicious cape jessamine, multitudes of altheas, bowers of the multiflora rose, and a great variety of vines and flowering shrubs peculiar to this climate of perpetual verdure and loveliness. The fields, the gardens, the fine houses, the sugar manufactories, &c., apparently move past you as you descend, like the images in a magic lantern.

You see, too, that this whole region is not destitute of the forms and institutes of Christian worship. The Catholics have numerous churches along the coast, and the spires, seen at the intervals of every six or seven miles, cheer the eyes of all who are not sceptics or bigots. Emerging suddenly from the sombre, sunken, moss-clad scenery of the Upper Mississippi into these enchanting regions of culture, wealth, and beauty, I was greatly excited.

On a beautiful morning near the close of February, we were landed at Lafayette, where the boat stopped to discharge a part of her cargo, about three miles above New Orleans. The passengers, impatient of delay, concluded to walk to the city. Leaving the levee, we took a circuitous route through unenclosed fields, which a few years before had belonged to a large sugar plantation. They were adorned with a carpet of green grass, where herds and flocks grazed in common. Here and there we passed a farm house in the midst of gardens, luxuriant shrubbery, and orange groves. The fruit was thickly scattered along the ground, like apples in the orchards of New England, when autumn pours forth her ample stores. The air was cool, inspiring, and scented with the flowers of early spring. The music of the thrush, and various other species of singing birds, saluted our ears with their sweetest notes. All things, as far as our eyes could reach, seemed like a paradise. These suburbs, then so radiant with rural charms, are now the site of a large portion of the buildings belonging to New Orleans, and contain, at the lowest computation, eighty thousand inhabitants.

With the beautiful and soothing sensations which such a morning and such scenery naturally awaken, my first entrance was made to the metropolis of Louisiana. I was cordially welcomed, and well provided for. The trustees formally waited upon me in a body. They struck me as being remarkably fine-looking gentlemen, with polished manners, and well-informed, but so cheerful, easy, natural, and agreeable in their conversation, that I concluded at once that they were not communicants of the Presbyterian church. In the course of our interview, I ascertained that such was indeed the fact. Not one of the number was a Creole of New Orleans. They were immigrants from various quarters of the United States and Europe, who had been led to unite in establishing a church for Mr. Larned, not to gratify any sectarian preferences, but to enjoy the society and teaching of one whom they admired for his personal qualifications only — his extraordinary genius, learning, and eloquence. They were so enthusiastic in their praises of my predecessor, that I not only despaired of being able, in any tolerable manner, to fill his place, but I felt that it would be presumption to make even an attempt to address an audience that had been accustomed to such an elevated style of pulpit exercises. I told them plainly that such were my feelings, and begged them to excuse me from preaching at all. Two of them immediately replied, "We once heard you preach at a watering place in Kentucky, and if you preach now as well as you did then, the people of New Orleans will be more than satisfied — they will be highly pleased." The occasion referred to has been already mentioned.

The next day — Wednesday — I was invited to dine with Dr. Davidson, an eminent physician, who belonged to the board of trustees. There were no gentlemen present but those of the medical profession. The company comprised all the American practitioners then in the place. They did not number, I think, more than half a dozen. The two doctors were present who attended Mr. Larned on his death bed. He had opened his church every Sunday from the beginning of the epidemic, though all his friends importuned him, in the strongest terms, to desist from his labors, and to repair to the pine hills, on the other side of Lake Pontchartrain, where the yellow fever had never been known.

"Last summer," said Mr. Larned, "when the epidemic broke out, I followed your advice, and ran away into the country. In my absence, both the French and English newspapers animadverted on the course which I took, and inquired if it were consistent with the character and obligations of a *Protestant* clergyman to desert his people in periods of calamity and general suffering. Catholic priests always remain at their posts, whatever perils assail them. I felt in my heart that these criticisms were just, and resolved that I would never leave New Orleans again in a sickly season. I must adhere to this resolution. Duty is ours, events are God's. Surely, a minister in his vocation should feel the ennobling principle of honor not less acutely than a military hero. The soldier of the cross should always act on the motto, '*Victory or death.*' It is as ignominious for a clergyman to flee from the approach of disease, as for an officer of an army to skulk on the field of battle."

In harmony with this sublime sense of duty, my predecessor encountered the epidemic of 1820. For more than two months, he exposed himself, wherever

the line of his profession called, to the shafts of the
dread enemy. From morning to night he was occupied with the sick and the dying, and in attending
funerals. Unsolicited he walked through the wards
of the Charity Hospital every twenty-four hours.
The 27th day of August Mr. Larned preached his
last discourse, at eleven o'clock, A. M. The weather
was beautiful, and the audience unusually large for
the season. It was observed that his countenance
was remarkably florid, as if flushed by some preternatural excitement. His delivery was uncommonly
animated and eloquent. This fact was noticed by
the whole congregation. His text was Philippians
i. 21, "For to me to live is Christ, and to die is
gain."

"We never heard him speak before," said Dr.
Davidson, "with equal impressiveness and solemnity.
In contrasting the burdens, frailties, and sufferings
of a mortal lot with the glories of immortality, he
seemed to be inspired. The bosoms of his hearers
were stirred with the strongest emotions of delight,
wonder, and astonishment. He intimated that his
own work on earth might be drawing to a close.
'I am ready,' said he, 'to meet a final hour; to
take a last look at the countenances of beloved relatives and friends; to see this fair and glorious scene
of sublunary shadows no more. For I have been
made certain through Jesus, that the universe of my
Father stretches far away beyond the islands, shores,
and oceans of earth's spreading continents. As I
see this audience with my bodily vision, so with the
eye of faith do I now gaze upon those higher regions,

where disembodied spirits are expatiating over the verdant, smiling fields of an everlasting life — a life unassailable by disease, toil, pain, infirmity, sin, temptation, or death. To me there is nothing dark or desolate in the entrance to a world of spirits. O, let me die, that I may go and live forever! O, welcome, thrice welcome the hour when the portals of the tomb shall open to receive these mortal remains, and the light of a better world shall break in upon my forgiven, redeemed, and emancipated spirit!' I do not mean to intimate that the above were the precise words used by Mr. Larned, but the general strain and import of his peroration, as described to me by many, who were present on the occasion.

" As soon as I came out of church," said Dr. Davidson, " I met a circle at the door, conversing about the sermon. All remarked the unusual redness of our pastor's face, and the unearthly eloquence of his words. In a few moments after reaching my residence, a message came that Mr. Larned was taken ill on his way home from church, and wanted to see me immediately. I obeyed the summons without delay. On inquiry, I found that he had been seized with a severe chill and pain in the back, — the invariable precursors of the yellow fever, — before daylight Sabbath morning. He ate nothing at breakfast, but drank two or three cups of strong coffee to relieve his head, before entering the pulpit. This stimulus, together with that of speaking, tended greatly to aggravate his fever. His symptoms were most unfavorable.

"'Doctor,' he inquired, 'do you call this the

yellow fever?' I replied, 'Your complaint is not yet sufficiently developed to enable me to give a positive answer to your question. By to-morrow we shall know better about it.' I passed most of the afternoon and evening with him. He grew worse rapidly. Early Monday morning, in a paroxysm of great suffering, he repeated the question, 'Doctor, have I got the yellow fever? Do not deceive me; I am prepared to know the whole truth.' And the truth was told him. 'I have another request to make,' he said — 'that whenever you consider me beyond the hope of recovery, you will let me know it.'

"The next day, on Tuesday, it became obvious that he could not live many hours. I remarked to him that it gave me great pain to say that his disease must soon terminate fatally. He received the intelligence with perfect composure, and rehearsed the text on which he preached for the last time — 'To me to live is Christ, to die is gain.' All company had been kept from visiting him. His wife, whose health was so feeble that she could not aid the nurses and attendants by personal coöperation, came into the room at his request. He bade her a most touching, affectionate adieu, and when she left the room desired her not to return, saying that he should soon meet her in heaven, and that he wanted to spend his few remaining moments in prayer and meditation. He was sensible to the last, never murmured nor complained, and was almost continually uttering sentiments like these: '*All is right; all is well; all is safe. Father, not my will, but thine, be done.*' His last words were addressed to a lady of the Methodist congregation, who was by his bed side during a great part of his sickness. She asked him whether his hopes remained unshaken. He replied, 'I know in whom I have believed, and that he is able to keep that which I have committed to him against that day. Without a doubt, fear, or misgiving, I resign my spirit into the hands of God, who gave it.'"

Dr. Davidson related to me a curious fact during our conversation at this time. He was a trustee, church treasurer, confidant, and bosom friend of Mr. Larned. During the ravages of the epidemic in 1820, Mr. Larned spoke to him, when returning one day from the sick room of a dear friend, about to die without what the Presbyterians call a religious hope, in the following strain: "I must either renounce the theology which was taught me at Andover and Princeton, or abandon entirely the practice of visiting the death beds of the irreligious. What can I say to the poor sinner about to draw his last breath, who confesses that he has led a worldly and impenitent life? Such was the condition of the sufferer whom I have just left with the chill of death upon him. Around the bed was a circle of mourning friends and kindred, stupefied with horror and heart-rending agony, whose solemn silence was broken only by the sighs and shudderings of grief and despair. I confess that our religion could afford them no words of hope or consolation. Could I tell them, what I had been led to regard as Bible truth, that death in every instance is the awful consequence of original sin? that it is a thick, overshadowing cloud, where God is present only in displeasure, unless the dying person has experienced a change of heart, and leans on the vicarious atonement made by Jesus as the only ground of salvation? Impossible! The young man on whom the mortal stroke has fallen, though amiable, has led a gay, thoughtless, worldly, fashionable life. He is dying with a character which cannot now be changed. It is too late. If there be not in the great Father a free, independent, unconditional, undeserved, unpurchased mercy for our lost race, then there can be no ground of hope for the sinners around us, who in crowds are entering the unseen world, without faith and repentance."

About this time, a great change came over Mr. Larned's preaching. This was admitted by all who attended his church. At the first prayer meeting which I attended in the vestry room none but the communicants were present. In the course of a free conversation on the prospects of religion in the Crescent City, the members of the Session and others present remarked that, much as they admired Mr. Larned for his personal accomplishments, genius, eloquence, and noble bearing, they could not but feel that he died at a fortunate moment, both with reference to his clerical fame, and the prosperity of evangelical faith in New Orleans. I was astonished at these words, and asked for an explanation. They replied, that during the last year of Mr. Larned's life, he scarcely so much as alluded to the distinguishing doctrines of Presbyterianism in the pulpit. His sermons were general homilies on the goodness of God, and the excellences and pleasures accruing from a religious life this side the grave. He also manifested, they said, a fondness for worldly society, which seemed incompatible with the character of a devoted minister of Jesus Christ. The deacons told me that they themselves, and nearly all of the communicants, had deserted the society, in a body, several weeks before the death of their late pastor.

At the same dinner party I had much talk with a Dr. Flood, at that day the oldest and most popular of the American physicians in New Orleans. He was a gentleman of great colloquial powers, and much originality of genius. Speaking of New Orleans, he said, " Sir, the Creole inhabitants, here, enjoy as large a share of health as falls to the lot of those who live in Boston, New York, Philadelphia, or any other northern city. It is a most palpable error which is circulating abroad, that the locality of New Orleans precludes even those who are born and brought up within its limits from the blessings of firm, full health. This idea is refuted by a thousand facts — by the exemption from diseases in general, which characterizes the native population; by the remarkable health of infants; by the entire absence of those local maladies which are almost universal in higher latitudes; and by the appearance of the population generally, which will compare most favorably with that of any other people, for all the indications of uniform and vigorous health. Even during the last summer, amidst all the afflictions, discomfort, and gloom of the epidemic, one could see at the St. Louis Hotel, every morning, among the old residents, who remain here permanently, as fine specimens of health as can be found any where on the continent. The same remark is applicable to Charleston, South Carolina, Jamaica, St. Domingo, Havana, and the West Indies generally. Let a man become acclimated, and let him adopt the habits of the old population, and he may be safely insured at as small a premium as in any part of the United States."

I received this statement then with utter incredulity; but now I can cordially subscribe to its correctness. During eight months of the year, New Orleans is blessed with an extraordinary degree of health. From the first of October to the ensuing summer, the weather is generally more agreeable and salubrious than that of any other place with which I am acquainted. Dr. Dewey somewhere says, "Whilst the disastrous days of the year are carefully recorded, preserved in memory, and often dwelt upon, its happy days are forgotten. They pass unnoted in the table of life's chronology, unrecorded in the book of memory, or the scanty annals of thanksgiving. My brethren, if, for a series of years, we could place before our minds the many happy months which have been swept beneath the silent wings of time; if we could call up, from the dark backward and abyss of years, the hours of ease, peace, health, beatitude, in which the current of life has flowed on, amid kind and blessed visitations of Heaven's beneficence, bearing us calmly and gently upon its bosom as the infant in its mother's arms; if we could make them stand up before us as vivid realities, and behold them as we do our faces in a mirror, — we should deeply feel that God has constantly lavished upon us the richest bounties, and that ingratitude is the most enormous and aggravated sin of which we are guilty." These remarks are applicable to those of every locality on the globe. Is not the healthiest spot within our borders often visited by the pestilence that walketh in darkness, and the destruction that wasteth at noonday? Not unfrequently, amid the bracing winds and snows of winter, fatal epidemics prevail in the healthiest parts of New England. It is thought by those well qualified to judge correctly about the matter, that consumption, in its various forms, causes a greater destruction of human life in Boston, during the space (we will suppose) of every ten years, than the yellow fever does in the same time in New Orleans. At the north, the ravages of this fearful scourge are almost unnoticed, because they are regular, unintermitted, and looked upon almost as a thing of course, belonging to the ordinary current of human events. But in the Crescent City, the enemy comes down in a moment, without warning, like an Alpine avalanche, exciting the notice, wonder, and sympathy of the whole land; and after having fulfilled his mission in the compass of six or eight weeks, mysteriously disappears as he came, and is followed by a period of singular and almost universal health, sometimes extending even to years. As to the cholera, it is not peculiar to New Orleans, but pervades the globe. It should be observed, also, that the yellow fever is confined almost exclusively to strangers. It is the process by which exotics become assimilated to air, climate, temperature, &c., different from, and, in some cases, almost antagonistic, to those where they were born and reared. So far as the arrangements of God are concerned, I believe that all over the globe, the blessings of the seasons, weather, climate, soil, scenery, and other means of physical happiness, are pretty equally distributed.

There is, indeed, no geographical position where a low-minded, debased, and licentious man can be happy. All the beauties of nature are lost upon his hardened, perverse, and misdirected soul. The outward world appears to such a person a dull, indifferent, commonplace, wearisome affair — a deep, narrow valley, hemmed in by inaccessible rocks, filled with the rubbish of dull cares and tiresome vanities. But to the eye of a good man, all nature is clothed in beauty. "It unfolds in the numberless flowers of spring; it waves in the verdant branches of the trees, and the green blades of grass; it haunts the depths of the earth and the sea, and gleams out in the hues of the shell and the precious stone. And not only these minute objects, but the ocean, the mountains, the clouds, the stars, the rising and setting sun, all overflow with beauty." The same may be said of the marsh, the swamp, the barren heath, the sandy desert; the shapeless rock and hanging precipice; the most rude, gross, and uncultivated parts of nature: every thing which a noble man looks upon — the clods of earth, the furrows of the field, the insensible rock — are to his eye emblematical of the grand and lovely attributes of an Almighty Father. I repeat it, that to a virtuous man, wherever he is, — on the Connecticut, Hudson, Ohio, or Mississippi, — nature presents, in constant and ever-varying forms, images of the fair, orderly, proportioned, and wise, filling his soul with rapture, and lifting it up to the infinite Parent. This is in accordance with Scripture. "The heavens declare the glory of God, and the firmament showeth his handiwork."

It is a common opinion that Louisiana is much inferior to the Northern and Middle States, with respect to the numerous advantages of climate, health, temperature, and natural scenery. A distinguished naturalist has endeavored to show that the inhabitants of Lapland, for example, all things considered, derive as much happiness from the physical influences by which they are surrounded, as those who reside in the verdant regions of the south, where reign eternal spring and summer ; where the seasons, as they revolve, let fall no blight nor chill upon the rich and smiling landscape. He contends that the peculiar advantages of every latitude have corresponding disadvantages, so that God's goodness shines as strongly on one spot as another.

When the native of Switzerland takes up his abode in the luxuriant and beautiful clime of the south, — those green, sunny regions, where the glory of former generations still glimmers on the falling monuments and crumbling columns of immortal art, where nature lives forever, and forever spreads its unfading charms, and the bosom of the earth is fair and fragrant through all the circling months, — he beholds nothing so interesting as the mountain tops covered with eternal snow — those rugged rocks and frowning precipices that distinguish the wild landscape endeared to him by the tender reminiscences of home and childhood.

Not long since, I met at Niagara Falls a French Creole family, intelligent and refined, who had never before wandered beyond the limits of their native state. Whilst they seemed to appreciate the new and glorious objects which almost continually greeted their sight, as they journeyed north and east, still they remarked, that they had seen no place which they would prefer, as a residence for life, to the spot where they were born. To their eye, no prospect was more pleasing than that widely-extended plantation, where they had lived from the beginning amid all the endearments of a happy home. "How poor," exclaimed they, " are the cultivated hills and narrow intervals of New England, compared with the luxuriant soil of Louisiana, loaded with the richest productions — rice, cotton, sugar cane, &c.!" In our gardens are the orange, fig, and olive, all sorts of elegant shrubs, and every variety of flowers. We are awakened each returning morn by the melodious notes of the birds, whose lives have been passed upon the spot where their existence began, and that seem almost to be a part of the family. How bland, balmy, fragrant, and salubrious, our atmosphere! One of the ladies belonging to the company applied to her native state the following lines of Byron: —

> "Know ye the land of the myrtle and vine,
> Where the flowers ever blossom, the beams ever shine?
> Where the light wings of Zephyr, oppressed with perfume,
> Wax faint o'er the gardens of Gul in her bloom?
> Where the orange and olive are fairest of fruit,
> And the voice of the nightingale never is mute?
> Where the tints of the earth, and the hues of the sky,
> In color though varied, in beauty may vie?"

CHAPTER V.

MY FIRST SERMON IN NEW ORLEANS. — EXTEMPORANEOUS PREACHING. — PECUNIARY CONDITION OF THE CHURCH AT MR. LARNED'S DEATH. — GENEROUS OFFER MADE BY JUDAH TOURO, ESQ. — HIS PECULIAR CHARACTER. — ADMISSION TO THE PRESBYTERY OF MISSISSIPPI. — ITS RESULTS. — MARRIAGE.

THE first time I preached in the Crescent City was on the morning of the last Sabbath in February, 1822. On the previous Saturday evening, a committee of the trustees waited on me, to ascertain upon what plan I intended to conduct the services of the church. They said, "In all probability, the next day will be one of the loveliest of the spring season; and if so, there will be an overflowing house. Notice has been published in all the newspapers that you are expected to preach in the Presbyterian church on Sunday morning. Besides," they remarked, "your name has been a subject much talked about among us the last week; great expectations have been raised. We have assured our friends that you are in every respect qualified to be a successor of our former lamented pastor. Now, we have one request to make: it is, that you will not attempt to read a manuscript sermon. The hearers will expect you to imitate Mr. Larned by speaking extemporaneously, and apparently from the inspiration of the moment. You might read in our pulpit the best-written sermon that was ever composed, equal to one of Chalmers's,

Robert Hall's, or Dr. Channing's, characterized by profound, original thought, neatness and purity of style, happy metaphors, language perfectly appropriate, and completely polished, yet the congregation would retire dissatisfied, saying, ' We have heard a discourse erudite indeed, and able, but it was not like one of Mr. Larned's, — free, unconstrained, persuasive, coming warm and natural from a heart replenished with ardent, impetuous feelings, poured forth with the fulness and rapidity of a torrent.' "

I promised to comply with their wishes, and do the best in my power to gratify a New Orleans audience, but begged them, in case of a failure, to allow me to steal away as silently as possible the next week, in some vessel bound for Boston or New York, where the reading of sermons is tolerated in all pulpits. The committee retired. It was near nine o'clock in the evening. I had prepared a written discourse on the immortality of the soul, being determined never again to attempt extemporizing in the pulpit. I was in despair. I knelt down, and prayed for divine guidance and support. Arising, I paced the room for some moments in a paroxysm of anxiety, during which many schemes for escaping from the dilemma passed through my mind. Finally, I came to the conclusion to commit to memory the principal heads of the discourse I had written, and some of the most prominent sentences under each division, and trust for the remainder to the spur of the occasion.

In performing this labor, I sat up till daylight, then threw myself upon a sofa, and slept till the servant called me to breakfast. I had become calm; but it was the calmness of despair; for I had abandoned, even, the hope of succeeding in my mission. When the bell rang at eleven o'clock, I went to the church determined and reckless. It was one of those delightful mornings which I have never seen any where but in Louisiana. The large house was crowded with the most noble-looking audience that I had ever gazed upon; for then, ladies and gentlemen in New Orleans dressed as finely to go to church as they did when they went to the opera, evening party, or ball room. There were a good organ and excellent singers. During the music, immediately before the sermon, I attempted to recall to mind the heads of the discourse which I had spent the night in committing to memory. Thoughts and words had alike vanished from the tablets of my soul. I could think of nothing but that "sea of upturned faces." If there had been before me some short notes of the substance of the discourse, I should not have looked on my condition with so much despair. I said to myself, "If the hearers are not *solemnized*, they will doubtless be *amused* at my awkward, clumsy, feeble, perplexed, embarrassed, and desultory efforts." A cold perspiration covered me. Conforming as nearly as was in my power to what had been said was the habit of my predecessor, when the music died away, I arose very deliberately, opened the Bible, and after reading the text, closed it and laid it aside, that there might be ample room for action.

The moment I looked upon the audience, the words I had learned by rote the night before came to my recollection. I found no difficulty in rehearsing them; but I felt certain that they sounded to my auditors stale, flat, and insipid, although they seemed quite attentive and absorbed. Every eye was fixed upon me; but I ascribed this attention to the politeness of my hearers. They were too noble and high-minded to manifest their indifference openly. I confess, with shame and sorrow, that I thought more of man than God in delivering that discourse. This was the real source of all my perplexity; and to the present day, I cannot go into the pulpit with becoming indifference to the opinions and criticisms of those whom I address. Touching the subject of popularity, I have a morbid sensitiveness, which betrays, if not an entire absence, at least an extremely low condition of personal piety. If ministers felt properly their responsibility to God, they would be able always to preach well.

When I descended from the pulpit, the same gentlemen who had given me their advice the evening before, grasped my hand warmly, and congratulated me on the brilliant effort that had been made. They said it was enough to establish my fame. It was almost impossible to believe in their sincerity. Could it be that they would deceive me on such a grave matter? The disclosures of Monday proved that they had expressed their sober convictions. The audience on that occasion was composed of the *élite* of New Orleans, with respect to refinement and intelligence. Among them were the ablest members of the bar, — those who had belonged to Congress, — physicians, enlightened merchants, many strangers

of distinction, and the conductors of the daily press.
In my commendation every voice was joined. Whilst
my vanity was soothed by this unexpected success, it
awakened appalling apprehensions as to the future.
I was now fully committed to the position of an extemporaneous preacher. But the excitement must
be kept up. Another Sunday would soon come.
The favorable sentiments which had been inspired,
unless maintained and deepened on the next occasion, might end in disappointment and disgust. I
thought of these lines of Pope: —

> "Unhappy fame, like most mistaken things,
> Atones not for that evil which it brings;
> Then most our trouble still, when most admired,
> And still the more we give, the more required."

But the Rubicon was crossed. Nothing but sickness
or death could withdraw me from the engagement
which had been made and ratified by the united
plaudits of the society.

In this quandary, it was requisite to act promptly
and decidedly. I first thought of writing out my
sermons in full, and committing them to memory. But I soon found that this course would make
an exorbitant demand on my time. I could not
master a manuscript sermon, so as to rehearse
it with ease and correctness, without several mornings' study. My predecessor had a remarkable fa-
cility of memory in committing his own compo-
sitions. He spent the whole week, from Monday till
Saturday afternoon, in out-door avocations. About
dark, he drank strong tea, and then went into

his study. Between that hour and ten or eleven o'clock, he wrote down completely his sermon for the next morning. When finished, he read it once over very attentively, before retiring to rest. He rose very late Sabbath mornings. About an hour before the commencement of the services, he read his manuscript a second time, threw it under his feet, walked into the pulpit, and pronounced the discourse precisely as it was written, in the easy, flowing, unembarrassed manner of animated conversation. This anecdote I had from Dr. Davidson, an intimate friend, who was well acquainted with his habits. I have heard of one great American orator and statesman who can do the same thing — the Hon. Edward Everett, of Massachusetts.

Incapable of making such an effort, I was compelled to have recourse to some other mode of preparation. There was then in New Orleans one of the most eloquent lawyers of his day. I obtained an introduction to him. In the course of conversation, I remarked, that as I was just beginning to speak in public, and experienced much difficulty in the process, I should be very much obliged if he would tell me what kind of previous preparation for delivering a speech he had found most effective. He replied, "I never speak without intense premeditation on my subject, unless compelled by some unforeseen exigencies. With respect to ideas, you cannot be too careful and accurate in your preparation; but if you write down every word, and commit it to memory, (I have tried this once or twice,) you will overdo the matter, and render your discourse heavy. In spite of yourself, it will appear stiff and unnatural, labored and cold. I am a very wicked man, but if I had to preach in your pulpit next Sabbath morning, I should select a subject to my taste, then make, as the lawyers call it, a *brief* of what I intended to say. This I should carry with me through the week, and during my leisure hours, even when walking along the streets, think closely on its divisions and subdivisions, till I had attained a full and distinct view of the matter which I wished to clothe in words, till I had become warm and interested in it, and made it perfectly familiar to my thoughts. Then I could enter your pulpit, and speak with fluency, earnestness, ease, and with the best ornaments of style, manner, and elocution, that my poor genius could command. What do you think of this plan of preparing sermons?" he inquired.

"It strikes me as admirable," I answered. "If you will try it next Sunday," he added, "I will be present, and honestly give you my opinion of the character of your performances." I retired to my room, chose a subject, made a brief, and faithfully followed his directions, — with one exception, — I did not take it into the pulpit with me. He kept his word, and came to church on Sabbath morning. Meeting me after the services, he said, "Sir, your discourse was natural, easy, simple, and magnificent; you laid down sentence after sentence, and paragraph after paragraph, entirely fit for the press; I did not notice that you tripped a single time, which you would have done, had you used a manuscript. You will make an extemporaneous speaker quite as popular and brilliant as ever Mr. Larned was." This gentleman communicated to me what was worth more, as to the secret of speaking well in the pulpit, than all which I had heard from the professors at Andover, or read in treatises on the subject.

The above plan I have followed sedulously all my life since. The first fifteen years of my residence in New Orleans, I was particular in writing my briefs. I had preserved a large basket full of them, which were all burned when I left the people of my charge, in May, 1856. For the last twenty years, I have made only mental preparation for the pulpit. Each of the sermons of mine published in the "Picayune" was written off from memory, at two sittings — one on the Sabbath evening after it was delivered, the other on Monday morning, before breakfast. Not one of those discourses was rewritten or revised.

I hope it will not look like presumption to give my opinion concerning a question which has been so extensively contested among the clergy, and remains still undecided — whether extemporizing or reading sermons is the most instructive and edifying mode of delivery. Surely I may be pardoned for expressing a judgment dictated by the results of thirty-five years' practice. I do not use the word *extemporize* to mean preaching without study, premeditation, and careful composition. It is an insult to an audience to go before them, if it can be avoided, relying entirely for utterance upon the spur of the occasion. Whatever be his native genius, no clergyman can succeed as a settled pastor, without fixed habits of the most persevering and energetic study. He should rise at four o'clock A. M. in summer, and five A. M. in winter, so as to secure an opportunity of from five to six hours of uninterrupted study, before he is liable to be broken in upon by company, or by applicants for parochial ministrations. This routine I have faithfully pursued during the whole of my residence at the south. Without such systematic, previous, regular application and toil, it is impossible for any clergyman to make suitable provisions for the spiritual nourishment and growth of a large promiscuous congregation.

Think what resources are wanted to preach even one good sermon; but a hundred are needed for a single year. Who is sufficient for these things? Can that man become adequately acquainted with the natural sciences; history, sacred and profane; the Bible, its exegesis; the science of human nature, of ethics, and of beauty, — can that man have a soul warmed and enriched with the profound and diversified topics which appertain to pulpit instruction and persuasion, who spends the most of nearly every day in visiting, running about to make lyceum speeches, and addresses at political meetings, in cursing our civil rulers, and scolding them about those awful derelictions of duty which threaten to ruin this glorious republic? What a pity the parsons were not allowed to sway a sceptre over all human interests, secular and divine! In that case, the millennium, no doubt, would soon be in its zenith.

Nevertheless, I am satisfied that if a minister consults his highest usefulness, he will not depend much upon his notes in the pulpit. If he reads entirely or chiefly, he cannot adopt an easy, natural, impressive, and unaffected manner. There is an infinite difference between written and spoken language. If I were to read to my people in New Orleans, from the pulpit, one of Dr. Channing's best sermons, it would strike them as cold, artificial, elaborate, dull, and uninteresting. Positively, it would have a narcotic effect upon them. But let me present the same thoughts in the style of vivid, unforced, agreeable conversation, and they would be kept wide awake, absorbed, and intensely interested.

The most effective pulpit style which I have witnessed at the north (if we except occasional tediousness, prolixity, and some other peculiarities,) is that of the Rev. Henry Ward Beecher, of Brooklyn, New York. In one part of his discourse, there is close reasoning; in another, familiar talk; in a third, grand declamation; in a fourth, a fine, original picture of the imagination; in a fifth, something that will send a laugh like an electric shock through the whole audience; in a sixth, an appeal to the sublimities of God, duty, and retribution, which makes all present feel solemn, and moved perhaps to tears.

In some instances, all these different manifestations are combined into a single paragraph. An orthodox " old fogy " would of course be shocked at one of his discourses, as it would seem to him utterly devoid of reverence, but he could not go to sleep under its delivery. For myself, I cannot but honor and admire the man who, in defiance of all the prudery and pedantry of church conventionalisms, enters the pulpit to pour out a Niagara of original thoughts on the great themes of Christian truth and duty, and social progress. I must say, however, that I have no sympathy with his peculiar views on slavery. Here I differ from him as far as the east is from the west. If all ministers, like Mr. Beecher, would abandon, but for an hour, their manuscripts, and speak in public as they do in private, we should not hear these universal complaints about cold, dead, dry, metaphysical sermons. But, generally, people would find the church a more interesting place than the opera, theatre, ball room, museum, or evening party.

A meeting of the society was called, on the third Sabbath after my arrival in New Orleans, to elect a permanent pastor. I was chosen to fill this office by a unanimous vote, both of the pew holders and communicants. I told the committee, who waited on me to ask my acceptance of the post to which I had been called, that I could not give them an answer till I had examined the pecuniary affairs of the church. The treasurer's books and papers were placed in my hands. By the aid of a young gentleman familiar with the routine of a counting room, I soon ascertained that the church indebtedness amounted to forty-five thousand dollars. They could show no assets whatever; there was not a dollar in the treasury. As soon as these facts were ascertained, I informed the committee that I was immovably determined not to accept their offer at all, unless the above-named debt were in some way liquidated.

The legislature of Louisiana happened to be in session at that very moment. The trustees applied to them for a lottery, which was then considered a justifiable mode of raising money for charitable objects. It was granted at once, and the same week the scheme was sold to the agents of Yates and McIntyre, New York, for twenty-five thousand dollars. The balance of the debt was raised by selling the church to Judah Touro, Esq., a merchant, originally from New England. The property was worth a great deal more than twenty thousand dollars. The sale of the church was looked upon as merely nominal, although it was purchased without any conditions, expressed or implied, or any pledges as to the final disposition which should be made of it. All had confidence in the general character of Mr. Touro, and were very glad to have the church put into his hands.

Mr. Touro was left an orphan about the age of ten, in his native place, Newport, R. I. After that time he lived in Boston fifteen years, and was trained to the pursuits of mercantile life. He immigrated to New Orleans in 1802, and never left it for a day till his death, with the single exception of marching to the battle field, at the time of the invasion, in 1815, to lay down his life, if necessary, (and he came near doing it,) for the preservation of our liberties. Did he not display a patriotism as noble and undaunted as that of Washington, Warren, Lafayette, or any others whose names are inscribed upon the brightest pages of American history? It is universally known what sort of a place New Orleans has been, especially for the last forty years, with respect to sudden, extraordinary reverses and fluctuations in commercial affairs. In rapid succession the storms of distress have desolated that emporium, sweeping away like a crevasse, in a few short hours, the hopes and possessions of hundreds and thousands, and producing a complete revolution in the community. I have seen the millionnaire of one year laboring in the next as a clerk in a counting room or bank.

Through all these " times that tried men's souls," Mr. Touro pursued the even tenor of his way, ever calm and self-possessed, and with his robes unstained. The poisonous breath of calumny never breathed upon his fair name as a merchant and upright business man. The most tempting opportunities of gain from the shattered fortunes which were floating around, never caused him in a single instance to swerve from the path of plain, straightforward, simple, unbending rectitude. He was uniformly just. " Justice," says Plato, " is the divinest attribute of a good man." I heard Mr. Touro once remark, that, in his whole life, he had never knowingly, deliberately injured a fellow-being, either as to his person, property, or reputation. Of all the glories which men have displayed in any age, none is more entitled than this species of excellence to our unqualified admiration. None is more rare. I heard a deacon of an orthodox church, in the interior of New England, who was largely engaged in selling goods to the surrounding farmers, say, a short time ago, that he had to keep a strict eye even on a majority of the church members with whom he dealt, or they would deceive him as to the quantity and quality of the various articles which were offered in the way of exchange. "Yet," continued he, "I do not doubt their piety."

This same gentleman, a moment before, had expressed a doubt whether it was possible for Mr. Touro to have been a pious man, because he was a Jew. I replied, that it was true, he was born, reared, and had lived, and died in the Hebrew faith. It was the faith of his father, who was a learned and most esteemed rabbi. It was the faith that had been handed down to him by a long line of illustrious ancestors, reaching back to the patriarchal ages of the world. It was the faith of Abraham, Isaac, and Jacob, to whom those glorious promises were first given, which embrace the final, complete, and everlasting exaltation of all mankind. It was the faith of Jesus himself, who was a Jew, and who declared that the religion of the Old Testament contains all that is requisite to guide us to eternal joy; that he came into the world not to destroy that faith, but to free it from corruptions, and send it forth in its divine, original, unimpaired vigor and freshness. "Besides," I added, "all admit that the moral character of Mr. Touro was spotless. He was one who was never guilty of prevarication, falsehood, libertinism, or the bartering of his conscience for filthy lucre." "All this," answered the deacon, "amounts to nothing, so far as the question of his piety is concerned. He may be perfectly just, good, true, and lovely, as to his moral conduct; yet he cannot be saved without faith in the Son of God." What a delusion! *Faith in the Son of God* is nothing more nor less than goodness of heart and life.

Dr. Chalmers once said, " All *right-hearted persons* are pious in the sight of God, whether Hebrew, Christian, Pagan, or Deistical in regard to mere creed or abstract opinions." A man who thinks himself more wise, more enlightened, more pleasing to God, or possessed of a fairer prospect of being admitted finally to the kingdom of heaven than his neighbors, because his creed is sounder than theirs, is not only guilty of a narrow, mean, exclusive bigotry, but deliberately tramples on that precept of the gospel which says, we "must by no means condemn a neighbor on account of his peculiar religious principles." " Who art thou that condemnest thy brother," &c. ? " To his own Master he shall give an account of himself, and be judged accordingly." It is awful to think of this violation of the law of charity among the various denominations in the United States. Multitudes of noble, high-minded men are kept from joining any particular church, from the conviction that such a step would expose them to the hatred and persecution of antagonistic sects. I have often heard Mr. Touro say, that, though an Israelite to the bottom of his soul, it would give him the sincerest pleasure to see all the churches flourishing in their respective ways, and that he was heartily sorry that they did not more generally *fraternize with, love, and help each other*.

This gentleman was the humblest man whom I have ever been acquainted with. A person overmodest is very seldom found, or rather is to be looked upon as an anomaly in this proud, selfish world of ours. But Mr. Touro was too sensitive on this subject. The most delicate, deserved, and timely expressions of esteem from particular, intimate friends and acquaintances, seemed to give him pain instead of pleasure. I remember being in his company once, when a friend proposed to read to him a paragraph from a Boston newspaper, which spoke of his character in terms of eulogy. He refused to listen to the perusal, and remarked, with apparently excited feelings, that "he would thank them to change the subject of conversation." Several times, when alone, I asked him some questions about the battle of New Orleans, in which he received such a dreadful wound. He declined making any particular remarks about it, further than to express his deep sense of the kindness of his friend, R. D. Shephard, Esq., who carried him from the field of conflict and saved his life. He is the only one of the veterans under General Jackson, on the plains of Chalmette, with whom I have conversed, who seemed to take no pleasure in describing the part which he acted on the ever-memorable 8th of January, 1815. Mr. Touro once said, in my hearing, that he would have revoked the donation given for completing the Bunker Hill Monument, on account of their publishing his name in the newspapers, contrary to his wishes, had it not been for the apprehension that his real motives would have been misunderstood and misrepresented. And most assuredly the fear was well grounded.

I wish here to record a few lines as to the character of Judah Touro's philanthropy. The name of John Wesley, founder of that large, respectable denomination, the Methodists, is enrolled on the list of eminent British philanthropists. For what reasons? Because, among other virtues, we are told that, by a life of the most unexampled economy, he saved, in the space of fifty years, one hundred and fifty thousand dollars out of his income, to be devoted to the cause of charity. Judah Touro, by habits of frugality not less strict and admirable than those of the eminent Christian just named, during a half century accumulated five hundred thousand dollars, to be used in promoting the same sublime purpose. Mr. Wesley is praised because he was so generous in his donations to the church that was nearest to his heart, and of which he was the principal originator. Mr. Touro gave to the church which he most loved not less than the great Wesley did to the Methodists — two hundred and twenty thousand dollars. I have never heard of but one religionist in the United States who can be compared with Mr. Touro, as regards the liberality of his benefactions to his own church; and he bestowed nothing on other denominations.

But Mr. Touro gave more to strangers than to his brethren. On the former he conferred three hundred thousand dollars; on the latter, but two hundred thousand. With a generous profusion, he scattered his favors broadcast over the wide field of humanity. He knew well that many of the recipients of his bounty hated the Hebrews, and would, if possible, sweep them into annihilation. In this respect, did he not recognize the principle upon which God himself distributes his bounties among men? For Jesus declares that the Father loves and blesses his enemies as much as he does his friends. So the person I am speaking of consulted not the ill-desert, meanness, prejudice, or sin, of those whom he was pleased to help, but only how they might be best raised from debasement and destitution. If God were to pour out on his foes vengeance instead of love, his throne would crumble, and the universe be reduced to chaos. Indeed, this feature of Mr. Touro's beneficence is so exalted, noble, and godlike, that I should but mar and obscure the bright ideal by the most impressive description that language could give. He once saw, when standing at the door of his counting room, a poor, lost inebriate, in the hands of the sheriff, passing on his way to prison for debt. Mr. Touro stopped him, and spoke kindly to him, as he had known him in better days. Ascertaining the sum for which he had been apprehended, he immediately paid it, and effected his release. It amounted, with costs, to nine hundred dollars. He said, "I do not much expect that it will be of any benefit to the individual himself, but I have performed the act for the sake of his family."

It was a time of great business depression in New Orleans, when Mr. Touro became the proprietor of the church edifice and grounds. Many of the society fell in the preceding epidemic. Some who were most prominent in settling Mr. Larned had just compounded with their creditors. The friends of the institution were few, feeble, impoverished, bankrupt, and pushed to the very brink of ruin. A noble Israelite snatched them from the jaws of destruction. From that day down to its destruction by fire, he held it for their use, and incurred an additional expense of several thousand dollars for keeping it in repair. For myself he professed the strongest personal regard, and showed it by giving me almost the entire income of the church — the pew rents — for about twenty-eight years. He might have torn the building down at the beginning, and reared on its site a block of stores, whose revenue by this time would have amounted to half a million of dollars at least. He was urged to do so on several occasions, and once replied to a gentleman who made a very liberal offer for the property, that " there was not money enough in the world to buy it, and that if he could have his way, there should be a church on the spot to the end of time."

This man was a Jew. Is there a *Christian* society in New Orleans that has ever offered the Unitarians the slightest assistance, or even courtesy? Is there one that would put forth a hand to help them to-day, if they were in danger of perishing? Is there one that would not rejoice in their complete, absolute destruction? The Unitarians have aided materially towards the erection of all the orthodox Protestant churches in the Crescent City. But when they were burned out, and asked for one of the orthodox churches to hold meetings in occasionally, the favor was denied on the alleged ground that by showing such a kindness, they might indirectly encourage the dreadful heresies which we were laboring to promulgate. It was this spirit that burned Servetus, that kindled the fires of the *auto de fe*, and has condemned to the wheel, rack, gibbet, or cross, the noblest benefactors of our race. But in this emergency, the aforesaid Hebrew came to our relief. He purchased a small Baptist chapel for us to worship in, free of charge, till he could put up a larger building for the use of the congregation.

The question is often asked, whether Mr. Touro was as liberal in the matter of private donations as in his public charities. We cannot give an arithmetical answer to this question, for he followed most scrupulously the injunction of our Lord, "Let not thy left hand know what thy right hand doeth." It has come incidentally to my knowledge, that since my settlement in New Orleans, the amount of his private benefactions has not been less than thirty thousand dollars. It no doubt far exceeded this statement. Touching this matter, did space allow, I could give many interesting anecdotes. Though Mr. Touro was exact, rigid, and methodical in his business transactions, this trait of character had not its origin in covetousness. When his impulses led the way, he poured forth his money freely as water. I was in his counting room one morning, when he told me, weeping, that he had just signed a document resigning his legal title to the entire estate of an only sister, recently deceased. It was worth, if I remember aright, about eighty thousand dollars. He refused to take the smallest fraction of it, and requested his friends at the north to distribute it for charitable purposes, in the manner which they thought would be most agreeable to her, were she still living. Had avarice been his ruling passion, would he have allowed such a windfall to escape his grasp?

It has often been said by persons in New Orleans, that Mr. Touro did not do for myself particularly, as much, all things considered, as I had a right to expect. But do they know the principles which governed and directed his acts of kindness to me and mine? He often said, " Mr. Clapp, you are altogether too profuse and indiscriminate in your charities. I admit that you are economical in your habits and mode of living; but were you to come into the possession of a fortune, you would give it all away in a year or two, unless you had an overseer appointed." I might have done so then, but I am sure that I should not do so now, if I had the chance. It was his honest conviction that I ought not to have access to much money at a time. But most of my friends are not aware of the magnitude of the benefits which he was actually pleased to confer on me. Besides allowing me to take nearly the whole income of the pew rent, he gave me in small sums, from time to time, not less than twenty thousand dollars. Whenever I told him that I was out of money, he always supplied me, saying, " that was the last he could let me have, for the church ought certainly to yield me enough." Indeed, it was entirely owing to the unwise profusion of my charities, that I did not leave New Orleans with an ample competence for life.

The title " Philanthropist " is the most honorable

surname on earth. It has been most justly bestowed on Judah Touro, and he will wear it till time is no more; it will be inscribed in light immortal on the diadem of his everlasting reward. I thank God for my acquaintance with this man; I thank God that he was my friend; above all, I would be thankful for the hope of meeting him in that brighter existence, where those who love each other will be separated no more.

Daniel Webster once said in an address before the Hebrew Benevolent Association of New York city, "We are indebted to the Jewish nation for revealed religion, for the most important blessings and refinements of civilized life, and for all well-grounded hopes of immortal bliss beyond the grave." It is a trite and commonplace remark, that charitable institutions have never been known to exist, except in those lands illuminated by the light of revelation. When we look along the shores of the old pagan world, we behold the relics of mouldering cities, pyramids, palaces, temples, villas, obelisks, military columns, spacious amphitheatres, and statues erected to immortalize heroes, poets, and scholars; but nowhere in those regions do we meet the remains of free public schools, orphan asylums, hospitals, retreats for the destitute and unfortunate, nor monuments intended to perpetuate the memory of those who consecrated their lives to the melioration of humanity. They are found only in those lands which have derived their ideas of glory from the Hebrew Scriptures, and from the life and teachings of Him who uttered the parable of the good Samaritan.

What a striking evidence of the divine origin and necessity of the Bible! This sacred volume has taught the world, that for man there is no heritage on earth worth the seeking, worth the asking, worth the having, but an upright and beneficent life. This is that building spoken of by our Saviour, that rests upon an immovable basis. When the rains descend and the floods rage, and the winds blow and beat thereon, it cannot be overthrown, for it is founded upon a rock.

The names of those who built the Egyptian pyramids are lost in oblivion. But if, instead of rearing piles of magnificence for self-aggrandizement, they had employed the same means in founding institutions for the deaf and dumb, hospitals, and other philanthropic establishments, their memories would have been preserved green and flourishing by grateful millions; they would have floated down on a gathering tide of glory to the last syllable of recorded time.

I staid in New Orleans this year, 1822, till the middle of May. The congregations were constantly as large as the house would hold. My extemporaneous style of preaching seemed to be generally acceptable. Some, however, did not like me at all. One gentleman of strong mind and great reading, and a confirmed Deist, stopping me in the street one day, spoke thus: " Since my settlement in New Orleans, I never went inside of a church till Mr. Larned came here. I attended his meetings every Sabbath, not because I believed in his ideas of religion, — they were revolting to me, — but to enjoy the indescribable charms of his natural eloquence. I heard you preach yesterday. As a didactic performance, your sermon was respectable, perhaps equal to an ordinary discourse of Mr. Larned; but your delivery is far less interesting. *He* seemed to speak because he could not help it; *you* speak in a labored manner, as if it was a very unwelcome task. There is nothing to interest me in your manner, and your doctrines I repudiate; but when you come across poor, sick, and suffering people, call on me; it will always give me pleasure to aid in relieving them."

He was as good as his word. I cannot tell how many hundreds he gave me, in times of public distress, to be distributed according to my best judgment. I offered to give — but he never would receive — vouchers for the faithful manner in which the funds intrusted to my hands were disposed of. For aught he knew to the contrary, the moneys given were used for my personal emolument.

Another gentleman, a Calvinist, communicant, and a constant attendant on church, urged upon me, every time I saw him, the importance of getting up in the Crescent City such revivals of religion as were flourishing at the north. "It makes me weep in secret," he said, "when I think of the number of unregenerate souls *here* that are hurrying to the regions of eternal woe." Yet this man, though he was wealthy, never could be persuaded to give me ten dollars to relieve a sick, indigent, dying family. But his creed was the very type of evangelical purity. He knew the Westminster Catechism by heart, and was eternally talking about justification by *faith alone*, man's utter inability to do any thing good, the glories of electing grace, and the certainty that eternal damnation must be the portion of all those who die in their sins. I have often revolved in my mind the question, which of these characters was most acceptable to God, the Deist, whose heart and life were full of goodness and mercy, or the Calvinist, whose belief and worship were in exact accordance with prescribed, accredited formulas, but whose daily walk yielded no fruits of purity or disinterestedness.

In general, I found the state of society in New Orleans more agreeable than I had imagined. Most of the gentlemen whom I became acquainted with were distinguished for superior refinement and wide knowledge of the world. Their frank, easy, open, and generous hospitality was truly delightful. Most of the families that I visited received me without ceremony, as a friend whom they loved and confided in; not as a person preëminently holy, so purified from the attachments of earth as to have no taste for the scenes and enjoyments of society. One day I was invited to take tea in a family of our congregation, and pass the evening with a small number of friends. Being called to attend a wedding, I did not reach the house till near ten o'clock. Instead of a few persons convened simply for an hour's conversation, there was a large, gay company, whose movements had resolved themselves into a dance, and were directed by a band of musicians. Now, if I had followed the advice of one of my venerable instructors at Andover, I should have instantly retired, that I might not, even in appearance, have sanctioned, for a moment, a species of recreation so inconsistent with the dignity and seriousness of a Christian life. But as I was politely conducted to a chair in the midst of a circle of ladies, who preferred looking on to an active participation in the festivity going forward, I determined to make myself at home, and commit what I had been taught to regard as a heinous, unjustifiable indulgence, by witnessing an entertainment pronounced, among Presbyterian clergymen generally, to be sinful and injurious. There was, however, in my heart, no sense of violated duty, no feeling of guilt. I realized then my accountability to God, and that were I to die instantly, my future interests would be just as safe as if called to draw my last breath in the pulpit, at a funeral, by the bed of the dying, or in the sacred seclusion of the closet.

I spent an hour or more in this cheerful circle, where all things to the eye and ear were refined, orderly, and decorous. The hearts of that company were visible only to the Omniscient One. I shall refer to the impressions made on my mind by their external appearance. Before me stood the young and happy, upon whose fates and fortunes the sombre shadows of adversity had not yet gathered; their minds were bright and buoyant, their steps elastic, their ears opened to the melodies of sound, their eyes radiant with pleasure. As I was meditating upon those comely brows, flushed with the bloom of early life; the fair forms of feminine grace and loveliness; the dignified, accomplished manners of those more advanced in years; the music; sprightly conversation, wit, love, gayety, and joyousness which characterized the whole scene, — a sweet, profound, unwonted perception of God's goodness captivated my soul. Such intense feelings of piety I had never before experienced. I said to myself " It has, indeed, pleased God, ' to make man but a little lower than the angels, and to crown him with glory and honor.' If he is so beautiful here, what will he not become in that future state, where our loftiest ideals and actual attainments both will regularly advance in a progression that is infinite!" I was rapt in delightful visions of a spiritual world. This thought took complete possession of my mind. God is too good not to provide for us something nobler, better, greater, more permanent, and more satisfying than the transitory possessions and pleasures of time. Can he present to us the chalice of existence, and then dash it from our lips just as we begin to taste its joys? Is not his infinite love a pledge that he will never treat us so cruelly? Would a kind parent promise his children favors which he never intended to bestow on them? Can God awaken irrepressible desires of continued, unending happiness, only to be crushed out and disappointed forever? Nothing in mathematics is more certain than the doctrine that the inherent, essential desires of our moral nature will be completely gratified. Can they be, if death is an eternal sleep?

If the Holy Spirit ever breathed on my heart, it was on that occasion, amid the music, thoughtlessness, levity, ceremonials, and sensuous attractions of an evening party. There, if ever, the inspirations of God touched and ennobled my soul. Said a lady who was sitting next to me, " Mr. Clapp, you seem to be in a brown study. Are you thinking out a sermon ? "

" No, madam ; but a glorious subject for a sermon has just entered my thoughts. We are cheated, we are deceived, by the very constitution of our nature, if the pleasures of this evening are not a prelibation and foreshadowing of purer and ever-increasing joy beyond the grave. If a bird or a beast could cherish a conscious desire of happiness, this fact would prove its title to an endless life."

" Indeed," continued the lady, " you have made a notable discovery — the seeking of happiness even in amusements demonstrates our immortality. Had you not better preach on the subject next Sabbath ? "

Her suggestion, though made facetiously, was followed. I took for my text Isaiah xxviii. 20 : *" For the bed is shorter than that a man can stretch himself on it, and the covering narrower than that he can wrap himself in it."* I began by saying, " O, the misery, depression of spirits, gloom, ennui, and despair of those who live below their highest capabilities and aspirations ; who live in a merely physical and sensual existence — a world of the bodily and animal senses ; who never soar to feel their divinity, by expatiating over the immortal regions of truth, knowledge, beauty, and virtue ! Whatever may be the good purposes for which the animal appetites and passions were given us, they are a source of continual sorrow and unhappiness to the pure and spiritual mind —

a mind that longs to rise to God, and live above the plane of animal sensation only, which is so fatal to honor, glory, and happiness, yet so inspiring and invigorating to vice. The unrestrained indulgence of a single natural desire, or passion of the physical man, is enough to darken, prostrate, and destroy the soul. This habitual neglecting to subject appetite to a sense of duty is the real source of all the sin and degradation on earth.

"Moreover, as intimated in the text, the person who gives himself up to self-indulgence is never satisfied. He chases a rainbow that is painted on a cloud, and retreats before him as he advances, till finally it vanishes forever from his view. Not one of all the irreligious millions who have lived, ever sat down for one moment contented with present attainments, without longing after some remote and inaccessible good. They spent their days only to be broken by toil, to be wasted by sickness, to be racked with pain, to be desolated by one surge of sorrow after another, till called to enter ' that undiscovered country from whose bourn no traveller returns.' Yes, my friends, like a pendulum, they were constantly vacillating between the ecstasy of hope and the lifelessness of possession — struggling, striving, and wearying themselves out, till the curtain of mortality fell, and their busy, restless, disappointed hearts, crowded with plans, cares, and anticipations, forgot to beat, and all their fluttering anxieties were hushed forever in the cold silence of the tomb. Without timely repentance, in like manner shall we all perish.

"What signifies this solemn fact, testified to by universal experience, that our material bed and covering are too small for us? What mean these immeasurable longings, which no earthly forms of beauty and bliss can satiate? They teach us, my friends, that at death we shall not be turned into cold clay or dry dust, lifeless, senseless, and thoughtless, forevermore; that the soul of man will last as long as the throne of God; that it will live through more years, ages, centuries, and cycles than there are drops of water in the ocean; and even then the morning of an endless existence will scarcely have dawned around us; that we have been created to tread the broad and boundless pathways of a destination that has no limits. Solemn, sublime, inconceivable, transporting thought! If we realized it, all the material possessions and glories around would seem to us but as worthless spangles in the dust we tread on — but as the baubles and playthings which little children use in the sports of a summer's afternoon. The pressure of sin would be removed from our bosoms; free, elastic, and joyous, we should stand upon the lofty eminence of Christian faith, and look out upon a perspective of loveliness, rising and spreading, in all the glories of immortality, beyond the dark ruins of earth and time."

Such, in substance, was the sermon suggested to my mind by witnessing the profusion, splendor, and beauty of a social entertainment. The lady above mentioned remarked to me the next day, that last Sunday's sermon was the best I had yet preached, in the judgment of all the congregation. "We had better make a party for you once every week." Incidents similar to the one just narrated, have given birth to most of the discourses which I have delivered in New Orleans. A settled minister cannot adapt his homilies to the wants of his parishioners, unless they are all embraced in his parochial visits; unless he is on terms of the most familiar, unreserved, and intimate intercourse with them, so that they are induced honestly to communicate to him the thoughts, feelings, doubts, fears, hopes, and secrets of their inmost souls. Never until I went to New Orleans had I any just conception of the best mode of preaching, nor the class of subjects which should be generally introduced into the pulpit.

On the 20th of May, 1822, indispensable business called me to leave the south on a jaunt to New England. I returned to my post of labor before the epidemic of that year had terminated. On my way up the river, I made a pause at Louisville, to take upon myself the vows of wedlock. I was married the 31st of May, 1822, to Miss Adeline Hawes, a beautiful and interesting young lady, originally from Boston, Massachusetts, but at that time a resident of Kentucky. For thirty-five years we have been sharers of each other's joys, consolers of each other's sorrows, and helpers together amid the allotments and vicissitudes which were ordained for us by a wise and merciful Providence. We have had six children; three of them — one son and two daughters — are in the spirit land; three sons survive. The eldest is settled in the Crescent City; the second is in

Chicago; the third and youngest is with his parents in Louisville.

We have reason to bless God for the degree of health and prosperity which have been bestowed upon us in perilous times gone by; that we still live in peace and competence; and above all, that we are permitted, through Christ, to cherish the glorious hope, that after having finished the eventful journey of human life, we shall meet in those eternal scenes of beauty and of bliss which await the children of God in a brighter and better world.

CHAPTER VI.

GENERAL REMARKS UPON THE EPIDEMICS WHICH HAVE PREVAILED IN NEW ORLEANS. — ASIATIC CHOLERA IN THE FALL OF 1832 AND THE SUMMER OF 1833.

THERE have been twenty very sickly seasons during my residence in New Orleans. The yellow fever raged violently in 1822, '24, '27, '28, '29, and '30. The epidemics that prevailed in '27, '28, '29, and '30 were extremely fatal. In 1829, more than nine hundred persons died from yellow fever alone; yet no report of these awful visitations was published in the medical journals of the day.

In the excessively warm summer of 1832, my strength was so much reduced, that a change of climate was prescribed by friends and physicians. I started with my family in a steamboat, bound for Cincinnati, intending to spend the remainder of the season at Niagara, Montreal, and Saratoga Springs. But when I reached Ohio, news came that the cholera had made its appearance at Quebec and other places.

It was travelling with great rapidity. In one short month this terrific pestilence walked unseen from the capital of Lower Canada westward to Detroit, and in a southern direction to Lake Champlain, Albany, and New York. It seemed to prefer following the courses of great rivers, like the St. Lawrence, Ohio, and Mississippi.

Dr. Drake, of Cincinnati, expressed the opinion that within a few weeks the disease would break out in all our principal cities. Fearing that New Orleans might be attacked during my absence, I immediately abandoned a journey which held out such an attractive prospect, and retraced my course down the river. I could not get rid of the presentiment that a period of unprecedented calamity impended over the Crescent City. The previous summer, in the month of August, a frightful tornado had swept over and inundated New Orleans. The Creoles said that this was the forerunner of some frightful pestilence. I proposed to leave Mrs. Clapp and the children with her aunt in Kentucky, till the overflowing scourge should pass through the land. But she declined acceding to the proposition, and quoted these memorable words of Scripture: "Whither thou goest, I will go ; and where thou lodgest, I will lodge; thy people shall be my people, and thy God my God. Where thou diest will I die, and there will I be buried : the Lord do so to me, and more also, if aught but death part thee and me."

We arrived at New Orleans, on our return home, about the 1st of September. The weather was most sultry and oppressive. To most of my friends our conduct appeared so unwise, that they hardly gave us a cordial welcome back. I said to them, " 'Though neither a prophet nor the son of a prophet,' I see a dark cloud suspended over us, which will soon discharge a tempest of unparalleled violence and destruction." That very week, several cases of yellow fever occurred in the Charity Hospital and boarding houses along the levee. It soon grew into an epidemic, and carried off hundreds during this and the succeeding month.

On the morning of the 25th of October, 1832, as I was walking home from market, before sunrise, I saw two men lying on the levee in a dying condition. They had been landed from a steamboat which arrived the night before. Some of the watchmen had gone after a handbarrow or cart, on which they might be removed to the hospital. At first there was quite a crowd assembled on the spot. But an eminent physician rode up in his gig, and gazing a moment, exclaimed in a loud voice, "Those men have the Asiatic cholera." The crowd dispersed in a moment, and ran as if for their lives in every direction. I was left almost alone with the sufferers. They could speak, and were in full possession of their reason. They had what I afterwards found were the usual symptoms of cholera — cramps, convulsions, &c. The hands and feet were cold and blue; an icy perspiration flowed in streams; and they complained of a great pressure upon their chests. One of them said it seemed as if a bar of iron was lying across him. Their thirst was intense, which caused an insufferable agony in the mouth and throat. They entreated me to procure some water. I attempted to go on board the steamboat which had put them on shore. But the staging had been drawn in to prevent all intercourse with people on the levee. Thence I returned, intending to go to the nearest dwelling to get some relief for the unhappy men, whom all but God had apparently deserted.

At that instant the watchmen arrived with a dray. Happily, (because, perhaps, they spoke only the French language,) they had no suspicion that these strangers were suffering from the cholera. If I had pronounced that terrific word in their hearing, they too might have fled, and left the sick men to perish on the cold ground. I saw them placed on the vehicle, and subsequently learned that they were corpses before eleven o'clock A. M. the same day.

I walked home, attempting to be calm and resigned, determined to do my duty, and leave the consequences with God. I said nothing to my family about the sick men whom I had met, though they thought it strange that I had taken so much more time than usual in going to and from the market, and observed that I looked uncommonly thoughtful and serious. I felt that the hour of peril had come. I said in silent, inward prayer, "O God, thou art my refuge and fortress; in thee do I trust. O, help me, and strengthen me, for vain is the help of man. His breath goeth forth; he returneth to the dust; in that very day his purposes perish. O, happy is the man that hath the living God for his help, whose hope is in Jehovah his God." I felt a delightful sense of my dependence; that Providence was my shield and buckler, and that nothing could befall me or my family, which, if we did our duty, would not work out results great and glorious beyond all thought and imagination. It seemed to me that, trusting in the Most High, I could trample under foot pain, sickness, death, and every other evil.

The weather, this morning, was very peculiar. The heavens were covered with thick, heavy, damp, lowering clouds, that seemed like one black ceiling, spread over the whole horizon. To the eye, it almost touched the tops of the houses. Every one felt a strange difficulty of respiration. I never looked upon such a gloomy, appalling sky before or since. Not a breath of wind stirred. It was so dark, that in some of the banks, offices, and private houses, candles or lamps were lighted that day.

Immediately after breakfast I walked down to the post office. At every corner, and around the principal hotels, were groups of anxious faces. As soon as they saw me, the question was put by several persons at a time, "Is it a fact that the cholera is in the city?" I replied by describing what I had seen but two hours before. Observing that many of them appeared panic-struck, I remarked, "Gentlemen, do not be alarmed. These may prove merely what the doctors call sporadic cases. We do not yet know that it will prevail to an alarming extent. Let us trust in God, and wait patiently the developments of another morning."

That day as many persons left the city as could find the means of transmigration. On my way home from the post office, I walked along the levee, where the two cholera patients had been disembarked but three or four hours before. Several families in the neighborhood were making preparations to move, but in vain. They could not obtain the requisite vehicles. The same afternoon the pestilence entered their houses, and before dark spread through several squares opposite to the point where the steamer landed the first cases.

On the evening of the 27th of October, it had made its way through every part of the city. During the ten succeeding days, reckoning from October 27 to the 6th of November, all the physicians judged that, at the lowest computation, there were five thousand deaths — an average of five hundred every day. Many died of whom no account was rendered. A great number of bodies, with bricks and stones tied to the feet, were thrown into the river. Many were privately interred in gardens and enclosures, on the grounds where they expired, whose names were not recorded in the bills of mortality. Often I was kept in the burying ground for hours in succession, by the incessant, unintermitting arrival of corpses, over whom I was requested to perform a short service. One day, I did not leave the cemetery till nine o'clock at night; the last interments were made by candle light. Reaching my house faint, exhausted, horror-stricken, I found my family all sobbing and weeping, for they had concluded, from my long absence, that I was certainly dead. I never went abroad without kissing and blessing them all, with the conviction that we should never meet again on earth. After bathing and taking some refreshment, I started out to visit the sick. My door was thronged with servants, waiting to conduct me to the rooms of dying sufferers. In this kind of labor I spent most of the night. At three o'clock A. M., I returned home, threw myself down on a sofa, with directions not to be called till half past five. I was engaged to attend a funeral at six o'clock A. M., 28th October.

In the progress of my round on this occasion, I met with a case of cholera whose symptoms were unlike any thing that I had before witnessed. The patient was perfectly free from pain, with mental powers unimpaired, and suffering only from debility and moral apprehensions. From his looks, I should have supposed that he was sinking under some kind of consumption, such as prevails at the north. He was an educated man, whose parents, when living, were members of the Presbyterian church. His will had just been made, and he believed himself to be dying, which was actually the case. I have said that his mind was uninjured; more, it was quickened to preternatural strength and activity.

When I took his hand in mine, he said, "The physicians assure me that I must soon die; I am unprepared; I look back with many painful regrets upon the past; I look forward to the future with doubts, fears, and misgivings. What will become of me?" I replied, "What, sir, is your strongest wish?" He answered, "That it may please God to forgive and save me, for Christ's sake." I added, "If this is the real wish of your heart, it will be gratified, no matter how wicked or unworthy you may be. Is your father living?" I inquired. He said, "No, sir; I saw him breathe his last in my native home. He died happy, for he was good. Never shall I forget that last prayer which he uttered in behalf of his surviving children." "Suppose," I continued, "you were absolutely certain that death would introduce you into the presence of that beloved parent, and that he would be empowered by the Infinite One to make you as happy as he pleased, and to receive you to his bosom and embrace forever; would you not most willingly, joyfully, and with perfect confidence, commit your fate for eternity to the decision of such a pure, kind, affectionate father?" He answered in the affirmative. I said, "Is it possible that you have so much confidence in an earthly parent, and at the same time can hesitate to commend your spirit into the hands of that heavenly Father, who loves you as much as he does himself, — whose love is transcendent, boundless, infinite, everlasting, — who cannot allow you to perish, any more than he could destroy himself?"

"I see I am in an error," he exclaimed. "O God, help me and strengthen me." I then made a short prayer. "Can you repeat with all your heart, as in the presence of God," I asked, "the words which I am about to utter? If you can, say them aloud, along with me. 'My Father, who art in heaven, thou hast promised that thou wilt evermore draw nigh to those who draw near to thee in true and earnest prayer; that thou wilt hear their cry, fulfil their desires, and help them, and save them. Have pity upon me, O God, according to thy loving kindness; according to the multitude of thy tender mercies, hide thy face from my sins, and blot out all mine iniquities. Create within me, a clean heart, O God; renew within me a faithful spirit; cast me not away from thy presence, and take not thy Holy Spirit from me. Carry me in thine almighty arms, and finally receive me into glory. Though my flesh and my heart fail, be thou, O God, the strength of my heart, and my portion forever. These blessings I humbly implore in the worthy name of Jesus Christ our Saviour; and unto Thee, the only wise God, the King eternal, immortal, and invisible, be ascribed praise and thanksgiving, glory and dominion, now and forevermore. Amen.'"

Every word of this prayer he repeated after me in a distinct and audible voice. At the close, he exclaimed, "It is finished;" then gazing with a fixed eye, as upon some object on the ceiling over him, he said, "God be praised, I see my father." Doubting as to what he meant to say precisely, I asked, "What father do you see, your heavenly or your earthly father?" He answered, "My earthly father. Can you not see him? There he is, (pointing upwards,) smiling down upon me, arrayed in splendid garments, and beckoning me to follow him to the skies. He is going — he is gone." On the utterance of these words, his arm, which had been raised heavenward, fell lifeless, and he breathed not again. There was a smile, and expression of rapture on his face which lingered there for hours. It was the only good-looking corpse which I saw in that epidemic. His form was magnificent, his breast large and arched, his whole appearance that of statue-like repose. There he lay before me, as beautiful as life itself. His countenance wore such a smile of ecstasy, I could hardly realize that his immortal spirit had fled. I laid my hand on his heart. It moved not.

This incident made a lasting impression on my mind. It deepened, it strengthened, immeasurably, my belief that the soul survives the body. "Who knows," said I to myself, "but every one of these hundreds that are dying around me, when they draw their last breath, are greeted by the disembodied spirits of those whom they knew and loved on earth, and who have come to convoy them to the scenes of a higher and nobler existence?"

Shortly after this, I was standing by the bed of a young lady in her last moments, when she called to me and her mother, saying, "Do you not see my sister (who had died of yellow fever a few weeks before) *there?*" pointing upwards. "There are angels with her. She has come to take me to heaven." Perhaps these facts are in harmony with the doctrines of modern spiritualists. One thing I know. There is not a more delightful, sanctifying faith than this — that as soon as we die, glorified spirits will hover about us, as guardian angels, to breathe on our souls their own refinement, and to point our way to the heavenly mansions.

The morning after the death scene which I have just described, at six o'clock, I stepped into a carriage to accompany a funeral procession to the cemetery. On my arrival, I found at the graveyard a large pile of corpses without coffins, in horizontal layers, one above the other, like corded wood. I was told that there were more than one hundred bodies deposited there. They had been brought by unknown persons, at different hours since nine o'clock the evening previous. Large trenches were dug, into which these uncoffined corpses were thrown indiscriminately. The same day, a private hospital was found deserted; the physicians, nurses, and attendants were all dead, or had run away. Not a living person was in it. The wards were filled with putrid bodies, which, by order of the mayor, were piled in an adjacent yard, and burned, and their ashes scattered to the winds. Could a wiser disposition have been made of them?

Many persons, even of fortune and popularity, died in their beds without aid, unnoticed and unknown, and lay there for days unburied. In almost every house might be seen the sick, the dying, and the dead, in the same room. All the stores, banks, and places of business were closed. There were no means, no instruments for carrying on the ordinary affairs of business; for all the drays, carts, carriages, hand and common wheelbarrows, as well as hearses, were employed in the transportation of corpses, instead of cotton, sugar, and passengers. Words cannot describe my sensations when I first beheld the awful sight of carts driven to the graveyard, and there upturned, and their contents discharged as so many loads of lumber or offal, without a single mark of mourning or respect, because the exigency rendered it impossible.

The Sabbath came, and I ordered the sexton to ring the bell for church at eleven o'clock A. M., as usual. I did not expect to meet a half a dozen persons; but there was actually a congregation of two or three hundred, and all gentlemen. The ladies were engaged in taking care of the sick. There was no singing. I made a very short prayer, and preached a discourse not more than fifteen minutes in length. It made such an impression that several of the hearers met me at the door, and requested me to write it down for their perusal and meditation. I complied with the request. Here it is. My text was the passage found in Isaiah xxvi. 3 : " Thou wilt keep him in perfect peace whose mind is stayed on thee, because he trusteth in thee."

I began by rehearsing the closing lines of Bryant's " Thanatopsis : " —

> " 'So live, that when thy summons comes to join
> The innumerable caravan, which moves
> To that mysterious realm, where each shall take
> His chamber in the silent halls of death,
> Thou go not like the quarry-slave at night,
> Scourged to his dungeon, but, sustained and soothed
> By an unfaltering trust, approach thy grave
> Like one who wraps the drapery of his couch
> About him and lies down to pleasant dreams.'

" My friends, death is a dispensation of love. Reflect that as many persons die every hour as there are tickings of the clock in the same time. All die. Not only the idiot, the fool, and the reprobate, but also the best, wisest, and noblest, are laid in the grave. That law which sweeps over all, irrespective of moral character, cannot be a punitive infliction. Man would die if he were as spotless as an angel. Were it not for the grave, how soon would this globe be filled to absolute repletion ! We die simply that we may awake to a new and nobler existence. We cease to live as men, that we may begin to live as angels. There is a certain animal that exists first in the shape of a worm. Its appropriate element is water. At length it sinks in insensibility and death. After a while, its grave opens; it comes forth from the grovelling dust a new being, an inhabitant of the air, with beauteous wings and plumage, to bask in the sunbeams, to sip the aroma of the flowery world; to move through the atmosphere, a creature of ethereal endowment and loveliness. In the same manner, the soul of man must drop its "mortal coil," that, disengaged from earth, sense, and sin, it may be transformed into a being adapted to the scenes of a higher and incorruptible existence.

Reflect upon the declaration of Jesus, that all who die shall be made immortal. He also teaches that in the immortal state they will sin no more, hunger no more, thirst no more, weep no more, die no more, but be like the angels of God in heaven. There is no difference between the good and the bad, as to the eternity of their duration. This is admitted by all orthodox divines of every school and denomination. There is nothing frightful in death, except to the unenlightened imagination. It is the slightest evil that crosses the path of human life. Nay, rather, it is not an evil; it is the greatest blessing. It is dust only that descends to dust. The grave is the place where we shall be permitted to lay down our mortality, weakness, diseases, sorrows, and sins, to enter upon a higher existence, with angels, and the spirits of the just made perfect. We are taught by the apostle Paul that it is impossible for either sin or pain to go along with us into the unseen world. "There the weary are at rest." Glorious prospect!

In the eternal state, there are no bodies, no sickness, no wants, no groans, no injustice, no forms of depravity.

"Yes, my friends, if we looked at the subject aright, we should rejoice in the thought, that before another setting sun, before we reach our homes to-day, death may come to release us from these burdened, tempted, frail, failing, corruptible bodies, that we may enter upon the wonders of a life immortal, whose progressions will constantly increase, in the freshness, extent, beauty, and plenitude of divine, unfading, and unimaginable charms. Do not be alarmed, my friends; death cannot hurt you. 'But,' you may ask, 'is there nothing for us to do, that we may die in peace?' Yes, in the language of Scripture, 'you must cease to do evil, and learn to do well.' If you are conscious of living in the commission of any sin, however dear, you must resolve, before you rise from your seats, to renounce it forever, and cast yourselves on that boundless mercy, revealed by Him who is the conqueror over Death, and saith to us all, 'He that trusteth in me shall NEVER, NEVER DIE.'

"Our eternal existence and bliss depend upon laws which we can neither create, cancel, nor modify. They will be brought about in God's own time and way; by influences just as resistless as those that produce day and night, the descent of rivers, the tides of the ocean, or the succession of the seasons. May the grace of our Lord Jesus Christ, the love of God, and the fellowship of their Holy Spirit, be with you all, to-day and forever. Amen."

In the above homily, I stated what I sincerely believed to be sound, scriptural views of death. Any doctrines calculated to inspire men with a dread of the grave are false, heathenish, and atheistical. The next day, a gentleman said to me, "I verily believe that your sermon, yesterday, saved my life. I went into church frightened, weak, in utter despair; I came out calm, resigned, full of hope, and able to tread cholera, death, and all other ills under my feet."

For several days after this Sabbath, the plague raged with unabated violence. But the events, toils, trials, and gloom of one day, in this terrific visitation, were a *fac-simile* of those that characterized the whole scene. A fatal yellow fever had been spreading destruction in the city six weeks before the cholera commenced. Thousands had left it to escape this scourge. So that, at the time of the first cholera, it was estimated that the population of the city did not exceed thirty-five thousand inhabitants. During the entire epidemic, at least six thousand persons perished; showing the frightful loss of one sixth of the people in about twelve days. This is the most appalling instance of mortality known to have happened in any part of the world, ancient or modern. Yet, in all the accounts of the ravages of this enemy, in 1832, published in the northern cities and Europe, its desolations in New Orleans are not even noticed — a fact which requires no comment. The same ratio of mortality in Boston, the next twelve days, would call for more than twenty-three thousand victims. Who can realize this truth? The same epidemic broke out again the following summer, in June, 1833. In September of the same year, the yellow fever came back again. So, within the space of twelve months, we had two Asiatic choleras, and two epidemic yellow fevers, which carried off ten thousand persons that were known, and many more that were not reported.

Multitudes began the day in apparently good health, and were corpses before sunset. One morning, as I was going out, I spoke to a gentleman who resided in the very next house to mine. He was standing at his door, and remarked that he felt very well; "but I wonder," he added, "that you are alive." On my return, only two hours afterwards, he was a corpse. A baker died in his cart directly before my door. Near me there was a brick house going up; two of the workmen died on a carpenter's bench, but a short time after they had commenced their labors for the day. Often did it happen that a person engaged a coffin for some friend, who himself died before it could be finished. On a certain evening, about dark, a gentleman called on me to say a short service over the body of a particular friend, just deceased: the next morning I performed the same service for him. I went, one Wednesday night, to solemnize the contract of matrimony between a couple of very genteel appearance. The bride was young, and possessed of the most extraordinary beauty. A few hours only had elapsed before I was summoned to perform the last offices over her coffin. She had on her bridal dress, and was very little changed in the appearance of her face.

Three unmarried gentlemen, belonging to my congregation, lived together and kept *bachelor's hall*, as it is termed with us. I was called to visit one of them at ten o'clock P. M. He lived but a few moments after I entered the room. Whilst I was conversing with the survivors, a second brother was taken with cramps. There was nobody in the house but the servants. They were especially dear to me because of their intrinsic character, and because they were regular attendants at church. We instantly applied the usual remedies, but without success. At one o'clock in the morning he breathed his last. The only surviving brother immediately fell beside the couch of the lifeless ones, and at daylight he died. We laid the three corpses side by side.

One family, of nine persons, supped together in perfect health; at the expiration of the next twenty-four hours, eight out of the nine were dead. A boarding house, that contained thirteen inmates, was absolutely emptied; not one was left to mourn.

Persons were found dead all along the streets, particularly early in the mornings. For myself, I expected that the city would be depopulated. I have no doubt, that if the truth could be ascertained, it would appear that those persons who died so suddenly were affected with what are called the premonitory symptoms hours, perhaps a day, or a night, before they considered themselves unwell. In this early stage, the disease is easily arrested; but when the cramps and collapse set in, death is, in most cases, inevitable. Indeed, that is death. *Then*, nothing was known of the cholera, and its antecedent stages were unnoticed and uncared for. Hence, in a great measure, the suddenness as well as the extent of the mortality.

Nature seemed to sympathize in the dreadful spectacle of human woe. A thick, dark atmosphere, as I said before, hung over us like a mighty funereal shroud. All was still. Neither sun, nor moon, nor stars shed their blessed light. Not a breath of air moved. A hunter, who lived on the Bayou St. John, assured me that during the cholera he killed no game. Not a bird was seen winging the sky. Artificial causes of terror were superadded to the gloom which covered the heavens. The burning of tar and pitch at every corner; the firing of cannon, by order of the city authorities, along all the streets; and the frequent conflagrations which actually occurred at that dreadful period, — all these conspired to add a sublimity and horror to the tremendous scene. Our wise men hoped, by the combustion of tar and gunpowder, to purify the atmosphere. We have no doubt that hundreds perished from mere fright produced by artificial noise, the constant sight of funerals, darkness, and various other causes.

It was an awful spectacle to see night ushered in by the firing of artillery in different parts of the city, making as much noise as arises from the engagement of two powerful armies. The sight was one of the most tremendous which was ever presented to the eye, or even exhibited to the imagination, in description. Often, walking my nightly rounds, the flames from the burning tar so illuminated the city streets and river, that I could see every thing almost as distinctly as in the daytime. And through many a window into which was flung the sickly, flickering light of these conflagrations, could be seen persons struggling in death, and rigid, blackened corpses, awaiting the arrival of some cart or hearse, as soon as dawn appeared, to transport them to their final resting place.

During these ineffable, inconceivable horrors, I was enabled to maintain my post for fourteen days, without a moment's serious illness. I often sank down upon the floor, sofa, or pavement, faint and exhausted from over-exertion, sleeplessness, and want of food; but a short nap would partially restore me, and send me out afresh to renew my perilous labors. For a whole fortnight, I did not attempt to undress except to bathe and put on clean apparel. I was like a soldier, who is not allowed, by the constant presence of an enemy, to throw off his armor, and lay down his weapons for a single moment. Morning, noon, and midnight, I was engaged in the sick room, and in performing services over the dead. The thought that I myself should be exempted from the scourge — how could it be cherished for a moment? I expected that every day would be my last. Yet, as I said before, I did not have the slightest symptom of the cholera. Two things render this fact very remarkable.

First, I took no regular meals during all this time, and really suffered a great deal from hunger. People stopped sending to market, and cooking, in a great measure. They were afraid to eat any substantial food. One day, passing by the house of a

Spanish gentleman, a total stranger, I smelt something savory, and took the liberty to go in. He, with two or three others, was dining. On the board there were shrimps, cabbage, and bacon, with a good supply of garlic. I told them who I was, and begged for something to eat. They treated me very kindly. I sat down, and gratified my appetite with fish, vegetables, boiled ham, garlic, and a glass of gin, and then went on my way refreshed. Meeting a physician at the next square, I told him what I had done. He exclaimed, "You are a dead man; you will be attacked with the cholera in one hour."

But I felt not the least inconvenience from the dinner I had eaten. I am satisfied that in cholera times, one may partake of any diet that he likes, in moderation, with perfect impunity. I have always acted on this belief. More are killed by medicine, starving, and fright, than from eating improper food. A mistaken opinion as to this subject has arisen from the fact that multitudes have been seized with cholera directly after receiving a breakfast, dinner, or supper, and have immediately ejected their food as it was taken. Hence they have fancied that what they ate brought on sickness. No. One of the invariable effects of the cholera is to suspend the process of digestion; and of course one of the peculiar consequences of the disease is falsely ascribed to the deleterious influence of some species of food. To be sure, gluttony and intemperance may bring on this epidemic; but they are hurtful at all times.

Secondly, my escape was wonderful, considered in another respect. For fifteen days in succession, the atmosphere was loaded with the most deadly malaria, and every species of noxious impurity. I had to encounter not only the general insalubrity which always infects the air when cholera prevails, but to this were superadded the constant inhalations of the sick-bed effluvium which emanates from corpses in every stage of decomposition, in which life had been extinct for days, perhaps, and the offensive smells of the cemetery. Most of the bodies laid in the ground had a covering of earth but a few inches in depth, and through the porous dust there was an unimpeded emission of all the gases evolved from animal matter, when undergoing the process of putrefaction. The sick poor were often crowded together in low, narrow, damp, basement, unventilated rooms.

Many times, on entering these apartments, and putting my head under the mosquito bar, I became deadly sick in a moment, and was taken with vomiting, which, however, passed off without producing serious effects in a single instance. Let the reader imagine a close room, in which are lying half a dozen bodies in the process of decay, and he may form a faint conception of the physical horrors in which I lived, moved, and had my being continually for two entire weeks. My preservation has always seemed to me like a miracle. It is true, some constitutions are not susceptible of the cholera. Some can never take the yellow fever or small pox. It is not improbable that my safety ought to be ascribed to some peculiar idiosyncrasy, which enabled me to breathe the air of this plague with impunity.

In 1822, I knew an unacclimated gentleman who slept on the same bed with an intimate friend, whilst he was sick of the yellow fever: on the morning of his death, he himself, his clothes, and the sheets, were absolutely inundated by a copious discharge of the *vomito*. After the funeral, he continued to occupy the same room, and had the best health all that summer and autumn. During the next thirty years, he never left the city for a day, and was never sick. I have known numerous instances of the kind. Such phenomena doubtless result from natural causes; yet they do not happen without the appointment and providence of our heavenly Father.

An atheist, in the midst of the first cholera, spoke to me, one day, the following words, in substance: "Mr. Clapp, you are laboring very hard among the sick and dying; I admire your benevolent and self-sacrificing spirit; you aid in imparting to the wretched victims medicine, nursing, &c. By these material agencies, I believe you have already saved some lives. All this is achieved in harmony with the philosophical relation of cause and effect. But do you really imagine that *your prayers* can accomplish any good whatever? The cholera has a certain mission to fulfil. It will march forward to its destined goal, regardless of the chants of choirs, or the prayers of saints. Its movements are determined by blind, undiscriminating, and resistless laws.

"When you ask God for favors in behalf of a sick man, which will be conferred upon him sooner or later by the operation of inevitable, necessary laws, your petitions are of course entirely useless. It is equally apparent, that when you implore that assistance of Heaven which cannot be granted consistently with the ordinances of nature, your prayers are utterly nugatory. They cannot avert the cholera, nor any of the innumerable ills to which we are liable, any more than by a word you could stay the cataract of Niagara, or arrest the planets in their course."

This gentleman was apparently as moral a man as I have ever met with. Just, sincere, self-denying, kind, exemplary in all his life and conduct, I respected his character and motives, and felt that I was bound to answer his interrogatories honestly. "In the first place," I replied, " we pray because we cannot help it, any more than we can help breathing. It is an irrepressible tendency of our nature. I have not seen a person die in this epidemic, in possession of his reason, who did not wish to have me pray for him. You cannot, by reasoning, prevent men from eating when they are hungry, or seeking the refreshment of nightly repose after the fatigues of the day. So neither can you dissuade them from praying in scenes of sickness, trouble, and death. They want prayer just as much as they want the light and air of heaven. Now, suppose it to be in point of fact, philosophically considered, inefficacious; still, it gives the sufferer, at least, temporary consolation. It makes him feel as if he were in the hands of a Supreme Being, who will take care of him, the ever-blessed and only potentate — potentate over the laws of nature, over the events of time, sickness, death, and the grave. Call it a delusion, if you please; yet it inspires the dying man with a soothing and unfaltering trust, which enables him to meet a final hour with composure, feeling the triumphant assurance that though death must destroy his body, it cannot separate his immortal soul from God, from the society of spiritual beings, nor from eternal communion with a beauty and grandeur infinitely surpassing those of the visible, material creation.

"Besides, I must say, that to me your reasoning is inconclusive. Your assertion is, that the universe is so organized, that the efficacy of prayer is an absolute impossibility. Now, prove it. Assertion is not proof. You take the ground that the laws of nature, forsooth, will not permit the Supreme to answer the just, sincere, devout, and reasonable petitions of his children. He is prevented from doing so by difficulties of his own creating. Allow me to ask, 'How do you know that such is the case? Have you seen every thing? Have you travelled quite through the regions of immensity? Have you visited all these worlds upon worlds that revolve in space? Can you tell what "varied being peoples every star"? Is your reason capable of receiving all truth? Is your knowledge the measure of all that is possible in a boundless universe? Can you stretch your inch of line across the theatre of our Creator's works?' Why, sir, you cannot prove it to be absurd for God to work *miracles* in answer to prayer. Yes, for the accomplishment of special purposes, and with reference to particular persons and exigencies, He may consistently, for aught we can show to the contrary, actually suspend the laws of nature, cause heat to lower instead of raising the mercury of the thermometer, rivers to ascend on an inclined plain, water not to drown, poison not to kill, fire not to consume, and cold not to freeze.

"But, waiving this point, to me it is plain, that without the aid of miracles the Almighty could answer prayer by the mere arrangement or instrumentality of nature's eternal and unchanging laws, as you call them. The power of arrangement simply may produce results to us vast and immeasurable. Take as an example what in the scientific world is called galvanism. This, as you know, is in nature identical with lightning. You are familiar with the effects of this tremendous agent. You also are aware that it is a power awakened by the mere using of certain arrangements of various substances. If a finite being can achieve so much by wielding nature's laws in a particular direction, what cannot the Infinite One accomplish by similar means? Remember that the cholera, or any other epidemic, is an effect. What is its cause? Some substance, poison or malaria, (call it what you please,) imperceptible to the senses, of whose nature and properties we are consequently ignorant. It is admitted that for every poison in nature there is an antidote; that is, some substance, which, if brought to bear upon it, can destroy or neutralize its deleterious tendencies. It is perfectly easy, then, for the ever-present, omnipotent Father, by the mere order or juxtaposition of different substances, to turn away disease, in answer to prayer from individuals, families, or cities. By the use of natural laws, it may please God to preserve *me* in this pestilence, which is now destroying hundreds on every side. Suppose that, with your limited intelligence, you had the power to arrange and direct the laws of nature throughout the State of Louisiana. In the exercise of such a commission, what could you not achieve? You might raise its inhabitants to heaven, or sink them to perdition. How easy, then, would it be for the infinite mind, by similar means, to answer the prayers of his children, from the angel who bends before the glories of the unveiled throne, down to the humblest believer that treads these low vales of sin and sorrow! Depend upon it, nothing is more reasonable than the doctrine that God hears and answers prayer. On this topic nothing is more absurd than scepticism. The largest faith, as to this point, is nearest the truth."

This argument against my unbelieving friend was strikingly illustrated and confirmed by what actually occurred in the city, a few days after our interview. The cholera had been raging with unabated fury for fourteen days. It seemed as if the city was destined to be emptied of its inhabitants. During this time, as before stated, a thick, dark, sultry atmosphere filled our city. Every one complained of a difficulty in breathing, which he never before experienced. The heavens were as stagnant as the mantled pool of death. There were no breezes. At the close of the fourteenth day, about eight o'clock in the evening, a smart storm, something like a tornado, came from the north-west, accompanied with heavy peals of thunder and terrific lightnings. The deadly air was displaced immediately, by that which was new, fresh, salubrious, and life-giving. The next morning shone forth all bright and beautiful. The plague was stayed. In the opinion of all the medical gentlemen who were on the spot, that change of weather terminated the epidemic. At any rate, it took its departure from us that very hour. No new cases occurred after that storm. It is certainly, then, in the power of God, not only by wind and electricity, but also by other means innumerable beyond our powers of discernment, to deliver a city from pestilence, in answer to the prayers of his children. Some one has said that " a little philosophy may make one an unbeliever, but that a great deal will make him a Christian."

I think it very wrong to apply disparaging epithets to any person on account of his honest opinions on religious matters. A minister should never denounce, but he may discuss, and entreat with all long-suffering and forbearance. I said to this gentleman, as he was leaving me, " Your philosophy may be right and mine wrong. You are a highly gifted man. I bow to the superiority of your genius. You are wise, prudent, and sagacious, as to all matters appertaining to the present world. You are noble and upright in your secular plans and enterprises. Yet allow me to assure you that, by neglecting communion with God in habitual prayer, you suffer a loss, a diminution of happiness, that no words of mine can depict. There is a higher wisdom in heaven and earth ' than is dreamt of in your philosophy.' Prayer would make you a happier being.

Prayer would impart to you, amid the mournful vicissitudes and trials of earth, a deep, calm, and immovable peace — a prelibation of that which is enjoyed in the spirit-land of the blessed and immortal."

The young man with whom I had the above colloquy was the son of a Presbyterian clergyman. He manifested great respect and love for his father, but complained that he would never allow him to reason about religion. He actually supposed that all the follies and absurdities of Calvinism were taught in the Bible. "I cannot believe in such a book," he said. I replied, "Neither could I, if your supposition were correct. But I cannot find a distinguishing doctrine of the Calvinistic system in the Scriptures."

It is a curious fact, that though this man died in unbelief, yet he sent for me to visit him on his death bed. He fell a victim of the second cholera, which occurred in June, 1833. Entering his room I found him in perfect possession of his faculties. He said, "I am about to die. My belief is unchanged. I hold that man is nothing after death. Yet I look upon my decease with no apprehension. I have no solicitude and no regrets. I am in peace with all the world. To me existence has been a great blessing. But I am willing to take my exit from the stage of life, to afford room for a successor. I shall soon close my eyes, never again to open them; never again to gaze on this beautiful and magnificent universe. I have sent for you because I love and respect you. I also wanted to have you see with what calm, conscious serenity I can submit to my fate.

> 'Like bubbles on a sea of matter borne,
> We rise and break, and to that sea return.'"

"Do you indeed love my society?" I inquired. "Now, suppose it was optional with you, when you die, either to be annihilated, or, leaving behind your lifeless dust, to pass off to a world destined to enjoy forever the highest means of both physical and mental happiness, where sin, pain, want, sorrow, and trouble cannot enter, where you would meet all the lost and loved ones of earth, to be separated from them no more, and where you would rise from one scene of knowledge, refinement, and bliss to another without ever reaching the ultimate boundary of improvement. You like to see me here — would you not like to see me hereafter?"

"I confess," he replied, "that a conscious, intelligent, continued, ever-progressive existence is the most glorious destiny which we can conceive of. It is a captivating ideal. It is so lovely that men cling to it in defiance of reason and argument. I conceive that we are so organized that we cannot help loving and longing for immortality."

"Do you not remember," I continued, "the lines of Addison, —

> ''Tis the divinity that stirs within us;
> 'Tis heaven itself, that points out an hereafter,
> And intimates eternity to man.'

Again allow me to recall to your recollection the words of the poet, whom you just now quoted, —

> 'He sees why nature plants in man alone
> Hope of known bliss, and faith in bliss unknown;
> Nature, whose dictates to no other kind
> Are given in vain, but what they seek they find.'"

"Yes," he went on to say, "poets and preachers agree in their charming descriptions of a higher and heavenly life beyond this vale of tears. But every grave which is dug refutes their unfounded theories." I then suggested this thought. "You hold that there is no God ; that some blind, unintelligent, resistless law caused you to be born, to grow up, to go through the mingled allotments of the past, and will, in a few moments, command you back to mix again with the elements whence you were taken. Now, what evidence have you that this same stern, unrelenting influence may not cause you, after death, (according to the metempsychosis taught by Pythagoras,) to enter the body of some brute, or to sink to lower and lower degrees of wretchedness throughout eternity ? If we are not in the hands of a Father whose attributes are infinite love, wisdom, and power, then we have nothing to hope for, and the worst to fear, then the doctrine of endless misery, which your good, venerable parent believed in, may turn out to be true at last."

As I perceived that he was fast declining, I stopped the conversation at this point, and requested the favor of bidding him farewell, as I did all my dying friends, by rehearsing a few texts of Scripture, and offering a prayer. I opened the Bible, and pronounced some sentences from different chapters, giving what I believed to be the true sense of the original, in my own words. "Jesus Christ has abolished death, and brought life and immortality to light in the gospel. For we know that when our earthly tabernacles shall be dissolved, we shall enter a building of God, an house not made with hands, eternal in the heavens. As the children of Adam must all descend to the tomb, so they must all one day be made alive in Christ. The future state will be the complete antithesis of the present.

"This side the grave all men are mortal; beyond it, they will all be immortal. Here, all are corruptible; there, all will be incorruptible. Here, all are in a greater or less degree sinful; there, all will be holy. Here, all are weak; there, all will be strong, incapable of fatigue or infirmity. Here, all are debased; there, all will be made glorious. All who die, both good and bad, just and unjust, shall be raised up again, and admitted to a resurrection state. And in that resurrection state, they shall hunger no more, thirst no more, weep no more, sin no more, die no more, but be as the angels of God in heaven. And there shall be no more curse, but the throne of God and the Lamb shall triumph over all evil."

This reading was followed by a prayer, in nearly the following words: "My Father, who art in heaven, I commend this beloved friend, from whom I am soon to be separated for a short time, to thy infinite love and mercy, through Jesus Christ our Lord. I thank thee for the assurance that he cannot be crushed nor hurt by the forces of time, nature, death, or the grave. I bless thee for the revelation of the gospel, that his soul is a germ of thine own infinite, eternal, uncreated, and unchanging life; that therefore it must live, and advance in knowledge, worth, brightness, and beatitude, long as thy ever-blessed throne shall endure. Amen." At the conclusion, he exclaimed, with a feeble but distinct voice, "So mote it be. I fear nothing." He spoke not again. Fifteen minutes afterwards, his pulse ceased to beat.

I cannot believe that this man was insincere in the views which he expressed concerning the soul's everlasting extinction. He gave every evidence of an undoubting assurance in the reality of those opinions which he avowed. He led a most moral, upright, and charitable life. He did not disbelieve on account of his great wickedness, nor because he was afraid of punishment in a future state, according to the usual representations of the pulpit. He was altogether too intelligent and noble to be actuated by a principle so debasing. His was a mind singularly earnest, honest, and conscientious. He met the final scene in this brief drama of existence with an unshaken equanimity, and expired as calmly as an infant falls to sleep in its mother's arms. I go so far as to say, that he left the world in the exercise of a humble and Christian spirit. As he was breathing his last, the image conveyed in the following stanza was forcibly impressed on my mind: —

> "How sweet the scene when good men die,
>   When noble souls retire to rest!
> How mildly beams the closing eye,
>   How calmly heaves th' expiring breast!
> So fades a summer cloud away;
>   So sinks a gale, when storms are o'er;
> So gently shuts the eye of day;
>   So dies a wave along the shore."

In all my experiences, I never saw an unbeliever die in fear. I have seen them expire, of course, without any hopes or expectations, but never in agitation from dread, or misgivings as to what might befall them hereafter. I know that clergymen generally assert that this final event passes with some dreadful visitation of unknown, inconceivable agony, over the soul of the departing sinner. It is imagined that in his case the pangs of dissolution are dreadfully aggravated by the upbraidings of a guilty conscience, and by the unwillingness, the reluctance of the spirit to be torn with ruthless violence from its mortal tenement, and hurried by furies into the presence of an avenging Judge. But this is all a picture of superstitious fancy. It is probable that I have seen a greater number of those called irreligious persons breathe their last, than any clergyman in the United States. Before they get sick, the unacclimated are often greatly alarmed; but when the enemy seizes them, and their case is hopeless, they invariably either lose their reason, or become calm, composed, fearless, and happy. This fact is a striking illustration of the benevolence of our Creator. If men's minds were not disturbed by false and miserable teachings, they would not suffer in death any more than they do when they fall asleep at night. Death is called a sleep in Scripture. "Death is the sleep of the weary. It is repose — the body's repose, after the busy and toilsome day of life is over." Even the convulsive struggles of the dying are not attended with pain, any more than the sobs and groans with which we sometimes sink into the slumbers of nightly rest. This is proved by the testimony of those who have been resuscitated after they became cold and pulseless, and restored again to life and breath. Their agonies were all seeming, not real, they tell us.

Persons without religion often die uttering words which indicate what are their strongest earthly loves or attachments, their "ruling passion." A young man of my acquaintance was once in that stage of the yellow fever superinduced by the beginning of mortification. Then the patient is free from pain, sometimes joyous, and very talkative. The individual I am speaking of was perfectly enamoured of novel reading. One of Walter Scott's romances was daily expected in New Orleans. Not many minutes before his death, it was brought to his bed by a friend whom he had sent to procure it. It was placed in his hands, but he was no longer able to see printing. The pages of the book, and the faces of his friends, were growing dim around him. He exclaimed, "I am blind; I cannot see; I must be dying; must I leave this new production of immortal genius unread?" His last thought was dictated by his favorite pursuit and passion. Men must carry into the other world the character which they possess at the moment of death.

I knew another gentleman, whose admiration for the Emperor Napoleon amounted to a monomania. He had collected all the biographies, histories, and other works tending to illustrate his life and character. This one theme had taken such exclusive possession of his mind, that he could neither think nor converse on any other subject. He was taken with the yellow fever. I went to see him when he was near his end. I took him by the hand, and hardly had time to speak, before he asked me what I thought of the moral character of Napoleon. The gentlemen standing by could not suppress a smile. I replied, that according to the representations of Las Casas, and others most intimately acquainted with him, Bonaparte was a firm believer in God, a divine providence, Jesus Christ, and immortality; and that it gave me great pleasure to believe in the correctness of their statements. He was of course delighted with the answer given. I read from the Bible. I then asked him if there were any particular subjects or favors which he would have embraced in my prayer. He answered, "There is but one blessing which I crave of Infinite Goodness — that after death, I may be conducted to those celestial regions where I can enjoy the sight and society of the greatest and best man who has lived — the late Emperor of France." Poor man! He could think of no higher, no nobler destiny.

It would be well were all to remember that great, glorious thoughts, habitually cherished, spontaneously fill the mind in a dying hour, to bear it aloft and buoyant over the dark gulf.

In all my experiences in New Orleans, I have met with no dying persons who were terrified, except church members who had been brought up in the Trinitarian faith. Let me not be misunderstood. I do not mean to insinuate that these individuals were not good Christians. They were perfectly sincere, and this very sincerity was the cause of their fear and apprehensions. One, to whom I allude, embraced the Calvinistic doctrine of election. He was a just, conscientious, most excellent man. I knew him intimately. His last words were, "I have no hope; all is dark. There is a bare possibility that I may be saved." This was the language of honesty. For he held that salvation would be conferred upon only a part of mankind, elected to this destiny by a decree of God — eternal, immutable, and altogether irrespective of character and works, and all the remainder would be doomed to eternal woe, without any regard to their merit or demerit. No honest man, with such a creed, could die without the greatest dread and anxiety. For if God has inflexibly determined to destroy a portion of his children, however pure and good they may be, no one can know absolutely, from his character, that he is among the saved; no one can feel certain of enjoying final, everlasting happiness.

When I first entered the clerical profession, I was struck with the utter insufficiency of most forms of Christianity to afford consolation in a dying hour. Paul says, the revelation of Jesus was given "to deliver those, who, through fear of death, were all their lifetime subject to bondage." Ancient pagan literature invariably represents death as the greatest calamity of human existence; it was denominated the stern, terrible, insatiate, cold, bitter, merciless "foe." It was the avenue to an eternal night; where the fair, the venerated, and the loved would be lost beyond recovery. If all this were true, we might justly say, "Speak not to us of consolation; there *is* no consolation; there is no support for such a lot as ours; nothing but dulness can bear it; nothing but stupidity can tolerate it; and nothing but idiocy could be indifferent to it." Jesus came into the world to announce the sublime doctrine that no one ever was, or ever will be, injured by death; that death is not so much as the interruption of existence; that death, indeed, is only death in appearance, while in reality the spirit's life is progressive, ever continued, and immortal.

Whoever, then, advocates those views of death, the belief of which tends to make its recipients afraid to die, ignores the messages of the gospel on this momentous theme. The great prominent truth of the Bible is, that, in every instance, " the day of one's death is better than the day of his birth." All these efforts to make death a scarecrow, to frighten men into the church, are as low and debasing as they are irrational and anti-Christian. Death is not the enemy, but the friend, of man.

Not the blue sky, not the richest landscape, not the flowers of spring, not all the charms of music, poetry, eloquence, art, or literature, present to our contemplation any thing so lovely and magnificent as death and its consequences, viewed through the telescope of the New Testament. Yet almost all the clergy, for fifteen hundred years, have employed their utmost genius, learning, and oratory to portray, in colors so appalling, that nobody who believes them can think upon the grave but with the deepest dread, dejection, and horror. It would be quite as wise to bring up our children atheists, as to corrupt their minds with the apprehension that the dissolution of the body may conduct them to everlasting evil. It would be better, safer every way, for our children to believe in annihilation, than in endless misery.

In the cholera of June, 1833, the disease first invaded our own family circle. Two daughters, the eldest four, and the youngest two years of age, died about the same time. I was so fortunate as to procure a carriage, in which their bodies were conveyed to a family vault, in the Girod cemetery, which had been constructed and presented to me, some years before, by the trustees of Christ Church, Canal Street — a church characterized for large, generous, and noble sympathies. I rode in the carriage alone with the two coffins. There was not a soul present but myself, to aid in performing the last sad offices. Most desolate and heavy was my heart, at the thought that they had left us to come back no more, —

> "No more would run to lisp their sire's return,
> Or climb his knees the envied kiss to share."

The chastening hand of the great Ordainer was so heavy upon me, that, chilled and discouraged, I should have sunk into the gulf of utter scepticism, without the supporting hope of meeting the lost and loved ones again, in a brighter and better world.

CHAPTER VII.

CHANGE IN MY THEOLOGICAL OPINIONS AND STYLE OF PREACHING. — LIBERAL COURSE PURSUED BY THE CONGREGATION, WITH RESPECT TO THESE MODIFICATIONS. — GENEROUS MANNER IN WHICH I WAS TREATED BY MY PRESBYTERIAN AND OTHER TRINITARIAN BRETHREN IN THE MINISTRY.

It is a truism among all the learned of the present day, that religious faith is produced by influences which we can neither create nor destroy. An honest man is no more accountable for his belief than he is for the movements of his heart and lungs, the features of his face, color of his hair. In general, it may be said that faith is the result of evidence. In some cases, it is brought about through those exercises of the mind which are by nature unavoidable. Thus faith in a great First Cause, in the existence of the soul, in justice, and immortality, is inseparable from human nature. It is not less essential to man, than to possess the prerogatives of perception, speech, memory, hope, fear, and desire. But many forms of faith are created by one's voluntary efforts. For example: faith in the Bible, in phrenology, mesmerism, homœopathy, democratic institutions, the Copernican system, geology, &c., is acquired by observation, study, and research.

In examining and weighing the facts and evidence appertaining to these subjects, one may be fair or unfair, just or unjust, impartial or prejudiced. If a man investigate Christianity itself, with no other motive than an earnest and sincere desire to obtain the truth, and honestly comes to the conclusion that it is false, he is not to blame for such a conclusion. He cannot help it any more than he can avoid the belief that two are less than eight.

When I entered the ministry, many of my opinions, though sincerely held, rested only on the principle of implied faith, or authority. In New Orleans, I had to encounter just, wise, and noble men, belonging to each of the different denominations in Christendom. For some years after my settlement, I was invited, almost every Sabbath, to preach on some particular subject. This fact imposed upon me the necessity of looking into the foundation of many doctrines, whose truth I had always before taken for granted. Hence I became a very hard student. When not engaged in out-door vocations, I was constantly occupied with my books and studies, in order to prepare myself for a wide and almost boundless range of pulpit discussion.

One day, it was incumbent to prove that Samson actually lived, and performed the extraordinary feats recorded in the book of Judges. The next Sunday, I was called to explain the cherubim and the four wheels, in the first chapter of Ezekiel, or the deluge, or the destruction of the Canaanites, or Jonah and the fish, or the case of Shadrach, Meshech, and Abednego, who came out unhurt from the midst of the burning, fiery furnace. Every biblical difficulty was brought to me for solution, and it was my especial province to elucidate all the dogmas which have been professedly derived from the sacred volume since the days of Tertullian. I noticed, indeed, no invitations but those which had the stamp of respectable names, and such as I had reason to believe were dictated by a worthy desire to obtain knowledge, and promote the advancement of Christian truth. These efforts to meet the wants of those who had a right to call on me for spiritual information enlarged my views, changed and rectified many of the opinions which had been imbibed from venerable teachers, and opened to me wonders and beauties which I never should have seen, had my life been passed in the regular, quiet, prescribed routine of ministerial duties in a New England parish.

I will illustrate this remark by relating an incident. The only university in Louisiana, at the time of my settlement there, was located in New Orleans. From the beginning, all the presidents, professors, and officers of the institution, had been of French extraction, either Creoles or foreigners. One of the most popular and efficient members of the board of administrators was an English gentleman, of splendid talents and acquirements. It was his wish to place some northern man at the head of this college, " in order," as he said, " to Americanize its usages, studies, and course of discipline."

The pastor of the Presbyterian church was recommended to him as a person qualified to fill the office. This was done without my knowledge or consent. It happened in the spring of 1824, Judge W. — the gentleman above mentioned — came to church one

Sunday morning to hear me preach, not (as he afterwards said) because he felt any interest about my religious tenets, but to form a general estimate of my abilities as an orator and scholar. The subject of the sermon on that occasion was the horrid dogma of endless punishment. It was taken up at the particular request of a lady, whose husband undisguisedly and strongly repudiated the doctrine. She said that he was a model of every virtue that could adorn home or society at large, but all this would be of no avail, unless he became a disciple of Christ. To become a Christian, and to embrace the Calvinistic creed, were things, in her judgment, perfectly coincident. For myself, I then thought that the doctrine of eternal suffering was true, and that a belief of it exerted a most salutary influence on the heart and life of its recipient. "Most happy," said the good lady, "shall I be, if you succeed in reconciling my husband to this solemn, sublime article of the Christian faith."

At the outset, I told the hearers that this doctrine was inexplicable to human reason ; that it was based entirely on the authority of revelation. So I confined myself simply to a rehearsal of those texts, which, as I imagined, taught the eternity of future woe. After the audience had dispersed, Judge W. remained, and was introduced to me. We walked home together. I found him learned, liberal, polished, and courtly in his manners. In the course of our conversation he remarked that he had once studied the subject on which I had been preaching, with special attention. It happened thus: After leaving the university, he endeavored to prepare himself for taking *holy orders* in the Episcopal church. But it was out of his power to find the doctrines of the Trinity, the vicarious atonement, endless punishment, plenary inspiration, and some other articles in the Bible. He therefore abandoned the idea of obtaining ordination, and became a student in one of the Inns of Court, London. Judge W. was a superior linguist, and well versed in the original Scriptures.

When parting with me that morning, he said, " Mr. Clapp, I have a particular favor to ask. You told us in the sermon just delivered that there are hundreds of texts in the Bible which affirm, in the most unqualified terms, that all those who die in their sins will remain impenitent and unholy through the ages of eternity. I will thank you to make me out a list of those texts in the original Hebrew and Greek. That some of such an import occur in our English version is undeniable; but I think they are mistranslations. I do not wish to put you to the trouble of multiplying Scripture proofs touching this point. Two, five, or ten will be amply sufficient." I replied, " Judge, it will give me great pleasure to grant your request. I can furnish you with scores of them before next Sunday." He smiled, saying, " I do not deny it," and politely bade me good morning. I was perfectly confident that the judge would be convinced that he had most egregiously misunderstood and misinterpreted the word of God. I rejoiced in the thought of his speedy discomfiture.

> "For fools rush in where angels fear to tread;
> Distrustful sense with modest caution speaks;
> It still looks home, and short excursions makes;
> But rattling nonsense in full volleys breaks,
> And never shocked, and never turned aside,
> Bursts out, resistless, with a thundering tide."

The very next day, Monday, before going out, I made, as I thought, the best arrangements for collecting the *proof texts* which had been solicited. A table was set in one corner of my study, well furnished with the appropriate books — lexicons, Hebrew and Greek, concordances, commentaries, English, Latin, and German, with standard works on the Pentateuch, the history and antiquities of the Jewish nation. I had no authorities in my library but those which were of the highest repute among Trinitarians of every denomination. With the help of Gaston's Collections and the references in the Larger Catechism of the Presbyterian Church, the access was easy to all the passages of Scripture which are relied on to prove the doctrine of endless sin and sorrow.

I began with the Old Testament in Hebrew, comparing it as I went along with the Septuagint and English version. I hardly ever devoted less than an hour each day to this branch of my studies, and often I gave a whole morning to it. Having been elected to the presidency of the New Orleans college, I was in the enjoyment of constant intercourse with Judge W. Almost every week he inquired, "Have you discovered yet the *proof texts* which you promised to give me?" I replied, "No, judge, I am doing my best to find them, and will accommodate you at as early a period as possible." During that and the succeeding year I read critically every chapter and verse of the Hebrew Scriptures, from Genesis to Malachi. My investigations were as thorough and complete as I could possibly make them. Yet I was unable to find therein so much as an allusion to any suffering at all after death. In the dictionary of the Hebrew language I could not discover a word signifying *hell*, or a place of punishment for the wicked in a future state. In the Old Testament Scriptures there is not, as I believe, a single text, in any form of phraseology, which holds out to the finally impenitent threats of retribution beyond the grave. To my utter astonishment, it turned out that orthodox critics of the greatest celebrity were perfectly familiar with these facts. I was compelled to confess to my friend that I could not adduce any Hebrew exegesis in support of the sentiment that evil is eternal.

Still, I was sanguine in my expectations that the New Testament would furnish me with the arguments which I had sought for without success in the writings of Moses and the prophets. I scrutinized, time and again, whatever in the Gospels, the Acts, and the Epistles, are supposed to have any bearings upon the topic, for the space of eight years. The result was, that I could not name a portion of New Testament Scripture, from the first verse of Matthew to the last of the Apocalypse, which, fairly interpreted, affirms that a part of mankind will be eternally miserable. But the opposite doctrine, that all men will be ultimately saved, is taught in scores of texts, which no art of disingenuous interpretation can explain away. Here I should say that at the time above mentioned I had never seen or read any of the writings of the Unitarian or Universalist divines, not even those of Dr. Channing, with the exception, perhaps, of one or two occasional discourses that had been sent to me through the post office. During the whole ten years my studies were confined to the original Hebrew and Greek Scriptures, and the various subsidiary works which are required for their elucidation. My simple, only object was to ascertain what "*saith the Lord*" concerning the final destination of the wicked. It is an important, most instructive fact, that I was brought into my present state of mind by the instrumentality of the Bible only — a state of mind running counter to all the prejudices of early life, of parental precept, of school, college, theological seminary, and professional caste.

My circumstances at the time furnish conclusive proof that I could not have been actuated by any selfish, mercenary, or improper motives whatever. I was well aware how much was hazarded by venturing to interpret the Bible for myself; that the public proclamation of the results which had been forced upon me would call down the severest anathemas of the church; that, naked and almost alone, I should encounter the bristling spears of that large army, which, though it repudiates the use of the wheel, the rack, and gibbet, still employs, for the purpose of preventing free inquiry, the more cruel engines of scorn, contempt, obloquy, and misrepresentation. It is sad to think that if in this land of boasted freedom a clergyman feels bound, in conscience, to interpret the Scriptures differently from the majority of the denomination to which he belongs, it is impossible to follow his private judgment without imperilling his good name, his standing in the ministry, and even his *Christian character*, without being driven like chaff before the storm of popular prejudice and persecuting clamor.

From this account the reader will perceive my meaning, in the remark that faith is, in a great measure, produced by causes which are entirely above and beyond human control. In March, 1824, it became my duty in the pulpit to avow a faith which ten years afterwards I was compelled by the providence of Almighty God to repudiate. I say *Divine Providence* constrained me to adopt this course; for my introduction to Judge W., his coming to hear me preach, the particular theme discussed on that occasion, the request which led to a new and thorough examination of the Scriptures, and to a decided revolution in my theological views, were the appointments of the Infinite Intelligence. As a parent takes his feeble, tottering child by the hand, when treading a rough, difficult path, so Heaven was pleased to guide me through the mazes of error and superstition, in which I had wandered from childhood, into the broad, beautiful fields of evangelical truth.

On the first Sabbath of July, 1834, I proclaimed distinctly from the pulpit, for the first time, my firm conviction that the Bible does not teach the doctrine of eternal punishment. It was the happiest day that I had ever experienced. I felt that now I could vindicate the ways of God to man. I felt that revealed religion, like the stars of the firmament, reflected the glories of our Creator. I kept repeating to myself for weeks the following lines: —

> "And darkness and doubt are flying away;
> No longer I roam in conjecture forlorn;
> So breaks on the traveller, faint and astray,
> The bright and the balmy effulgence of morn.
> See Truth, Love, and Mercy in triumph descending,
> And nature all glowing in Eden's first bloom;
> On the cold cheek of death smiles and roses are blending,
> And beauty immortal awakes from the tomb."

Some of my friends wonder that I should be so much attached to New Orleans. One reason is, that it is endeared by those sacred associations which assure me that my origin is divine, and my destination eternal life. It is natural that I should love a place where I was permitted, for the first time, to catch glimpses and revelations of the infinitely Beautiful — where, amid perplexities, discouragement, and despair, the Holy Spirit came to my relief, and enabled me to gaze upon the outspreading glories of an everlasting, universal Father, the unchanging, almighty Friend of man, however low, fallen, dark, or depraved; the place where, in the twinkling of an eye, I became a new man, was born again, and with indescribable rapture looked out upon another and more glorious universe than that which addresses the senses.

Yes, it was in the Crescent City, (and I can never forget it,) not in my native place, not in New Haven, Boston, or Andover, but in New Orleans, where I learned to take shelter from all the ills with which earth can assail us, under the brooding wings of Ineffable Goodness. Yes, there, amid " the pestilence that walketh in darkness and the destruction that wasteth at noonday," it was my privilege to feel the heart of Infinite Love beating close to my heart, and to be assured that it will throb forever through all the pulses of my mental and deathless being. Can I ever forget the place or time when I actually felt the arms of everlasting Power, Wisdom, and Beneficence clasping me about as the fond mother hugs the babe to her bosom to soothe its grief and hush its sighs? To me the mysterious problem of life was solved on the banks of the Mississippi. There I was first led to repose on the bosom of my God, and to say, " Thou wilt guide me with thy counsel, and at last receive me into glory. Whom have I in heaven but thee, and whom on earth do I love in comparison with thee? Though my flesh and my heart fail, God is the strength of my heart, and my portion forever. My soul thirsts, longs, lives, prays, and toils to become one with thee, for assimilation to thee, for the constant unfolding and enlarging of those mental powers which constitute thy glorious image."

As it is natural to be thrilled at sight of the widely extended prairie, the firmament of heaven, or the boundless expanse of the ocean, so the heart remembers the spot where it was first warmed and lifted up by those unfailing hopes, which, crossing the gulf of death, the line of time, and the boundaries of the visible creation, connect our fates and fortunes with the wide, boundless scenes of an imperishable hereafter. I can recall a single day, in New Orleans, during which I received an amount of happiness more than sufficient to counterbalance all the sufferings of my life; nay, more, which enabled me to regard these very sufferings as instruments by which Heaven is working out for me kinds and degrees of good inconceivably great and glorious. But this spiritual enjoyment to which I allude never entered my soul until I had been brought to see that God is incapable of destroying his own children, or, which is the same thing, allowing them to be destroyed. One of an opposite faith may be a very sincere Christian, but he can no more taste the peculiar delight which I am now speaking of, than a blind man can perceive the beauties of the rainbow.

In conjunction with a more thorough knowledge of the Scriptures, the peculiar events of my professional career had an extensive influence in modifying and changing the theological opinions which had been imbibed in New England. It was among the sick, prostrate, and suffering that the true interpretation of the Bible began to dawn upon my mind. I felt that the teachings of nature, providence, and grace must be harmonious. I had been reading books from a child, but as yet had not studied profoundly the mysteries of human life. Upon the principles of faith acquired at Andover, I saw the crowds around me hurried, by an unseen, resistless power, through the ordinances and appointments; the sudden alternations of health, sickness, prosperity, and adversity; the scenes of endurance, privation, and disappointment; the painful sunderings of the ties of friendship, affinity, and affection; and the other indescribable vicissitudes, fates, fortunes, and trials, which are condensed into the short span of this momentous existence between the cradle and the tomb, only as preparatory to a final residence in the dark regions of inconceivable, unbounded, and hopeless ruin. The more I thought upon the subject, the more deeply was the idea impressed, that such a destiny was utterly irreconcilable with infinite love. I used often to say, "If God be our Father, could he expose us to an evil that has no limits, and which no finite power can avert?" It was conceded on all sides that we could not save ourselves.

The very best are more or less sinful and unworthy at the moment of death. No degree of virtue, then, attainable on earth, can prepare us for immortal blessedness. True, I had heard, all my life, that the only basis of salvation spoken of in the gospel was the grace of God through Christ. But the doctrine had been uniformly presented to my mind in such a shape, and with such surroundings, that I had never discerned its genuine character and bearings. Constantly was I reminded that we could do nothing towards saving ourselves, and yet, at the same time that faith, repentance, and holiness before death, were the indispensable prerequisites to eternal life. Upon this ground, it appeared to me self-evident that the vast majority of my fellow-beings must perish everlastingly. No hopes could be rationally entertained for the final deliverance even of those who die idiots, or those who sink into the grave during the period of infancy.

Whilst in this state of perplexity and distress, I was called one afternoon to visit a remarkably interesting young man, sick of the yellow fever. I had often met him in company, and enjoyed his conversation. Every body admired him for his extraordinary talents, and the moral charms of his life and character. One of the deacons of the church happened to be in my study when I was sent for, and being an intimate acquaintance of the afflicted family, he accompanied me to the sick room. The usual services were performed. Within five minutes afterwards he expired. The mother uttered shrieks of grief and despair, enough to melt a heart of adamant. I tried to make some soothing remarks, but she refused to be comforted. As she was a communicant of the church, and beyond all question a very pious lady, I referred her to the inexhaustible riches of a Saviour's mercy.

"But the mercy of God," she replied, "is limited. Our beloved James is now, I fear, in a world where the blessings of a Creator's love will never be known. He was noble, kind-hearted, faithful, true, and good, but he was not religious. A few days ago he told me that he did not believe in the Trinity; that in his opinion the Son of God was inferior, subordinate to, and dependent on the Father. Dying with such sentiments, how can I entertain the faintest hope of ever meeting him in a better world?"

I replied very promptly, and perhaps with too much warmth, "Madam, in the unseen world, the catechism of our church is not the criterion by which persons will be acquitted or condemned. You say your son was honest, and most exemplary in the discharge of all his duties. What more could he have done? If he is lost, who then can be saved?"

"Do you mean to intimate," she inquired, "that one who expires disbelieving the supreme divinity of Christ, will ever be admitted to the kingdom of heaven?"

"I hope so," was the answer; "nor do I read any thing in the New Testament which forbids such a hope." But this thought was more shocking than consolatory to her. In a few weeks she left our society, and went to another church. A purer, more affectionate, or conscientious woman I have never known; but the sentiment "had grown with her growth and strengthened with her strength," that the gospel holds out no promise of forgiveness and restoration to those who leave the world in error and unbelief. The reflection arose in my mind, "Can that be true religion, which represents death as a calamity so great and terrible, that it excludes, of necessity, a great part of mankind from entertaining even the hope of a better and blessed life beyond the grave?"

As we were returning home, my friend the elder remarked that it seemed to him quite unaccountable that *infinite* mercy should be limited by any thing whatever — by time, nature, space, death, human folly, or corruption. "Can *Infinite Mercy* be gratified if a single child be left to wander forever in sin and unhappiness? Has this young man gone to a world where he will have no further opportunities of acquiring truth and becoming holy? Was such a doctrine really taught by Jesus Christ? How dark and desolate, then, the prospects of that future state! But I suppose it must be so. The clergy ought to understand this subject." These questions opened for me the way to another field of inquiry, analogous, indeed, to the one I had been exploring so long, but of a somewhat different phase.

Reaching my study, I took down Cruden's Concordance to the Holy Scriptures, and turned to the word *probation*. To my great surprise, I found that there was no such word in the Bible. Yet the following phrase is contained in almost every sermon: "*Probation* will end with the present life." I had heard Dr. Woods assert that if a man's accountable existence on earth was not more than twelve months, in this short space of time he must establish a good character, or he would be eternally ruined. No opportunity will be afforded a person after death to qualify himself for a happy immortality. It struck me that nothing could be more absurd than the sentiment that Infinite Wisdom had endued us with the capacity of an endless being, in which there could be no progression after the dissolution of the body. I had already prepared a complete list of the passages adduced in support of the doctrine of everlasting woe. They were constantly spread out on my table, like a map or chart which a ship master consults in navigating his vessel through difficult and dangerous waters. I looked them over and over most carefully, through the winter of 1833 and 1834, to see if they contained the affirmation, or any thing which in the remotest degree savored of it, that the state of man in the present life is *probationary* — a season of moral trial, upon the proper improvement or abuse of which depends our eternal weal. I found not a Bible argument in support of this dogma. On the contrary, I read therein that " God doth not punish forever, neither is his displeasure eternal. For as high as heaven is above earth, so great is his mercy. As far as the east is from the west, so far hath he removed our transgressions from us. He will not deal with us according to our sins, nor reward us according to our iniquities. Even as a father pitieth his children, so doth the Lord pity the sons of men. For he knoweth our frame, he remembereth that we are dust. As for man, his days are as grass; as a flower of the field, so he flourisheth. The wind passeth over it, and it is gone, and the place thereof shall know it no more. But the mercy of the Lord is from everlasting to everlasting, and his goodness to children's children. God is rich in mercy, plenteous in mercy, delights in mercy. Mercy shall triumph over justice. He will not afflict forever, because he delighteth in mercy. He is gracious and full of compassion, infinite, immutable, and everlasting in his benevolence. Mortality shall be swallowed up of life;" and so on to an indefinite extent.

How large, how cheering, how magnificent are these views of man's ultimate destiny! In the theory of theologians, the grace of God is jejune, narrow, circumscribed, inefficient, conditional, contingent, liable to be frustrated by the obstinacy, blindness, follies, whims, and caprice of feeble, fallible, erring, and unhappy mortals. In the Bible, it is an impartial, universal, almighty, ever-living, ever-present tenderness; a sea of compassion, in which all the guilt, sin, and unworthiness of our race will be lost and absorbed as a drop of rain is lost, when it falls into the ocean, and is seen no more.

Having reached what seemed to me an important crisis in my theological career, I could not reconcile it with the principles of honor to conceal from the church the new phases of my spiritual position. For ten years I had been employed in revising my faith. I had searched the Scriptures anew, unbiased by fear or hope, in regard to the final results. All this was done in the sacred seclusion of my heart and study, alone with God, and the enrapturing beauties of divine, eternal truth. There was no clerical nor lay friend with whom I could converse with respect to the new direction of my researches, and their effect in enlarging my intellectual and moral horizon.

Besides, it appeared to me wrong to communicate to others the change of sentiments towards which I was drifting, until they had assumed the shape of clear, full, and undoubting convictions. No doubt a sagacious, observing, regular attendant on my ministry might have detected the fact that I was not standing still, — that I was passing through a mental revolution of some kind or other. An intelligent Presbyterian — a noble, generous, constant hearer — said to me one day, "There has been of late a great alteration in your style of preaching; I cannot divine the cause." In reply, I said, "I am not conscious of any such change. Will you be so good as to describe your impressions touching the matter?"

He answered me thus: "In your addresses to sinners, your tone is more mild, gentle, and persuasive than formerly. It seems as if you do not look upon their guilt as quite so awful and aggravated as it is represented to be in the Bible. I want to have you speak to these godless, desperate men in your old-fashioned way. You should lighten, anathematize, and pour out upon them the denunciations of an offended Heaven. You should speak to them oftener of the horrors of that future world, *where the fire is not quenched, and the worm never dies.*"

During this transition, I had no books to aid me, written by liberal divines. And really I did not require them. Among all the Unitarian and Universalist writings which I have seen, no work, as to expansion or liberality of spirit and sentiment, is comparable with the New Testament, especially the Sermon on the Mount, the Acts, and the Epistles. Finding myself firmly fixed in the new views to which I have alluded, I determined to state them explicitly from the pulpit. Accordingly, on the first Sabbath of July, 1834, I arose in my place after prayer, and remarked, " that I could no longer believe in, avow, teach, or defend, the peculiar doctrines of the Presbyterian church." These doctrines were specified as follows: *particular election, the vicarious atonement, original sin, physical inability, and endless punishment.*

It was said that I was unable to find these sentiments in the Bible; that my reason ignored them; and that hereafter I should deem it my duty to wage against them, both in and out of the pulpit, a war of utter extermination. I then selected the subject of future punishment as the theme of my homily at that particular time. My discourse was unwritten, though I had before me copious notes of Scripture references. In conclusion, I gave them my new creed, in plain, simple, unambiguous terms.

I will here transcribe it. "There are not three persons in the Godhead; there is but one Being in the universe, of infinite, uncreated power, wisdom, and love — the Father of all mankind, the Father of a boundless majesty. Jesus Christ was not merely a teacher, exemplar, martyr, for the truth, but he was literally and verily *God manifest in the flesh — officially*, not actually a God. He came to enlighten, forgive, and sanctify all men; to immortalize the race; to carry them buoyant over death to the fellowship of saints and angels in glory. He knows all hearts, and in the redemption of mankind, performs actions which require divine attributes; so that we are certain that God was in Christ Jesus, (as there is a finite spirit in my body, now speaking to you,) 'reconciling the world unto himself, not imputing to men their trespasses.'

"All mankind are brethren, equally dear in the sight of God, and will eventually be saved by the renewal of their hearts through faith, repentance, holiness, and the forgiving grace of which Jesus Christ is the channel and dispenser. In this life, men are under a system of perfectly just and equitable rewards and punishments. No sin can ever be forgiven, until he who committed it has suffered a deserved retribution, and heartily repented of the same.

"Pure religion and undefiled consists in loving God with all the heart, and our neighbor as ourselves. It is happily expressed by the three terms *piety*, *purity*, and *disinterestedness* — proper feelings towards God, holiness of life, love, and kindness, and brotherly affection for all.

"The Holy Scriptures are the record of a divine inspiration. By inspiration, I mean a supernatural influence, which qualifies its recipient to set forth moral and religious truths, free from material, fatal, or essential errors. These articles constitute the platform on which I now stand, and hope to maintain so long as I live.

> 'He who these duties shall perform,
> Faithful, and with an honest heart,
> Shall safely ride through every storm,
> And find, indeed, that better part.'"

The principles embraced in the above creed are my faith to-day, essentially, and have been for the last twenty-two years.

When I came out of church, my friends gathered round me, especially the trustees and elders of the society. They were all astonished; some were pleased; many were alarmed; but none were offended. One of the most influential members present remarked, "Mr. Clapp, I cannot subscribe to the declaration which you have made this morning, but I think you have taken the only right, honorable course. You have shown your colors; you have frankly avowed your real sentiments; we know who you are, and on what to depend, and what you mean to teach in future. But I am afraid that, if the truth be on your side, you are at least fifty years in advance of the age. Christians in general will struggle desperately, and a long time, before they will part with the doctrines which you have openly rejected. Consequently, those of us who adhere to you will be branded, all over the United States, as errorists and dangerous heretics." Others addressed me in terms equally kind, noble, and forbearing. Nothing of a bigoted, scornful, censorious, or self-righteous spirit was manifested. Indeed, New Orleans is the most tolerant place in Christendom. All the misrepresentations abroad touching my character and opinions have been set afloat by strangers and non-residents.

Before this out-door assembly dispersed, it was proposed to postpone all action on the subject till I had delivered a course of sermons on this new gospel, as it was called. To this I joyfully acceded. I commenced the very next Sabbath, and kept on uninterruptedly till Christmas. My congregation gave me a fair, candid hearing, and said repeatedly that they would support me if convinced that I was right, however much it might subject them to public odium and unpopularity. The members of my society were singularly independent. With them, the authority of great names did not amount to much — " names which serve to guide the multitude as the bellwether guides his willing, faithful sheep, all of which will jump just as high as he does, even after he has knocked the fence flat on the ground." To pursue calmly, honestly, the investigation of truth in its most retired, latent recesses; to confess it when it is in disgrace; to endure contempt and ridicule in its behalf; to suffer for it with a martyr's unflinching constancy, require a firmness, a greatness of soul, a superiority to all selfish considerations, which is the very essence of moral heroism.

My friends supported me with an undaunted, unshaken, unwearied resolution. Most of them are now gone. Forever fresh and sacred will be their memories in my heart. They have their reward. Only a small number at that time — I think not more than half a dozen — left me; but a great many more joined the society on account of the stand which I had taken. It is natural for free men to love a free church, whose spirit is as wide and expansive as the heavens over us. And the seceders, too, were good men, true and conscientious. Those of them who are living at this day are my warm, steady, faithful friends. Indeed, I did not make an enemy by my Declaration of Religious Independence. Those who most dissented from me in opinion respected my candor and fairness. Here, as in every other department, it holds true that "honesty is the best policy." Those clergymen make a fatal mistake who suppose that an honest avowal of their opinions, however latitudinarian they may be, will detract a particle from their good standing in the public estimation — will lessen in any considerable degree their influence and usefulness, or diminish the number of their friends and patrons.

Many persons have thought that the doings of the Mississippi presbytery towards me in the emergency just spoken of were cruel, bitter, and vindictive. This opinion I could not indorse without many qualifications and apologies for my opponents. With one exception, I believe that all the members of that body, in their measures with respect to myself, and the church over which I presided, were actuated by pure and worthy motives. The relations between us had been most cordial and friendly. They felt no hostility to me personally, but were alarmed at what appeared to them the shocking errors into which I had fallen, and was endeavoring, by all means in my power, to propagate. Had I been in one of their places, I should have acted just as they did. I concede to others the same rights which I claim for myself.

A clergyman of great celebrity passed through New Orleans in the autumn of 1834. He called to see me, and spent several hours in my study. In the course of our conversation, he said, "Depend upon it, the doctrine of *God's infinite, eternal wrath* is a main pillar in the gospel of our Lord. What is there in the Bible, as you interpret it, which is fitted to restrain, alarm, arouse, and convert the base, ignorant, hardened sinner?"

I replied, "The doctrine of endless woe, as I believe, since its first promulgation, has never prevented a single sin, a single species of crime, nor reformed a single sinner. On the contrary, it has operated, immeasurably, to multiply and increase the very mischiefs it was intended to suppress. To pure, conscientious persons it has been a rack of torture, a source of unutterable anxiety, gloom, and despair.

Instead of reclaiming the wicked from the paths of turpitude, it has made them more reckless, desperate, and depraved. The unfounded tenet that the Creator is capable of frowning upon his children forever, and following them with his curse and displeasure through interminable ages, for the sins committed in this frail, erring, imperfect state of existence, has contributed, more than all the other corruptions of Christianity combined, to swell that tide of vice, crime, and immoralities, which for ages has rolled its dark and troubled billows, foul as the recesses of the Stygian pit, across this footstool of Jehovah.

"To me it seems more corrupting than any other idea that has ever afflicted our weak, sinful, unhappy, and misguided race. It represents the Father of all as inexorable, a boundless fountain of cruelty itself, gives him a character darker than Erebus, and presents him in that light which must, of necessity, prevent the believers thereof from cherishing one sentiment of cordial affection for their Creator. And whoever does not love God will be sure to sin against him. The very thought of *almighty vengeance* is enough to cover earth with sackcloth, and spread over the face of heaven the gloom of absolute despair. We cannot be more perfect than the God whom we adore. Whatever we look upon as superior, we assimilate to. If we embrace a sentiment which represents the Creator as cruel, partial, or revengeful, this belief, in spite of ourselves, will tend to harden and destroy all the finer feelings and sensibilities of our nature; make us, though ever so sincere, sour, morose, exclusive, and bigoted ; and impart to our characters the most harsh, stern, and repulsive features. As the stream cannot rise higher than its fountain, so no one can surpass, in moral excellence, the Divinity at whose shrine he makes the continual offerings of supreme homage and adoration."

The clergyman continued, " By what arguments, motives, or inducements, then, do you expect to reclaim the erring, sinful, and incorrigible ? "

I answered, " They can be subdued by nothing but the power of gentleness, the melting influence of compassion, the omnipotence of love, the control of the mild over the turbulent and boisterous, the commanding majesty of that exalted character which mingles with disapprobation of the offence the sincerest pity for the offender. A depraved heart will yield to nothing but love." Let me illustrate my idea by relating a couple of anecdotes.

Some time ago, I was called to visit a man confined in the calaboose of this city for murder. He had been tried, and was condemned to be hanged. The sheriff of this parish was a very humane person, and always procured a priest or minister to repair to the cells of those who were about to suffer the death penalty. The individual I am speaking of had been reared in the Protestant faith ; so the duty devolved upon me to administer to him the consolations of religion. I found him intelligent, shrewd, but most fearfully hardened and reckless. I asked him if he entertained any expectation of being pardoned by the governor. I found that he had no hopes of this kind. When I urged upon him the importance of making some preparation for the great change he was to pass through so soon, I was met with the assertion that he wanted not the prayers, the instructions, or the counsels of any clergyman. "I know as much about the future world," said he, "as you do, and am qualified to do my own praying." I had the New Testament in my hands, but he refused to hear me read a word of it. He said that he had solicited the sheriff, as an especial favor, not to allow him to be annoyed by the intrusion of ministers of any denomination. He was a native of Europe, an educated, well-informed man, and a confirmed, scoffing atheist. Seeing that my presence was not agreeable to him, I rose to depart.

When I took him by the hand, he said, "I perceive that you are a sociable man. I feel very lonely, and should be most glad to see you often, if you will not obtrude upon me the subject of religion, which I utterly abhor." I promised to call every morning at ten o'clock, till the day fixed for his execution. Walking home, I said to myself, "There must be some good thing which this poor man loves. I will try to find out what it is, and make it the subject of some moralizing which will be agreeable to him, and perhaps may indirectly reach and soften his heart." When I visited him the next morning, I told him that I had not called as a clergyman, but as a *friend*, and should indeed be happy to say something that he could listen to with gratification and profit. I began the conversation by making some inquiries about his family. His mind at once reverted to his childhood, youth, and early home; his parents, brothers, and sisters; his first warm loves, and first bright hopes, ere he had wandered from innocence into the dark regions of sin and ruin. In a few moments he sobbed and wept like a child. I wept with him; it was impossible to refrain from it. The prisoner was a young man, not over twenty-five years of age. He had ardently loved a young lady of his native place, who was married to a rival, and he ascribed his fall to this disappointment.

When I left him that morning, he seemed to be a new being. His countenance had lost its haggard and ferocious aspect, and become humanized, mild, and gentle in expression. "Pray," said he, "bring to-morrow some book to read, which may help to divert me from the terrible thoughts that prey upon my heart." On the third day, I took along with me Campbell's Pleasures of Hope and Thomson's Seasons. In the space of twenty-four hours, his mind was so changed, that he said, "Sir, I am sorry for the manner in which I treated you during our first interview. I recant the declarations which I then made, and hope you will forget them. Last night I dreamed that I was in my native place and home. The rapture I enjoyed aroused me from my sleep to consciousness, and the bitter certainty that I shall never see that home again. O that I could cherish that hope of meeting my beloved relatives and friends once more! O, I shall lose my reason before the hour of punishment arrives! O, pray for me! O, teach me! Are there no powers above to pity and bless me?" I knelt down and offered a prayer, to which he heartily responded amen.

From that day forward, he gave himself up implicitly to my guidance and direction, and became, I believe, a sincere penitent. Yet not one word was ever said to him about the anger of God, or future punishment. The very morning that he was doomed to suffer the sentence of the law, I passed a good deal of time in his cell, besides witnessing the awful catastrophe. Among other things, he said, "If I had known from early life that God was my Father, that he truly loved me, as a devoted mother does the babe of her bosom, and desired only my present and everlasting welfare, I should have been saved from a sinful life, and from this shocking and ignominious fate."

I will mention another incident to illustrate the point, that genuine repentance chiefly springs not from fear, but from the thought of the horrible ingratitude towards Supreme Love which the commission of sin evinces. Several years ago there was a lady — a mother — residing in one of the Northern States, distinguished for her wealth, social position, and her religious character. She had a favorite son, for whose advancement in life great efforts had been made. But notwithstanding, he became a profligate and vagabond. I had known him in our school-boy days. The mother addressed to me a letter concerning her lost child. From the latest information, she believed that he was wandering in the Southern States, and besought me, if I should meet the hapless fugitive, to acquaint her with the facts, and extend to him such offices of kindness as I might judge expedient.

A few days after the receipt of this letter, the young prodigal made his appearance in New Orleans, and found his way to my study. He was in a most woful plight, both physically and morally. In manners he was rude, audacious, and grossly profane. He wanted money. "Money will do you no good," said I, "unless you reform your life." "Reform!" replied he; "'tis impossible; it is entirely too late. I have no hopes; I can never retrieve my steps. I have nothing to live for. I am the execration of all who know me. I have not a friend left in the wide world." On his saying this, I went to my desk, and took out the above-named letter from his mother. Showing him the superscription, I asked him if he knew the handwriting. He replied, with a changed, thoughtful air, "It is my dear mother's." I opened and read to him one paragraph only. In a moment he seemed as if struck by some unseen, resistless power. He sank down upon his chair, burst into tears, sobbed aloud, and convulsively exclaimed, "O God, forgive my base ingratitude to that beloved mother!"

Yes, the thought of that fond parent in a far distant and dishonored home, who cherished for him an undying affection, who overlooked all his baseness, who never failed to mingle his outcast name with her morning and evening prayers, saying, (and this was the sentence I read to him,) "O my heavenly Father, I beseech thee to preserve, forgive, and redeem my poor lost child; in thy infinite mercy be pleased to restore him to my embrace, and to the joys of sincere repentance;"—the thought of such tenderness broke his obdurate heart, and the waters of penitence gushed forth. To make a long narrative brief, from that hour he was a reformed man, and is now an inhabitant of his native place, shedding around him the blessed influences of a sober, useful, and exemplary life.

Now, I ask, what, probably, would have been the effect upon that young man's destiny if a letter from his mother had been read to him couched in a style directly the reverse — a letter which breathed only of scorn, indignation, wrath, hatred, and menace; which uttered only the harsh tones of bitter upbraidings, reproach, and denunciations? Would it not have operated to harden his heart still more? to have given increased vigor and intensity to his desperate passions, and to have plunged him hopelessly into the abyss of ruin and degradation?

If all sinners could be brought to see that the Father in heaven actually cherishes for them a tenderness infinitely greater than that of this mother for her son, that he truly pities them, and pleads with them to return, by all the wonders of Calvary and all the sufferings of Jesus, and that he wills nothing but their highest good, — however contemptuous, proud, haughty, selfish, and unfeeling they might be, they could never again lift the puny arm of rebellion and disobedience against a love so amazing, so boundless, and ineffable.

Love only can overcome evil. A man is not truly penitent in the highest degree till he can say, in the words of Paul, "For I am persuaded that neither death, nor life, nor angels, nor principalities, nor powers, nor things present, nor things to come" — no being, no event, no created thing, no enemy, not even my fearful guilt and unworthiness — shall be able finally and forever to separate me " from the love of God which is in Christ Jesus my Lord." Every thing else may fail; friends may die; the earth, with all that it contains, be dissolved; but the throne of Divine Love will remain unmoved. The waves of eternity may beat thereon; they have no power to weaken, overthrow, or sweep it away. The above scene has been described in words as like those which were actually uttered as my memory is able to recall. I can vouch only for the substantial truth of what is recorded in this chapter.

CHAPTER VIII.

EPIDEMICS OF 1837 AND 1853. — REMARKS ON THE POPULAR VIEWS AS TO THE INSALUBRITY OF NEW ORLEANS. — THE CAUSES OF YELLOW FEVER, AND ITS REMEDIES. — ITS BEARINGS ON THE MORALS OF THE CRESCENT CITY.

It is not necessary for the purpose of the present work that a detailed account, in chronological order, of the epidemics which I have witnessed in New Orleans should be spread before my readers. I have dwelt with some particularity on the great cholera of 1832. I have virtually passed through the same scenes of toil, anxiety, and suffering, at least twenty times. To describe my experiences minutely, during each of these periods of trial and hardship, would lead me into useless repetitions. I should only be exhibiting to spectators a succession of pictures of one uniform, unvaried, heart-sickening, and depressing gloom. There is a wonderful sameness in the sombre realities of the sick room, the death struggle, the corpse, the shroud, the coffin, the funeral, and the tomb.

Let me ask the reader to pause here a moment, whilst I attempt to suggest a general but very inadequate idea of my labors and sufferings in each of the campaigns above referred to. The term of a sickly season in New Orleans has never been less than six weeks. In a majority of cases it has extended from eight weeks to ten. In 1824 it began early in June, and did not entirely disappear till the November following. On an average, it is within bounds to say that the duration of each epidemic spoken of in these pages was at least eight weeks. Multiply eight by twenty, and the product is one hundred and sixty. Hence it follows that since my settlement in Louisiana I have spent over three entire years in battling, with all my might, against those invisible enemies, the cholera and yellow fever. In those three years I scarcely enjoyed a night of undisturbed repose. When I did sleep, it was upon my post, in the midst of the dead and wounded, with my armor on, and ready at the first summons to meet the deadly assault.

A gentleman of New Orleans, who was in the battle of the 8th January, 1815, on the plains of Chalmette, by which General Jackson became immortalized, was one of my neighbors during the first cholera. He stood his ground manfully *one day*. The next morning I saw him making all possible despatch to cross Lake Pontchartrain into Florida. As I was passing by to attend a funeral, he spoke to me thus: "I consider it no sign of cowardice, but common prudence, to run away from the enemy that is now desolating our city. On the battle ground, under Old Hickory, we could see the enemy, and measure him, and cope with and resist him, with visible, sure, and tangible means. But here is a foe that we cannot see, with his fatal scythe mowing down hundreds in a day. When contending against the British, also, we had this advantage; every night there was a complete cessation of hostilities; and by sound sleep we were recuperated, and awoke each morning ready for the struggles of another day." He then repeated the following stanza from Campbell: —

> "'Our bugles sang *truce*, for the night-cloud had lowered,
> And the sentinel stars set their watch in the sky,
> And thousands had sunk on the ground overpowered,
> The weary to sleep, and the wounded to die.'

"But this terrible conflict allows no truce. The enemy is as active at night as in the daytime. I have chartered a schooner, and shall be off with my family in a few moments. I have always had the reputation of being a man of nerve and courage. But you see now how pale and trembling I am. I can stand unblenching to receive the assault of sword, bayonet, musket or cannon balls; but this dark, unseen, infernal enemy makes me as feeble and timid as a child. I am afraid we shall be nabbed, some of us, at least, before we get into the pine woods. Farewell; I never expect to see you again."

But on his return at Christmas, he found me in good health, and learned, with surprise, that I had not experienced a day's illness all the preceding summer. Though this man was not a member of any church, and rather sceptical in his religious tendencies, he became one of the firmest friends and supporters I ever had in New Orleans. He used to say, "Mr. Clapp, I neither know nor care any thing about your theology, but I know that there is something in your bosom that makes you intrepid in times of peril, disaster, darkness, and death. I know, sir, that no array of terrors can drive you from the post of duty, and that, consequently, you are the very minister for New Orleans."

In addition, let the reader admit to his imagination another important particular, essential to even a *distant* and faint impression of the endurance allotted me in those " times that tried men's souls." The exercises of our minds in sleep and dreaming are determined, in a great measure, by the nature of our employments through the day. An agreeable day's work lays up a stock of delightful thoughts and sentiments for the silent, peaceful hours of the succeeding night. What, then, think you, must have been the images before my mind during that portion of each night, when an epidemic was prevailing, in which I attempted to sleep? As to perfectly sound, dreamless sleep, it was almost a total stranger to me. Under the most favorable circumstances, I could only doze; and the various sights, horrors, and shudderings of the previous day, or week, or month were constantly passing in review before me. In those disturbed hours I often talked aloud, or prayed over and soothed and encouraged the dying sufferer. At another time I would pronounce a soliloquy in view of some broken-down, scathed, and bereaved widow, with her fatherless children, and earnestly supplicate the blessing of Heaven in their behalf. If I had seen during the day an uncommonly severe case of agonizing and dying, the terrific image haunted me without intermission for a long time, awake or sleeping. Perhaps there is no acute disease actually less painful than yellow fever, although there is none more shocking and repulsive to the beholder. Often I have met and shook hands with some blooming, handsome young man to-day, and in a few hours afterwards, I have been called to see him in the black vomit, with profuse hemorrhages from the mouth, nose, ears, eyes, and even the toes; the eyes prominent, glistening, yellow, and staring; the face discolored with orange color and dusky red.

The physiognomy of the yellow fever corpse is usually sad, sullen, and perturbed; the countenance dark, mottled, livid, swollen, and stained with blood and black vomit; the veins of the face and whole body become distended, and look as if they were going to burst; and though the heart has ceased to beat, the circulation of the blood sometimes continues for hours, quite as active as in life. Think, reader, what it must be to have one's mind wholly occupied with such sights and scenes for weeks together; nay, more — for months, for years, for a whole lifetime even. Scarcely a night passes now, in which my dreams are not haunted more or less by the distorted faces, the shrieks, the convulsions, the groans, the struggles, and the horrors which I witnessed thirty-five years ago. They come up before my mind's eye like positive, absolute realities. I awake, rejoicing indeed to find that it is a dream; but there is no more sleep for me that night. No arithmetic could compute the diminution of my happiness, for the last forty years, from this single source. Setting aside another and better world to come, I would not make such a sacrifice as one epidemic demands, for all the fame, pleasures, and gold of earth. What, then, will you think of twenty?

A clergyman said to me not long since, "You have indeed had a terrible time in New Orleans. You will be rewarded for it some time or other, but not *here*, not *here*. A suitable remuneration awaits you in the kingdom of God, beyond the grave."

I shocked my friend exceedingly by saying, " I neither expect any such remuneration nor desire it. I have had my reward already. Virtue is its own reward. I am no more entitled to a seat in heaven for all I have done, (supposing my motives to have been holy,) than the veriest wretch that ever expiated his crimes on the gallows." I repeat it, every person who does his duty receives a perfect recompense this side the grave. He can receive nothing afterwards, except upon the platform of mercy. For the good deeds done in the body, there is no heaven but upon earth. When will Christian ministers learn this fundamental truth of the gospel?

> "The soul's calm sunshine, and the heartfelt joy,
> Is virtue's prize: a better would you fix?
> Then give humility a coach and six,
> Justice a conqueror's sword, or truth a gown,
> Or public spirit its great cure — a crown."

In my efforts and struggles in New Orleans, I cannot presume to say that duty was always uppermost in my mind. Duty is to me an important, but a cold word. Yet I can assert, unqualifiedly, that I was not actuated by selfish, mercenary considerations — by any regard to the advantages of earth and time. I did but follow the impulses of my nature. I love my fellow-beings, and when I see them in want, pain, sickness, and destitution, I fly to their relief because I cannot help it any more than water can help running downwards, or fire can help burning. I deserve neither praise nor reward for acting in this manner. It is but a necessary carrying out of those spiritual principles which God has given me, and the very exercise of which is heaven itself — is the " divinity stirring within my soul." The persons who speak of Christians as not being fully rewarded in this life, it seems to me, have yet to learn the alphabet of revealed religion.

Again, during these seasons of trial, there is a constant drain on one's sympathies, which does not operate to lower or dry up their current, but to make it constantly more deep and rapid. It is often said that the power of sympathy is blunted and benumbed by familiarity, and being frequently exercised in the same way. This opinion has been expressed by the great Dr. Paley, of England, a divine whose defective powers of sensibility and imagination rendered him utterly incompetent to discuss many of the most interesting topics belonging to our spiritual nature. My own experience testifies that the oftener a professional man, either a physician or a clergyman, witnesses the distress and pain of a fellow-being, the greater will be his sympathy for suffering. As a general fact, the old physician has a much larger stock of tenderness than that with which he began his professional career. The medical gentlemen of New Orleans are to a remarkable degree humane, sympathetic, and charitable. Every picture of woe and agony which experience has hung up in the gallery of their memories has added to the nobleness of their hearts.

But it is said that increase of sympathy is of course increase of happiness. I doubt the truth of this proposition. To sympathize, in cases of distress and misfortune, is to have a correspondent feeling of *pain* experienced by another. I have often seen a man come into a room where his intimate friend was dying of the yellow fever, and in one minute after reaching his bedside, turn pale, faint, and become violently affected with nausea and vomiting. I have seen the mother repeatedly go into convulsions at the sight of spasms in her beloved child. I might mention instances of this kind to an indefinite extent. Is such sympathy a source of happiness? To be sure, this part of our nature is divine, and prompts us to deeds of magnanimity, of heroic sacrifice. And a magnanimous, self-sacrificing mind is happy, compared with one that is coarse, selfish, and unfeeling. Yet sympathy with sufferers is in every instance a painful emotion. A physician once said to me, "I had some time to sleep last night, but was kept awake by a painful remembrance of the agonizing scenes I beheld yesterday afternoon."

I will illustrate the position of a minister in New Orleans with regard to this matter, by relating a single item of my own experience. I was called one afternoon to attend the funeral of a gentleman who died of the yellow fever. He was a total stranger to

me. I had never heard of him in his life. I was
introduced to the widow, who was sitting in the same
room with the corpse. She had the stare, the
ghastly face, and wild expression of a maniac. I
tried to speak some fitting words to her. I said,
"Madam, it is our privilege to be assured that whatever befalls us in this life, however cruel and mysterious it may appear, is the ordination of God, and is consequently intended to subserve our happiness."
At this point, she interrupted me, saying, with loud, excited tones of voice, "Do not speak to me of a God or Providence. Behold that corpse," (pointing to the remains of her deceased husband.) "If there was a good God controlling human affairs, he would not have robbed me of my children first, and then taken away my husband — the only stay, prop, and support left me on earth." I could say nothing more. After a very short service, the funeral procession moved off. A gentleman who lived next door to the deceased rode with me in the same carriage to the cemetery.

From him I learned the little that was known of the history of the deceased. He arrived in New Orleans the last of May, three months before his death, perfectly destitute; he obtained a situation that yielded him a bare competence, by obligating himself to stay the whole year in the city. The epidemic broke out. He was a man of honor, and would not leave his post. He had two interesting children, a son and daughter, who died but a few days before him. The widow was left without a dollar, and had not a single female acquaintance to sympathize with her. On my return from the funeral, I called at the house to see her again, hoping by that time she would be more tranquil. I found her lying on a mattress, in the same room where her husband had expired. She herself had just been seized with the yellow fever. There was one hired servant in the house, and a colored nurse, who were preparing to leave immediately, because they had not been paid for their services. I assumed the debt which they alleged was due, and persuaded them to remain till the lady died or recovered. They said there were no provisions in the house, no fuel, and no comforts. I gave them enough to carry them through the night, promising the amplest remuneration for the future, if they would but faithfully take care of the sick woman. On my way home, I called a physician to her aid.

When I saw her early next morning, she was exceedingly ill. Finding that there was nobody to do any thing for her but myself, I started off at once on a begging tour, for my own means were exhausted. After running two or three hours in a blazing sun, I obtained the requisite assistance. At that time there were no Howard societies, no benevolent organizations, in the city. There was no concerted action with respect to objects of charity, but every thing was left to the spontaneous generosity of individuals. Yet, when I reported that a family was in want, it was easy to procure the needed aid, by giving my personal attention to the matter. But this took up a vast deal of my time. To the credit of New Orleans be it said, that her inhabitants have always been munificent in their donations for the relief of the sick and indigent.

This unfortunate lady, after a most severe attack, became convalescent. The hand of charity paid all her expenses — house rent, servants' hire, undertaker's bills, &c., till the return of autumn. Then a sufficient sum was raised to send her, with the remains of her husband and children, to her distant relatives. I mention this incident, not as any thing extraordinary; it was with me an every-day occurrence. But it may serve to show what kind of happiness accrues from the exercise of Christian sympathy. There is certainly something in it superior to mere selfishness. I have kept myself in a state of pauperism by benefactions of the kind above named. My charities for thirty-five years, in New Orleans, were not less, on an average, than one hundred dollars a month, or forty-two thousand dollars in sum total. And this was expended upon persons abject, poor, unknown, and unhonored, who could make no return except that of a thankful heart.

The moral history of the lady I have been speaking of is so interesting, that I cannot pass it by entirely unnoticed. When restored to health, she became very much attached to me, and very communicative. Her intellect was of the highest order, and her reading extensive. In person she was not beautiful. But she, as well as her late husband, was a confirmed sceptic. On a certain time, she said, "My own history is sufficient proof that there is no God. I look back upon a life of unintermitted sorrow and disappointment. I married against my parents' consent, and they disowned me. My husband became a bankrupt, and at last we immigrated here to retrieve our shattered fortune.

"You know the sequel. I often say to myself, 'Why did I not die in infancy? Why was it that I have been subjected to the terrible, crushing burdens of such an adverse lot? Now I have neither husband, nor children, nor family, nor means, and no friend to help me, except yourself. Let the fortunate praise their kind Creator; but I am a wretch doomed to eat the bread of a bitter and neglected lot — to walk sadly and alone through this cold, unkind, uncongenial world, till permitted to enter upon the repose of the tomb.'" By conversation and the help of appropriate books, I endeavored to inspire her with higher, more ennobling, and more cheering sentiments; with what success will appear from a passage in a letter which she wrote to me some years afterwards. In the succeeding winter she returned to her native place, taking along with her the remains of her husband and children. She was kindly received by her relatives, contrary to her anticipations, and became comparatively a happy and a truly pious woman.

She wrote me many times after her departure, but is now an inhabitant of the spirit world. In one of her last letters she recorded the following words: "Suffering has humbled my pride and softened my heart. I remember when you first told me that human life was not intended to be a scene of enjoyment, but a school of discipline, where, by a series of trials and instructions, the higher and nobler capacities, which the Creator has implanted in the soul, might be developed and brought into activity. I now look upon the losses which I sustained in New Orleans as in reality the greatest blessings. Had my husband and myself lived there till we had become prosperous and wealthy, free from trouble, I should never have known that there was any higher good than the pleasures of time and sense.

"But now I behold and commune with an infinite Father. I no longer look upon my existence as a mystery, a curse, or a misfortune; but I feel that each passing day spreads before me glorious opportunities to be improved, and glorious forms of happiness to be enjoyed. My health is feeble, and the physicians have pronounced me to be in a hopeless decline. Yet I am happy, and take much exercise abroad. My family bestow upon me every possible kindness and attention. Every pleasant evening I walk to the cemetery, and linger, till the setting of the sun, around the tombs of my husband and children. I have no doubts, no fears, no despondency. The graves of those I love are upon the summit of a beautiful hill. From this spot I look out upon the calm splendors of the departing day; the golden and azure beauty of the skies, with the inspiring faith that beyond them are those brighter regions, where I shall soon meet the true, good, and beautiful whom I have lost, to be separated from them no more. Under God, you were instrumental in bringing me out of darkness into the light of a pure and happifying faith." I could relate instances of a similar description, sufficient to fill a volume. And I have referred to the subject simply to enable the reader to form a faint idea of the peculiar scenes in which my professional life has been passed.

But imagine what was, usually, my condition after the termination of an epidemic. Health reigns again throughout the city; absentees, with strangers, are rushing back in crowds. The weather is as charming as that of paradise. All is stir, bustle, cheerfulness, gayety, and hope. Were one unacquainted with New Orleans, to drop in upon us at this moment, he would conclude that we were among the happiest of communities. No hearses are seen wending their way to the burying grounds. The doctors are comparatively at leisure. The posts of employment, made vacant by the recent mortality, are soon filled by strangers, as young, ardent, hopeful, and sanguine as were their predecessors, and destined, most of them, to share the same fate. But there is one class of persons whose hands and attention are still occupied by the melancholy duties devolved upon them by the epidemic which has just closed.

The work of the clergyman, occasioned by this visitation, is protracted through the succeeding winter, the year, and perhaps many succeeding years. Poor families, in greater or less numbers, have been left destitute and dependent. They have none to look to but the minister, who stood by, in the dark hour, to pray, soothe, and support them, when their beloved husbands and children were consigned to the grave. They conclude, as they ought to do, that "pure religion and undefiled before God and the Father is, to visit the widow and the fatherless in their affliction." Though entire strangers, simply because I was with them in the season of sorrow and bereavement, they would come to me for counsel and aid, with as much confidence as if I had been a brother by the ties of natural affinity. I was regarded as the common friend and benefactor of the unhappy of every age, church, character, clime, and complexion. I have labored as much for those belonging to Orthodox and Catholic societies as for poor heretics and outsiders. I have always felt that any one who could say, " I am a man," had a sacred and imperative claim to my sympathies and kind interposition. Neither God nor mortality hath any respect of persons.

From Monday morning to Saturday night this class of sufferers used to besiege my doors, and draw upon my pecuniary resources. Young children had places provided for them in asylums, or private families. Older boys, of a suitable age, were apprenticed to some merchant, mechanic, or planter. But there is a great demand for such situations after an epidemic is over. There is often much difficulty in obtaining them. I could not tell how many weeks I have spent in hunting patrons for fatherless, forsaken, indigent boys. Then the widows were to be taken care of, and their wants, taste, capacity, and even whims could not be disregarded. Some had never been trained to any useful employment whatever, and had not the requisite skill to use the needle. What could be done for them? Why, they would tell me that they were able to manage a boarding house in excellent style, and there was one close by which they could procure, if they had only two or three hundred dollars to start with. Mr. Somebody would advance the funds, if I would be so kind as to indorse a note for them.

The note is executed; the establishment is opened under apparently favorable auspices. But, in the space of a few months, through mismanagement, it fails, and to prevent being protested, I have the note to pay. The lady, then, perhaps, finds a second husband, and embarks once more upon the dangerous sea of matrimony. In a short time, she comes to me with some doleful story of maltreatment and desertion, and wishes me to put her upon the way of obtaining a divorce. Another, who had an excellent situation in a good family as a seamstress, had some misunderstanding with the lady of the house, and she has resolved not to live there another day. She modestly asks me to get another place for her, and she expects me to attend to it without delay.

A third walks into my study when I am absorbed in meditating a discourse for the next day, and informs me that the man to whom I lately married her, and who seemed to be the very pink of morality, is not as good as he ought to be — is quite latitudinarian, indolent, and intemperate in his habits. The landlord threatens to turn her out of doors, unless the rent is paid before sundown. To prevent this catastrophe, she wants a loan of twenty dollars, which she will certainly return some day next week.

She obtains her request, and has hardly left the room before a fourth calls, to let me know that her son, for whom I got a place in a certain store, warehouse, or counting room, is overworked, besides being subjected to indignities which his father would not allow him to submit to an hour, if he were alive. His month is out, and she is determined that he shall never set his foot in that establishment again. It would be better for him to be in his grave than longer to endure such ill usage.

She is succeeded by a fifth visitor, who, addressing me with much warmth and a look of upbraiding, says, "You, sir, recommended a certain family as the best and safest place for my daughter in the whole city. But she is not only made a menial of, instead of being treated as one of the daughters, but the gentleman who, you said, was so pious, meeting her yesterday alone, offered her a gross insult; and I have taken her home that she might not be absolutely ruined."

In this way I am, perhaps, interrupted all Saturday morning, till the hour for dining has arrived. Next day, in all probability, the weather will be delightful, and I shall have to speak to a large audience, and among them will be many strangers of distinction, who have lately arrived; I am entirely unprepared. These thoughts weigh heavily upon my mind, and make me sick. I am so nervous that I can neither eat nor sleep till the labors of the Sabbath are over.

Heaven have mercy upon a clergyman incessantly molested by trials and importunities like these.

They make the salubrious months of the winter almost as undesirable as the preceding autumn, which was so saddened with pestilence and death. When a man is buried, he can trouble you no more; but these survivors of the conflict may follow you to your grave.

Yet these unfortunate persons are not to be blamed for the course they take. They can do no better, as a general fact. Upon every principle of honor and religion, the community is bound to take care of them. In New Orleans this obligation is recognized. A few years ago some charitable ladies belonging to the different religious denominations of the city, Protestant and Catholic, started an institution called the Widows' Home. It was fostered by benevolent individuals, and by the legislature of the state. Dr. Mercer, formerly of Natchez, Mississippi, but now of New Orleans, a man not only of wealth, but munificence, — another Poydras, Touro, or Lawrence, — has taken this establishment under his especial patronage. He has already bestowed on it fifty thousand dollars, and is prepared to increase his benefactions, if they shall be needed. This gentleman has higher and nobler aims than to make his fortune merely subservient to his physical enjoyment — to the throwing around him, in the greatest superfluity, the luxuries and refinements of genteel life. He gives bountifully to churches, schools, missions, almshouses, and other institutions. He does all that becomes the opulent friend and helper of humanity to elevate it in knowledge and virtue, and animate it with hopes of a more glorious destiny hereafter.

The two most fatal yellow fevers which I have witnessed were those of 1837 and 1853. In the former year there were ten thousand cases of fever reported, and five thousand deaths. The epidemic broke out about the middle of August, and lasted eight weeks. This is the greatest mortality which was ever known in the United States, if we except that which occurred in the cholera of New Orleans, October, 1832. The year 1837 is memorable for the introduction of what is called the quinine practice. It is now, I am told by the physicians, generally abandoned. By some persons abroad, our doctors have been much blamed for thinking to overcome the yellow fever by the above-named medicine. For myself, I do not wonder that they made such an attempt. It had been recommended by the most celebrated practitioners in the West Indies, and in other tropical regions. New Orleans has always been blessed with the most learned, skilful, and competent physicians; but they are neither omniscient nor omnipotent. The cause of yellow fever is to this day a profound mystery. It has been said that this is a true but humiliating confession by Dr. Dowler, of New Orleans. I quote from an article of his, published in the New Orleans Directory in 1854: —

"Heat, rain, moisture, swamps, vegeto-animal decomposition, contagion, and numerous other alleged causes are altogether inadequate and unsatisfactory. This might be shown by travelling over hundreds of inconclusive and contradictory volumes, filled with special pleadings, diluted logic, theoretical biases, and irrelevant facts.

"It is most certainly the duty of every writer on yellow fever to explain the cause of it, if he can; but it is equally his duty not to sin against the decalogue of logic, any more than against the decalogue of Moses. Fortunately, the *conditions*, if not the *causes*, of yellow fever are to a considerable extent known. For example, it is known to be connected — no matter how — with the warm season of the year, with unacclimated constitutions, with aggregations of people in towns and villages, &c. It rarely attacks rural populations unless they crowd together so as to become virtually towns.

"A correct appreciation of these conditions is next in importance to the discovery of the cause of yellow fever. Probably the former may prove, after all, the more important; for the discovery of the cause by no means warrants the conclusion that it is necessarily a removable or remedial one. The seeds of plants taken from Egyptian mummies contain the vital principle after the lapse of thousands of years, and will grow when the proper conditions shall be present, as heat, moisture, and earth, while the vital cause is in the plant. It is, therefore, a fundamental error to require a writer to explain the *ens epidemicum*, or to receive the alleged doctrine of contagion as the only alternative, when he cannot show what the cause *is*.

"It is better to acknowledge ignorance than to advocate an error. It is better to keep a question of this sort open, than dogmatically to close it against investigation. In the former case, the truth may be discovered; in the last, never. To *know* ignorance is preferable to *ignorance* of ignorance. To know that as yet we do not know, is the first step to be taken. Despair is not philosophical. The possible who can limit? If the cause of yellow fever has not been discovered, it may yet be; and when discovered, it may, or may not, be controllable. If it should never be discovered, any more than the cause that produces on the same soil a poisonous and a nutritive plant, it is probable that at least its essential laws and conditions may be ascertained, so as to afford advantages and protection equal to those derivable from the knowledge of its true cause. All the lessons of philosophy teach that yellow fever has a cause, without which it cannot appear, and with which it cannot fail to appear. Its antecedents and sequences must prove, when known, as invariably connected and simple as any part of physics.

"The diversity of opinion on this subject among the learned is wonderful. Dr. Rush and others affirm that the plague left London as soon as coal was introduced into the city as fuel. Now, the part of New Orleans most severely afflicted with yellow fever in 1853 was in the neighborhood of the founderies, where vast quantities of coal were used. Sometimes the firing of artillery in the streets and public squares has been followed by the retreat of the epidemic; at other times it has added an impetus to its march, as the eating of a salt herring was once followed by the recovery of a Frenchman and the death of an Englishman. The same is true of tar-burning. Milk, coffee, London porter, and various other articles have sometimes cured the black vomit, at others they only helped on the disease. A process which has cured the yellow fever one year, the very next will destroy all the patients."

Consequently, when an epidemic sets in, the physicians are in a quandary. They begin, perhaps, with medicine that was most efficacious in a former year; but it kills rather than cures. In this case what can they do? They must practise empirically. It is inevitable. They must travel blindfold, in a great measure. If they knew the cause of the complaint, they could apply medicines with skill and success, and avoid painful, and often most fatal mistakes. I have always sympathized with the physicians in New Orleans. Their duties in a sickly season are most arduous and responsible. Often have I seen them in a few weeks reduced to their beds by anxiety, toil, watchings, and disappointment; and multitudes, instead of thanking them, have cursed them, because they did not at once expel the epidemic from the city, which they could no more control than they could raise the dead.

Lately, our physicians have repudiated the use of drastic medicines in the treatment of this disease. They rely upon gentle remedies, the keeping up a constant perspiration by rubbing, and various external applications. The system of therapeutics at present adopted in New Orleans, with respect to diseases in general, approximates, in many particulars, to that prescribed by the homœopathic faculty. It is certainly much more successful than the practice which was prevalent some years ago. In one of the earlier epidemics, I saw a physician, in his first visit to a patient, who had been ill but four hours, take from him, by the lancet, fifty ounces of blood at one time. The sick man was bled till he fainted. He then ordered him to swallow, at once, three hundred grains of calomel and gamboge. So the physician himself testified. This sort of practice now would be regarded as certainly inevitably destructive of life.

In May, 1853, I went to Boston, Nahant, and Niagara, for my health. When at the Falls, I heard, by the telegraph and private letters, that the yellow fever had again become epidemic in New Orleans. This was in the warmest weather of July. Leaving my family, I immediately hurried home by the most expeditious route. I went in a steamer to Charleston, thence by railroad to Montgomery, on the Alabama River. From that place I took the mail route to Mobile, and reached the levee in about one week from New York. I was put out at the depot just before daylight.

This is on the banks of the river, about a mile from the centre of the city. Whilst waiting to get my baggage, I could smell the offensive effluvium that filled the atmosphere for miles around, resembling that which arises from putrefying animal or vegetable matter. As I rode upwards towards the heart of the city, I became quite ill, and on reaching my residence was seized with fainting and vomiting. I took a bath, and was partially relieved. I then ordered some tea and toast, intending to spend the next twenty-four hours in my room, for I was completely overcome by fatigue and want of sleep. But the hackney coachman knew me, and, contrary to his promise, spread the news of my arrival.

Before I had time to change my apparel, I was called on for professional services. In about one hour after entering my domicile, I left it to breathe the pestilence of a sick room. Here I found a physician, who was one of my parishioners and intimate friends. He exclaimed, " I am very sorry to see you here. I did not suppose that you could commit such an imprudent act as to come directly from the salubrious regions of New England into this charnel house, this receptacle of plague and death. It will cost you your life." From that day forward till November, I was enabled to attend to my duties every day. I was not seriously ill for an hour.

At this time, the city was full of moisture. It had been raining more or less every day for two months. And this falling weather lasted till the 20th of September. Some medical gentlemen thought that the severity of the epidemic was owing to the excessive rains of that summer. But the constant showers washed the gutters every day, and kept them clean. Besides, immense quantities of lime were strewed along the streets, yards, and squares, the exhalations from which were supposed to be antiseptic. It is a curious fact, that in 1837 the season was remarkably cool, clear, and dry. The weather resembled that of the so-called Indian summer. Yet the pestilence was never more destructive. And this very year, the fever was as virulent in the balmy, delightful weather of October, as it had been in the preceding rainy months. I judge, therefore, that the yellow fever is not affected, one way or the other, by meteorological changes.

On the day of my arrival, it rained incessantly from morning till night. In the space of twelve hours, the interments were over three hundred. The same day, I visited two unacclimated families belonging to my own church, who were all down with the plague. In these families were nine persons; but two of them survived. I knew a large boarding house for draymen, mechanics, and humble operatives, from which forty-five corpses were borne away in thirteen days. A poor lady of my acquaintance kept boarders for a livelihood. Her family consisted of eight unacclimated persons. Every one of them died in the space of three weeks.

Six unacclimated gentlemen, intelligent, refined, and strictly temperate, used to meet once a week, to enjoy music, cheering conversation, and innocent amusements. They had been told that it was a great safeguard, in a sickly summer, to keep up good spirits, and banish from their minds dark and melancholy thoughts. They passed a certain evening together in health and happiness. In precisely one week from that entertainment, five of them were gathered to the tomb. One of the most appalling features of the yellow fever is the rapidity with which it accomplishes its mission.

There is some difficulty in arriving at the true statistics touching the epidemic of 1853. It was supposed by the best informed physicians that there were fifty or sixty thousand unacclimated persons in New Orleans when the epidemic began, about the

1st of July. From that time to the 1st of November, the whole number of deaths reported were ten thousand and three hundred. Of these, eight thousand died of the yellow fever. The physicians estimated that thirty-two thousand of those attacked this year were cured. Of course, if this calculation be true, the whole number of cases in 1853 was forty thousand.

The horrors and desolations of this epidemic cannot be painted; neither can they be realized, except by those who have lived in New Orleans, and have witnessed and participated in similar scenes. Words can convey no adequate idea of them. In some cases, all the clerks and agents belonging to mercantile establishments were swept away, and the stores closed by the civil authorities. Several entire families were carried off — parents, children, servants, all. Others lost a quarter, or a third, or three fourths of their members, and their business, hopes, and happiness were blasted for life. The ravages of the destroyer were marked by more woful and affecting varieties of calamity than were ever delineated on the pages of romance. Fifteen clergymen died that season — two Protestant ministers and thirteen Roman Catholic priests.

They were strangers to the climate, but could not be frightened from their posts of duty. The word *fear* was not in their vocabulary. Four Sisters of Charity were laid in their graves, and several others were brought to the point of death. It is painful to dwell on these melancholy details, but it may suggest profitable trains of thought. Set before your imaginations a picture of forty thousand persons engaged in a sanguinary battle, in which ten thousand men are killed outright. One thousand persons will fill a large church. Suppose ten congregations, of this number each, were to be assembled for worship in Boston, on the 1st day of July, 1858, and that on the first day of the following November, in the short space of four months, all should be numbered with the dead. This mortality would be no more awful than that which I have witnessed in the Crescent City.

In a letter which was written by myself to the Rev. Thomas Whittemore, September, 1853, are the following lines: "Let us look for a moment at a rainbow of beauty spanning this dark cloud of pestilence. During the past season of gloom and affliction, the inhabitants of New Orleans have displayed a degree of heroism, a power of philanthropy, to me absolutely unparalleled. Families of wealth and ease, instead of going over to the delightful watering places in this vicinity, on the sea shore, to enjoy themselves, have passed the whole summer in the city, and devoted their days and nights to the taking care of poor, stricken-down, forlorn strangers, who had no claims to their charities but the ties of our common humanity. I know one gentleman and lady in independent circumstances, who have had under their charge, in the course of the summer, as many as thirty poor families, and all strangers to them. These they have taken as good care of as if they had been of their own kith and kin. Such things have been common all over the city, and in all classes of our heterogeneous population. The members of the Howard Association have achieved miracles of benevolence. I hesitate not to say, that this city, in the late fearful visitation, has given to the world an example of Christian philanthropy as lofty as can be found in the records of all time. I have often thought, that if our northern brethren could have been in New Orleans the past summer, they would no longer entertain a doubt but that a slaveholder may be *a Christian — the highest type of man, the noblest work of God.* Every means which ingenuity could devise or benevolence suggest has been employed to avert and mitigate the evils of the plague. More than two hundred children have been made orphans, and the ladies within and around the city are making clothes for them, and doing every thing possible to promote their welfare.

"Another thing which has deeply impressed my heart is, the northern sympathy which has been displayed towards New Orleans, notwithstanding the people of the free states are so widely separated from us, in opinion and feeling, with respect to the subject of slavery. Laying prejudice and antipathies aside, they have shown that divine benevolence which disdains all the limits dictated by selfishness, and looks upon every human being within its reach as having a sacred and imperative claim to its kind offices. What more could have been done for us than has been done? I should like to shake hands with Mr. Gerritt Smith, and thank him with all my heart for his munificent subscription for the relief of the sufferers in our late epidemic. And Boston, the metropolis of my native state, has given for us, I believe, a larger amount, in proportion to her population, than any other city. Massachusetts should be the first in all noble and illustrious charities, as she is confessedly preëminent in the glories of science, social refinement, and pure religion." Such were my impressions of these scenes, which were committed to writing at the time they occurred, in the autumn of 1853.

Thucydides has bequeathed to us a tragic and striking description of a plague which, in his day, took place at Athens. He tells us that demoralization raged there equally with the epidemic — that all the ties of friendship, of affinity, of moral responsibleness, of honor and religion were dissolved. All the refinements of civilized life, according to his statement, were swept away by a deluge of licentiousness — wild, frantic excesses, neglect of the sick and dying, the plunder of houses, murder, and other atrocities too awful to mention. The narratives of the plagues which have prevailed in Europe in modern periods contain similar statements. Are they credible ? If so, then it is certain that mankind are infinitely better now than they were in the olden times.

In the epidemics which I have witnessed, instead of unusual depravity, an extraordinary degree of benevolence has prevailed, shedding a heavenly light upon the dark scenes of the sick room, the death bed, the coffin, the funeral, &c. Yet, with respect to this subject, New Orleans has been most shamefully misrepresented. In the summer of 1824, an English officer came into our city on his way from Jamaica, West Indies. He was an intrepid, well-informed, interesting man, and was induced to visit New Orleans simply to gratify his curiosity. It happened that he came to our church one Sunday morning; after the services, I had the honor of making his acquaintance. He said he was glad to be with us in days of mourning, disaster, and death, for he wished to become acquainted with all the phases of suffering humanity, and had much rather see New Orleans in the sickly season than in the healthy period of winter. He accompanied one of our physicians to the Charity Hospital, and walked with him through all the yellow fever wards. He used no precautions, and seemed to be entirely superior to fear. We admired his courage, equanimity, and gentlemanly bearing. After a fortnight's sojourn, he left us in good health.

On his return to England, his travels in the United States that summer were published. A copy of the work fell into my hands. In turning to that portion of the book descriptive of his experiences among us during the time just mentioned, I was astonished at the assertion, that New Orleans, in the midst of a dreadful epidemic, was full of merriment, intemperance, and gayety. He says the sick were neglected and abandoned; that crowds rushed every night to balls, operas, and theatrical amusements; and that intoxicated persons were often seen uttering profane and ribald language when employed in burying the dead — in performing the last sad offices which humanity calls for. Words more false, defamatory, and unjust could not be written. Similar fictions are propagated in our northern cities concerning New Orleans every time an epidemic prevails there. Yet the fact is, that in the darkest days its inhabitants have deported themselves nobly, and recognized the sacred claims of religion and humanity. Many of these libels are circulated in letters professedly written by persons who were eye and ear witnesses of the scenes which they described.

It seems to give some men peculiar delight to depreciate and vilify human nature. It is easy to be severe, harsh, satirical, and disparaging in commenting on the behavior of our fellow-beings. But no one was ever too charitable in his views of other men — their motives, principles, character, or conduct. It has been my lot, for the last forty years, to reside in what are reputed to be the worst places in the civilized world; yet to this day I have not met a person so hardened, so brutal, as to be capable of treating with indifference, neglect, or levity, the suffering forms of humanity within his reach. In New Orleans, I have been often struck with admiration to see persons in the lowest walks of life making every possible sacrifice of time, ease, and money in attending on the sick, soothing the dying, and providing tombs and a decent burial for those who were absolute strangers, and utterly destitute. I go so far as to say, that I have never, in a single instance, seen poor and wicked people (as they are called) declining to perform all the offices of charity in their power to the ill and distressed around them. This most terrible form of sin has sometimes, perhaps, been manifested in the higher circles of humanity. I have never beheld it even *there*.

When I hear human nature run down, — prayed, preached, or talked against, — I feel that it amounts to a virtual impeachment of God's own perfections. It is but a depreciation, a slandering of his own glorious work. I have witnessed noble and disinterested actions among all classes of mankind, not excepting the rudest and most vulgar. I knew a woman, herself impoverished, and so ignorant that she did not understand the meaning of the phrase " *self-sacrificing benevolence,*" take a sick child from an adjoining house, whose father and mother had just died of the yellow fever, and watch over it till worn out with fatigue and anxiety, without the slightest hope of any reward, and when even her own children were dependent upon her daily labor for subsistence. I saw much of this woman, on whom the proud and fashionable, perhaps, would look only with contempt. She was faithful, sincere, truth-loving — the just, conscientious, generous friend of the poor, cast down, forgotten, and suffering, who could make no return for her kind doings. Yet she had never been a member of any church, and could not read her Bible.

I have seen poor young men, standing on the vestibule of mercantile life, close their stores, suspend all business, give their days and their nights, their toil and their money, to the relief of sick, indigent, and helpless strangers, from whom they could neither wish nor hope for the smallest remuneration. I have known them to carry on this work of charity, till their health was undermined, and their lives were offered up as a sacrifice on the altar of philanthropy. And these persons were not members of any Christian church. What is religion, or philosophy, falsely so called, arrayed against such facts as these?

I was once at Niagara when a man was carried over the falls. For fifteen long hours he clung to a log jutting out from between the rocks in the middle of the cataract. Thousands were spectators of the awful scene. What was their conduct? The sufferer was a mere youth, about twenty years of age, one of the laborers engaged in excavating a canal, — a foreigner, without a relative near, — in the humblest possible condition and circumstances; yet the multitude looking on wrung their hands, sighed, struggled, and wept, as if he were united to them by the tenderest ties of affinity and love. What efforts were made for his deliverance? Had it been practicable, almost any sum of money might have been raised to effect his rescue. For what? Because his life, on selfish principles, was of the least value to any person present? A gentleman from the Southern States offered a reward of one thousand dollars to any individual who would suggest a feasible plan for saving him. Shame on the traducers of man's heaven-descended nature. They simply felt that the sufferer belonged to the great brotherhood of humanity. This was the secret of their excitement, their sympathy, their tears, and labors for his salvation.

Now, during the prevalence of an epidemic, the people of New Orleans act in the same way. They are in the highest degree earnest, excited, serious, anxious, ready, one and all, to pour out their treasures and their hearts' blood, if it could avail, to save the victims of disease from the jaws of destruction.

The pulpit, literature, philosophy, and even poetry, lend their combined influence in helping on the work of misrepresenting and blackening the glorious traits of our holy nature. The preacher sometimes tells us that there is no real goodness outside of the church. Who were the three hundred men that laid down their lives at the Straits of Thermopylæ, to vindicate the liberties of their native land? Who were the thousands that have labored, toiled, and died, in New Orleans, in the cause of benevolence? What estimate would be formed of their characters, if they were tried by the line, square, and compass of the Westminster Catechism? Call up from the mists and shadows of bygone ages those noble and sublime forms, those right, enlarged, generous, philanthropic men, who poured out their lives for the common weal. These men, in our day, would not, on examination as to their creed, be admitted to the communion of any Orthodox church. No, nor would the Son of God himself. The church has done more to propagate mean conceptions of human nature than all the other influences which have tended to corrupt, darken, and debase our misguided race.

I repeat it, our books of travel, our history, poetry, romance, — the entire body of our literature, — newspapers, reviews, works on political economy, &c., all aid the pulpit in undervaluing and caricaturing human nature. I have never seen a letter, published in the northern religious newspapers, purporting to be a picture of the moral state of things in New Orleans, which was not a gross libel. Every one is exclaiming, "See, behold, how awfully wicked the world is!" I cannot join in this hue and cry; I long to exclaim in and out of the pulpit, "Behold how good and noble mankind are!"

I have mixed and conversed with the operatives of Birmingham, Manchester, and Glasgow, and other manufacturing cities of Great Britain. I have seen the lazzaroni of Naples, and the most depressed classes of Europe; among even these I witnessed the manifestations of disinterested love, which Jesus Christ defines as constituting the essence of true religion. The very worst person has something of this nobleness in his bosom. It is a perfection, the idea of which, however dim and undefined, is more or less the germ and element of every human soul. Go to any state penitentiary, collect its inmates, set before them the picture of a man "who loves the most unlovely of his fellow-beings, as God himself does; who is accustomed to sympathize with the most ignorant and debased; to give to the most uncharitable, if in need; to forgive those who are actuated only by revenge; to be just to those who would rob him of every farthing, if they had an opportunity; to repay ceaseless hate with never-sleeping love;" would they not gaze upon the portrait with the profoundest satisfaction and delight? But all know that it is impossible for a human being to sympathize with any virtue, unless he has in his own bosom some true perceptions of its charms, and a capacity to become clothed therewith. I have often come across the heroism of divine love in the humblest walks of life, in the very lanes and hovels of society. And on such occasions I always thank God and take courage.

Cicero, in one of his moral treatises, remarks that our affectional nature constantly improves. Beginning with the tender sensibilities of home, it imperceptibly enlarges, from the love of parent, brother and sister, to those more expanded regards which embrace the vast society of human kind. Pope has thus paraphrased the thought: —

> "Self-love but serves the virtuous mind to wake,
> As the small pebble stirs the peaceful lake:
> The centre moved, a circle straight succeeds;
> Another still, and still another spreads
> Friend, parent, neighbor, first it will embrace,
> His country next, and next all human race."

Setting aside the Bible, with all its propitious influences, I have long thought that the progress and experiences of human life, themselves, without any other instrumentalities, except the Holy Spirit, which operates on every heart, often inspire the soul with those meek and gentle affections that are the essence of evangelical holiness. I have been in the habit of asking persons, in their dying moments, whether they could, with all the soul, forgive their enemies — their bitterest enemies. Invariably they have answered in the affirmative. "We forgive all, as we hope God will forgive us." I ask, Do not all such persons die in possession of the right spirit? For Jesus declares the forgiveness of enemies to be the highest type of love. He tells us that in heaven love is the only, the universal, and all-controlling principle of action. It has glowed, and been growing more intense, in the bosoms of angels, from eternity. Here we may be neglected, forgotten, despised, injured, and trampled upon. But be not discouraged. All things will come out right at last. Raise your eyes, saith Jesus, to that spirit land where all things are radiant with the beams of an unbounded benevolence. There we may anticipate perfect love and confidence, the interchange of beneficent deeds only; a complete union of tastes and feelings, hearts and fortunes. There we, and all whom we love, are destined to become more intimate and endeared, beauteous and refined, as long as eternity shall last.

To me it is plain that the gospel affirms this doctrine: that no creed, no scheme of redemption, no power of faith, or repentance, is sufficient to insure one's salvation who hates his brother. Equally positive is it in asserting, that all who die in the exercise of a forgiving spirit will go to heaven. This category embraces all mankind, excepting infants and idiots. I know the clergy generally teach that death, of itself, has no power to change or improve the moral character. A more erroneous doctrine was never taught. Mere dying does more towards sanctifying a man than all the preceding acts, events, and influences of his life. It is the furnace by which he is purified, and prepared to enter, some time or other, upon the scenes of a purer and nobler existence, with angels and the just made perfect.

CHAPTER IX.

THE STATE OF RELIGION IN NEW ORLEANS THIRTY-FIVE YEARS AGO. — THE ROMAN CATHOLIC CHURCH OF LOUISIANA. — ITS AUSPICIOUS INFLUENCE ON THE HIGHEST WELFARE OF ITS VOTARIES, MORAL, SOCIAL, AND SPIRITUAL. — THE PECULIAR DIFFICULTIES WHICH CHRISTIANITY ENCOUNTERS IN NEW ORLEANS AT THE PRESENT DAY.

MULTITUDES suppose that genuine Christianity was not introduced into New Orleans till after its cession to the United States, the beginning of the present century. The first American missionaries, who visited the place shortly after the close of the last war with Great Britain, in their published letters and reports, expressed the opinion that the preaching of the gospel was as much needed in New Orleans as in any other spot in the whole world. They affirmed that *there* the pure faith of the New Testament was unknown and untaught. Yet the Catholic religion had been flourishing in that place from its commencement, one hundred years previous. Churches, schools, asylums, nunneries, and other institutions, such as are usually found in Catholic communities, had been built, with great labor and expense.

When deliberating on the expediency of making a settlement in New Orleans, I was told by divines of my own denomination, that if I went there, the most formidable *enemy* of the gospel would be arrayed against me — namely, the Papal church. From a child I had been taught to regard Popery as the man of sin, the great adversary of all goodness, described in the Epistles and the Apocalypse by St. John. In the chart of interpretation, pronounced orthodox at the north, numbers, dates, persons, places, and events were particularly laid down, to prove that all the evils, woes, and calamities mentioned in the book of Revelation were the maledictions of Heaven, denouncing the Roman Catholics. My instructors assured me that the Catholic faith was rapidly spreading in the western and southern parts of our country. It should be counteracted, they said, as far as possible, by sending out Protestant missionaries, and establishing Sunday schools throughout the great valley of the Mississippi.

One can hardly imagine how strong, blind, and hateful were the prejudices against this Christian sect which deluded my mind when I began a professional life in New Orleans. I had been there but a few weeks before I was invited to dine at the house of a liberal gentleman, where I was introduced to several Catholic priests. I found them intelligent, enlarged, refined, and remarkably interesting in conversation. Not a syllable was uttered about the differences of our faith. I was charmed with their style of manners. They left their clerical robes at home, and deported themselves with all the ease, elegance, and affability characteristic of well-informed and polished laymen. Before we separated, I was assured that they would be happy to see me at their private residences any time, and in the most free and

unceremonious manner. Gladly did I avail myself
of an opportunity to cultivate their acquaintance.
I wanted to obtain some personal knowledge of their
peculiar faith, principles, and ceremonies. Hereto-
fore, all that I had learned concerning these topics
had been derived from Protestant writings and conversation. I was anxious to hear them speak for
themselves.

In this respect my desires have been completely
gratified. The first time that I was alone with a
Catholic priest was an epoch in my existence. I was
encouraged, contrary to my expectation, to propose
whatever questions I chose in regard to his religion.
I did so, and was always answered with apparent
candor, directness, and sincerity. It seemed to
afford him great pleasure to impart the information
which I was solicitous to acquire. In a long conversation we discussed the principal articles of the
Catholic creed — the authority of the pope, the
worship of images, transubstantiation, the infallibil-
ity of the church, auricular confession, &c. During
this interview I was struck with the fact that the
objections to these tenets usually made by Protestant
divines were met by explanations which I had never
before seen or heard of. For example, the charge
of worshipping images was denied, and refuted in
the following manner: "All persons," observed the
priest, "love to look on the picture of a deceased
friend, who was the object of their highest esteem
and affection when living. This is a universal trait
of human nature. The Catholic church, true to
this instinct, has employed art to preserve and trans-

mit to other times, to bear onward from age to age, the forms and expressions of those noble sufferers, heroic apostles, and bright models of virtue that flourished in the antecedent periods of the Christian era. Who would not like to behold a perfect portrait of the Son of God, an exact representation of his person, when he tabernacled in flesh? Would not the sight warm, interest, and quicken our souls? Would it not exalt the tone of our piety?

"It is not true," he continued, "that we offer divine adoration — the homage due only to the Supreme Father — to these productions of human genius, not excepting the Madonna, the image of the Virgin Mary. We hold that the disembodied saints of former and later times are really with us, beholding our actions, and hearing our words, and helping us to lead a good life. Is not this doctrine asserted by Paul, in the following words? 'Wherefore, seeing we also are compassed about with so great a *cloud of witnesses*, [meaning, as all concede, departed saints,] let us lay aside every weight, and the sin which doth so easily beset us, and let us run with patience the race that is set before us; looking unto Jesus, the author and finisher of our faith, who, for the joy that was set before him, endured the cross, despising the shame, and is set down at the right hand of the throne of God.' Now, with this beautiful, inspiring faith, is it not both natural and proper to request them to pray for us and bless us, as we ask those holy persons whom we daily converse with in the flesh, to remember us in their thanksgivings and supplications to God? This is the head and front of our offending. And for such a simple, scriptural practice we are stigmatized as idolaters. Do you think, sir, that this is fair and just?"

I cannot resist the desire to relate an explanation, given at the same time, of that sublime mystery, transubstantiation — the supposed conversion of the bread and wine in the eucharist into the body and blood of Christ. "We do not teach," he said, "that there is any actual change in the elements perceptible to our reason or our senses. The substances, after consecration, are, externally and visibly, the same as they were before; but we maintain that then the body and blood of Christ are mysteriously (in a manner incomprehensible to human reason) present with the substance of the bread and wine. So much Luther and his compeers professed to believe. So much is admitted by the Lutheran divines of our day. Indeed, we defend transubstantiation by precisely the same reasoning which is employed by Protestant ministers generally in support of the Trinity. Jesus says, 'This is my flesh and my blood.' We stagger not at the declaration of God through unbelief. We do not undertake to solve the mystery upon philosophical principles, but receive it on the authority of revelation, with a cordial, reverential, and implicit faith. In the same manner your clergy remark concerning the Trinity. *For there are three that bear record in heaven — the Father, the Word, and the Holy Ghost, and these three are one.* Not *one* literally, they say, not *one* to the eye of human reason — that is impossible; but one in a glorious, transcendental, spiritual sense, at present inexplicable to our narrow, benighted, gross, and sensual minds. Am I not right?" inquired the priest.

It was not in my power to return a negative answer to the question. In a manner equally fair were the other peculiar articles of the Catholic faith simplified and explained. At the close of this interview, and, indeed, ever since, I have felt that a reception of the theology which was at that time taught at Andover required as much faith in what seems to the natural mind irrational or absurd, as that of any doctrine taught by the church of Rome. I have no space to pursue this topic further. Its full unfolding would require a volume. But no Protestant *Trinitarian* can consistently object to the Papal church, that its doctrines are repugnant to reason. They are not a whit more so than many of those which *he* most strenuously advocates.

I have often witnessed the celebration of high mass, not only in New Orleans, but also in various parts of Europe. There is not on earth another ceremony so august, solemn, and impressive. When the bell rings, at the instant of transubstantiation, the whole audience fall on their knees simultaneously, in silent, profound prostration before the altar, praying for the forgiveness of their sins, believing with all the soul that the body and blood of Christ are that moment before them, offered as a complete expiation, if they are truly penitent, not only for the sins they may have committed the past week, but during the whole of their past lives. The effect is thrillingly, ineffably sublime. There is nothing in our Protestant churches superior to it, as it regards impressiveness. I was once, on a beautiful Sabbath morning, in St. Peter's, at Rome, and during this part of the worship I could not help kneeling myself upon the tessellated pavement, to recognize my relation to that cross which speaks a universal language, which sheds the only light that shines on this dark world of sin — that cross which is both the emblem and pledge of our final triumph over death, and admission to the realms of everlasting life and happiness. If I had been brought up from childhood in the Roman Catholic fold, no modification of my theological views, nothing this side the grave, could tempt me to stray away from a worship whose forms and ritual are so simple and significant, yet, at the same time, grand, elevating, divine, and pure. I do not wonder that to those who have always been accustomed to a Roman Catholic church, our Protestant meetings should seem so unedifying, and even irreverent. Were I to become a Trinitarian this year, I should, with all possible sincerity and earnestness, seek for immediate admission to the most holy Catholic church, "which is built upon the foundation of the apostles and prophets, Jesus Christ himself being the chief corner stone."

I rejoice that some of the Protestant divines of our day seem willing to acknowledge that there are good and beautiful things even in Catholicism. Dr. Dewey, in his Journal of a Tour in Europe, writes as follows: " Nothing in Rome has astonished me so much as her three hundred and fifty churches. Any one of them is such a wonder and beauty as, if placed in America, would draw visitors from all parts of the country. The entire interior walls of many of these churches are clothed with polished antique marble. They are hung round with paintings, and filled with marble pillars, statues, tombs, and altars. These altars, built often of jasper, porphyry, and the most precious stones, are commonly placed in recesses or chapels on each side of the church, so that they offer some retirement to the votary.

"I confess that I seldom enter these churches without an impulse to engage in worship. My companions both agree with me. We have often said, that if it were not for the air of pretension it would have to any of our acquaintances who might chance to pass, we should certainly do it. As we were walking in St. Peter's to-day, one said, '*It does not signify. I do wish in serious earnest that I could be a Catholic.* I like their forms. These ever open churches, these ever ascending prayers; the deep seclusion and silence; the dim religious light; the voices of morning mass or vesper hymn; the sacred themes depicted upon every wall and dome; and again and evermore these holy altars, whose steps have been worn by the knees of pilgrims of ages past, — all these things commend themselves, not merely to the imagination, but to the most profound, unaffected sentiments of devotion."

Again he says, "One of the interesting services in the Catholic calendar consists of a periodical celebration of the virtues and sufferings of the saint or martyr to whom any particular church is dedicated. There are appropriate prayers and thanksgivings, anthems sung in commemoration of former days and deeds; the church is illuminated and clothed with decorations, to make the ceremony as attractive and interesting as possible. While many things ancient and venerable are passing away, I would lay my hand on the records of ancient glory, and preserve them. The virtues of the world are the treasures of the world. I would enshrine them in sacred rites; I would embalm them as the bones of the saints are actually preserved, in the very altars of the sanctuary. To praise virtue is to commend it to the respect of others. But we never respect it so feelingly and deeply as when we behold it clothed with the beauty and power of example. Let, then, I would say, goodness and good men be remembered by appropriate times, seasons, and services; let holy rites set forth, let holy words recount, their deeds and sufferings; let their virtues be borne upon the breath of music, an offering and a thanksgiving to Heaven.

"And a festival in Catholic countries to commemorate all *saints* — all *good men* — a season around which is gathered the mighty host of those who, in faith and patience, in suffering and triumph, have gone to heaven, — this, I confess, strikes my mind as something most meet, suitable, and hallowing. Our Protestant religion is too naked of such associations. We are too reserved, I think, even in expressing our regard towards living worth; we are not likely, then, to give too much expansion and expression to our enthusiasm for the heroism and sanctity of former days. It teaches a useful lesson to those who are struggling against the tide of this world's temptations; it teaches a beautiful lesson to the young, the ardent aspirant after virtue, to know that the piety and fortitude which, in their day, were humble and cast down, and fearful and despised, have at length come to live amid anthem and prayer, in the everlasting memory of all generations." How vehement, passionate, and stirring, as well as just, is the eloquence of the above quotations!

Since my acquaintance with Louisiana began, there have been, I believe, at no time, less than twenty priests stationed in New Orleans. Besides performing clerical functions in churches, chapels, convents, asylums, and hospitals, they have founded and kept in vigorous operation numerous schools and seminaries of learning for both sexes. In these respective vocations they have displayed the most unflagging zeal, and ardent, persevering industry. No Protestant ministers in the United States, of any denomination, accomplish as much hard service as they do. Morning, noon, and night, at all seasons, whether healthy or sickly, they are engaged in the prosecution of their arduous and responsible labors. Apparently, they live as if each day were their last, and as it becomes those to live who know not what a day, what an hour, may bring forth. Like the sun, which never pauses and never goes astray, so they revolve in the orbit of duty, a light, a charm, an ornament, and a blessing, to all who are embraced in their spiritual guardianship.

In addition to the duties common to churches of every name, they are required to keep their places of worship open, not on the Sabbath only, but during each day of the week. At every altar, mass is performed at least once a day. Then, the labor involved in the duties of the confessional is inconceivable to one who has not lived among the Catholics. I have known a priest engaged from daylight till noon, uninterruptedly, in receiving penitents, and that in the most inclement weather. All this time, he sits in a small place like a sentry box, applying his ear, in a stooping posture, to an aperture in the surrounding lattice work, which separates him from those who are making their confessions to him. This toil is unintermitted and everlasting. In the intense heat of July and the cold of December, (they have no fires in their churches,) it imposes a drudgery more severe than that of the poorest operative in secular life, whether he rolls the barrel and bale in the city, or digs and toils on a plantation.

In the cholera of 1832, I was the only Protestant clergyman that remained in the city, except the Rev. Mr. Hull, of the Episcopal church, who was confined to his house by a lingering consumption, and unable even to leave his room. This gentleman never left the city in sickly seasons, but fearlessly continued at his post, however great and alarming the mortality around him. So it was that in the first cholera I had no coadjutors but the Roman Catholic priests.

One of these, Father K., was among my most intimate personal acquaintances. He often dined with me, and spent hours at a time in the seclusion of my study. A better man I have not known. He was as liberal in his theological views as Dr. Channing or Bishop Fenelon, and yet most ardently attached to the Roman Catholic church. He was a firm disbeliever in the doctrine of endless misery, but did not advocate this view of futurity in his public discourses. His charities, like his soul, were large and unbounded. He inherited a handsome property, which enabled him to gratify his benevolent desires. In his labors during the cholera, this gentleman gave his services to all, indiscriminately, who needed the consolations of religion, whether Protestant or Catholic sufferers. "I feel," he said, "that all men are my brethren, and heirs of the same immortality. I spend all my time among the sick, irrespective of their character or creed.

"I am not allowed, indeed, to administer the rite of extreme unction to unbelievers. I do not attempt it. But with respect to such cases, I have a peculiar service of my own devising, dictated by the condition and circumstances of the sufferers around me, and which is not in any respect incompatible with my relations to the priesthood. I propound one question only to the departing sinner. I ask him if he believes in Almighty God, his Creator. If he answer affirmatively, (as all have hitherto done, without an exception,) I then offer this short prayer: May that merciful Creator, in whom you exist, forgive and bless you, and conduct you finally to those immortal joys which Jesus has procured for all men in that 'undiscovered country from whose bourn no traveller returns.'" Could any thing be more simple, appropriate, or sublime? He added, tears starting from his eyes with the utterance, "If it were in my power to prevent it, not one of these unhappy victims would be finally and forever lost." Will not, then, infinite, everlasting, and immutable mercy ultimately achieve their deliverance?

This excellent man lost his life in carrying out an enterprise of benevolence. He undertook to establish an asylum and school for orphan boys on the Bayou St. John. He had collected quite a number of fatherless children, and made suitable arrangements for their maintenance and education; and when every thing, to human view, promised a rich harvest of success, the enterprise was suddenly blasted by the ravages of a tornado. It commenced about sundown, and before midnight caused the waters of Lake Pontchartrain to rise several feet, and flow towards the city like the incoming tide of an ocean. At the dead hour of night, Father K. was aroused by the rushing of the waters into his room. He made all possible haste to awaken the boys, and placed them under the direction of a tutor, who soon conducted them beyond the reach of danger. Then he took some servants with him to the stables, to save a fine stock of cows from drowning. This object was accomplished, but with great difficulty. The good man waded and swam in the water so long that it brought on a chill and typhoid fever, which in a few days terminated his invaluable life and labors. To the community in general, and to myself in particular, his death was an irreparable loss. Our views on religion, and our tastes in general, were singularly harmonious. Strong and deathless were the sympathies by which we were united. I have not known a clergyman of my own persuasion whom I loved with a purer, intenser affection.

It is a wide-spread opinion that Roman Catholic priests practise *certain immoralities*, not only with impunity, but with the entire approbation of their parishioners, which, in Protestant communities, would blast completely and forever the reputation and influence of a minister. It affords me great pleasure to testify, that in New Orleans, just as much as in Boston or New York, a spotless moral life is a qualification indispensably necessary to the good standing of any clergyman, whether Protestant or Catholic. Priests are never seen in Louisiana at balls, theatres, private dancing parties, or operas even.

They do not teach that these amusements, abstractly considered, are sinful, but that, such are the weakness and prejudices of large classes in every community, they look upon it as incompatible with the spirituality and refinement of the priesthood to participate in their enjoyment. In their public deportment, the Roman Catholic priests of New Orleans are models of clerical wisdom, decorum, and propriety. They are sufficiently grave, serious, and dignified, and at the same time free from affectation, simple, natural, condescending, agreeable, and unconstrained in their intercourse with persons of every age, character, and condition in life. I have sometimes been present when their religious peculiarities have been assailed by unjust, gross, and insulting insinuations, and beheld with profound admiration their imperturbable equanimity, meekness, and forbearance. Happy would it be if all who profess to be the ministers of Christ should faithfully follow the example of Him "who did no sin, neither was guile found in his mouth; not rendering evil for evil, or railing for railing, but contrariwise blessing; who, when he was reviled, reviled not again; when he suffered, threatened not; but committed himself to Him that judgeth righteously."

Shortly after my settlement in New Orleans, I was called to reside for two years in the lower part of the city, in the midst of a population exclusively Catholic. There was hardly a single Protestant family within half of a mile from our domicile. When we took up our abode there, we expected to be quite solitary and lonely. But very soon our neighbors became acquainted with us, and showed the utmost civility and attention. We found them sincere, warm-hearted, polite, affable, and as kind when we were in sickness and trouble as if they had been united to us by the closest ties of natural affinity. It struck me that persons so agreeable and exemplary in private life and the domestic circle must have a religion not entirely devoid of exalted and ennobling influences. Hence I determined to avail myself of the opportunity afforded me of becoming thoroughly acquainted with the religious habits and practices of the laity in every-day life, as well as in the cathedral.

It was my good fortune to be admitted to a most confidential and familiar footing with a Creole family occupying a fashionable and distinguished position in society. The lady was a native of New Orleans, and had never been out of the State of Louisiana.

She had not been personally acquainted with any Protestant minister except myself. She had never read any of our religious books. She had breathed a Roman Catholic atmosphere only, from the cradle upwards. As to every particular, I have not seen, in the whole course of my life, a more charming woman. Her personal attractions were of the highest order, set off with that indescribable ease, simplicity, and elegance peculiar to French ladies, and which render their style of manners so fascinating. Her mind had been carefully cultivated. Besides music and other accomplishments, her knowledge of books and the world enabled her to shine in conversation.

She was an example of industry and economy in the management of her domestic affairs. No married lady of New England was ever superior to her in this respect. She presided at the dinner table with unsurpassed grace and dignity; and before the guests were seated, invariably called on some one to supplicate the blessing of Almighty God upon the entertainment. It is no exaggeration to say, that this lady possessed those rare excellences and properties of a good wife so graphically described in the last chapter of the book of Proverbs.

But what seemed to me most wonderful in the person I am speaking of, was the superiority of her attainments in spiritual excellence. She commenced each day with prayer, reading, and meditation. On one occasion, she was so obliging as to invite me to examine her oratory, as she called it — the little chapel appropriated for her private devotional exercises. Upon a table on one side of the room lay her most favorite religious books. Among these were the Bible, and the Imitation of Christ, by Thomas à Kempis — a work praised and used by Protestants of all denominations. It has been translated into all modern languages, and republished more than a thousand times. Indeed, this work is the storehouse whence Dr. Doddridge drew his principal materials in the composition of that celebrated manual called the Rise and Progress of Religion in the Soul. I remember this work more particularly, because its leaves were soiled, and almost worn out by constant use, like the *horn book* in which little children learn their letters and rudiments. Indeed, she said that for years she had been in the constant habit of perusing this volume, along with the sacred Scriptures. Of all uninspired productions, it had the warmest place in her heart.

I learned one fact from this lady, which illustrates the superior wisdom and efficiency of the Roman Catholic religion. The whole routine of her everyday life was particularly marked out and prescribed by the rules of the church; so that, by this means, every moment and hour were occupied with that faithful discharge of duties which consecrated the whole scene of her existence, filling her soul with an approving conscience, heavenly peace, and virtue pure — " sacred, substantial, never-failing bliss." But the Protestant minister contents himself with meeting his communicants once or twice a week only, in the church. Here he expounds to them the principles and rules of a holy life. After the benediction they disperse, and he sees them not again till the succeeding Sabbath. He cannot tell whether, during the intervening days, they have lived like heathen or Christians.

But the pious Catholic, during the whole time passed out of the church, feels that he is in the presence not only of Almighty God, but also of the priesthood. For every Sunday morning he expects to render his father confessor an account of his doings for the week just finished. The lady above mentioned, speaking of the advantages of frequently confessing to a priest, remarked, " Why, if I were not in the habit of making a moral reckoning with myself every week, but were to put it off to that unknown, distant, imaginary period, called the day of judgment, with the sincerest intentions, I should be at the best but a feeble, languid, vacillating Christian." Memorable words! Well would it be for every Protestant to ponder their import with deep attention. The Methodists have in their class meetings a sort of substitute for these weekly confessions. Hence this church deservedly enjoys a distinguished reputation for earnest, efficient, and every-day piety.

One evening I was at her house, when the conversation turned on the topic of there being no salvation out of the pale of the Catholic church. She expressed her opinion touching this matter in terms like these: " I believe that true religion consists in qualities of the heart, not in ceremonies merely — *in loving God with all the soul, and our neighbors as ourselves.* They who are actuated supremely by these sentiments must be saved, whether Catholics, Protestants,

Jews, Mahometans, or Pagans." A priest, sitting by, exclaimed, "That is right! Why, even Mr. Clapp may be saved upon our own principles, for it is a canonical doctrine among us, that any honest errorist will be accepted on the ground of invincible *ignorance* — an ignorance which he had no adequate means of overcoming." In the preceding paragraphs I have given a true, unexaggerated, but imperfect portrait of one woman who adorned the Catholic communion. There are thousands like it in different parts of our beloved land. Would to God that every woman in this republic had essentially the same beautiful character.

Never, till I went to Louisiana, did I behold that living and most perfect exemplification of a Christian spirit exhibited in the conduct and benefactions of those denominated Sisters of Charity. Look at them. They were, in many instances, born and bred in the lap of worldly ease and luxury. But, in obedience to a sense of religious duty, they have relinquished the pleasures of time for the charms of a life consecrated to duty and to God. There, calm and gentle as angels, they stay at their posts amid the most frightful epidemics, till death comes to take them to a better world. What a spectacle! Their whole existence is passed in watching the sick, and performing for them the most menial offices. They, indeed, fulfil the injunction of the apostle, "Honor all men." They glorify our common humanity. They feed the hungry and clothe the naked. When I have seen them smoothing the pillow, and whispering the consolations of religion for some unfortunate fellow-being, in his last moments,—dying among strangers, far from home, never again to behold the face of wife, child, relative, or friend this side the grave,—I could hardly realize that they were beings of mortality. They seemed to me like ministering angels sent down from the realms of celestial glory. O, how immeasurable the disparity between one of these noble spirits and a mere creature of the feminine gender, devoted exclusively to the follies and vanities of fashionable life, who makes a dazzling show for a few hours, and then sinks to be seen no more. These angels are seen in all our hospitals, both public and private, and in other places where their services are required, irrespective of the distinctions of name, religion, party, clime, or nation.

Indeed the Roman Catholic church is infinitely superior to any Protestant denomination in its provisions of mercy and charity for the poor. They seek to inspire the most wretched and forlorn with those hopes that point to a better world. When I was in St. Peter's Church at Rome, on a Sunday morning, I saw the poorest, most obscure and neglected persons kneeling on its splendid pavement, by the side of the most noble inhabitants of the Eternal City. In that cathedral, there is no place assigned for the exclusive use of fashionable people, any more than there is in heaven. All meet on the same level, as children of one common Father; as dependent on the same pardoning mercy; as travellers to the same grave; as partakers of the same promises, and heirs of the same immortal glory. Throughout

Catholic Europe, the doors of the churches are kept open day and night, from year to year, and century to century. There, at any hour of the day, the forsaken outcast, on whom the world has ceased to smile, can repair, and falling down before the altar of his God, feel supported by the sublime faith that he has in heaven a better and everlasting inheritance. I may say that Catholic churches are the homes of the poor. In countries enjoying this form of Christianity, the most fallen are incomparably less degraded than the worst of those who live in Protestant lands.

Besides, they all, without distinction, participate in the sacraments of religion. No one is permitted to die without the rites of the church. So it should be. Few Protestants know what is the nature of that last benediction, which the priest pronounces over the dying man. It runs, if I have been correctly informed, in a strain somewhat like the following: "Go forth, O thou immortal spirit, in the name of the Father who created thee, in the name of the Son who died to redeem thee, and in the name of the Holy Spirit that sanctifies thee; and when thou leavest the body, may the resplendent multitudes of angels greet thee; may the spirits of the just, clad in their white robes, embrace thee, and conduct thee to the everlasting mansions of the blessed." Could there be any thing more appropriate, more beautiful, touching, and grand? But with us the poor die without a clergyman, without a prayer, without a friend, without any recognition of their immortality, as if they were about to lie down with kindred brutes, in the same ditch, to exist no more forever.

No Protestant denomination, with the exception of the Methodists, have suitably remembered the poor. This remark was once made by a distinguished prelate of the church of England. In our Northern cities, New York, &c., there is an actual rivalry as to which church shall be the most exclusive. And one congregation has erected a separate building for the poor to worship in. Churches are constructed on purpose to shut out the poor. The pews are sold, like the boxes of a theatre, to the highest bidder. The poor can never enter there. O, what a commentary on the Christianity of our times! After spending the week in folly and dissipation, the aristocratic among us can repair to a fashionable place of worship on the Lord's day morning, to gratify a love of dress, to indulge that wicked, pitiful vanity, which one act of true religious worship would annihilate forever. I do not know where all this will end; but I do know that Protestantism will soon go down into the dust and darkness of death, unless it changes its entire ecclesiastical plans and policies. Eternal honor be to the Roman Catholic church, for practically observing the distinctive precept of our religion to remember and bless the poor. For the larger the charity of a church, the nearer it is to God.

Now, the Catholic church, as I have described it, went along with the first colonists, who settled themselves on the banks of the Mississippi. It has grown with their growth and strengthened with their strength, and the religious wants of the people of Louisiana have been as well supplied as those of Massachusetts, all things considered. I never go abroad without being compelled to listen to the utterance of the most disparaging and unjust remarks about my adopted state.

Travelling in Europe in 1847, when introduced to distinguished literary gentlemen as a resident of New Orleans, they almost invariably said, " We have always been told that your city is the most wicked, immoral place in the United States." One distinguished author, speaking of Louisiana, observed, " Its physical resources are undoubtedly very superior; but, alas! you have no literature and no history — the only things which can shed glory on a state. This is the first time I have ever met an educated gentleman from New Orleans. I am really glad to see you. Has Louisiana yet produced any scholars, poets, orators, or *savans*, worthy of note?" This question was asked, as I thought, in the spirit of sneering and sarcasm. It seemed intended merely to wound my feelings; for, a moment before, I had remarked that the first log cabin on the spot where New Orleans is built, then a wretched swamp, was erected within a century, and that nearly all the improvements in the state had been made within the last fifty years.

I ventured to reply thus : " Sir, you are familiar with the circle of human history. Did you ever read of an instance in which a nation only one, two, or three hundred years old had enriched itself with original works of science and literature ? It took nearly one hundred and twenty years to build St. Peter's Church. What a long succession of ages was requisite to produce the cities, temples, palaces, and galleries of art, which adorn England, France, and Italy! Hitherto, the people of Louisiana have been occupied, of necessity, in reclaiming and fortifying their lowlands against the annual inundations of the Mississippi, building houses, turning cypress swamps into beautiful plantations, and providing themselves with the various physical accommodations and improvements upon which the superstructure of civilized life every where rests. At present, for the most part, they import their books, not because they want the genius, but the time and other means essential to the creations of art and philosophy. As to our history, it is very recent, but contains some items of interest. You have heard, I suppose, of the invasion of New Orleans by your countrymen in 1815, and remember the results."

"True," he said, "the victory to which you have referred must be classed with the most brilliant displays of military skill and bravery recorded in the annals of time." He was surprised to learn that the conquerors of Napoleon were subdued by a patriot band of peaceful planters and merchants, who fought for their homes with the same undaunted, invincible spirit which has inscribed the names of Leonidas, Miltiades, and Washington on the tablets of immortal glory. Charles Gayarré, late secretary of the State of Louisiana, has given to the world a noble work upon our history. It is replete with narratives of wild, romantic, and thrilling interest. The author is a Creole, thoroughly acquainted with the character of Louisiana, deeply enamoured of its beauties, and has painted them in elegant and polished language.

When I travel in New England, too, I am often pained by hearing Louisiana spoken of in terms of disparagement and vituperation. Last summer, a clergyman of Massachusetts observed to me that he could hardly conceive of a greater calamity than for a pious and enlightened minister to be compelled to spend his days in Louisiana, where Christianity was encumbered by the corruptions of the Roman Catholic church. I have already given my opinion concerning the practical Christianity displayed by the priests, and their care for the poor, the outcast, the sick, and the dying.

There is indeed less religious display in Louisiana than in some other sections of our Union; but if what Paul asserts in the thirteenth chapter of First Corinthians be admitted, that the essence of Christianity consists in generous affections and sympathies towards our fellow-beings, I contend that the inhabitants of Louisiana have quite as much religion as those of Massachusetts, New York, or any other northern state. Charity, says the apostle, as above quoted, is the only thing absolutely needful in order to our acceptance with God, the charm and glory of the intelligent universe, the very soul, life, and breath of heaven itself. I would simply ask our traducers whether they can see our hearts, and positively pronounce them to be destitute of those noble sentiments denominated *charity* in the New Testament. I would invite them to remember and act in accordance with the following words of Jesus: "Judge not, that ye be not judged. For with what judgment ye judge, ye shall be judged; and with what measure ye mete, it shall be measured to you again. Who art thou that judgest another man's servant? to his own master he standeth or falleth." If gospel benevolence proves the existence of Christian principles, it is certain that true religion reigns and flourishes as vigorously in Louisiana as on the banks of the Hudson or Connecticut.

Some reader may feel inclined to say, "If the above statements are true, would it not be best for us all to join the Roman Catholic church immediately?" I should answer, "Yes, provided you can honestly subscribe to its theological opinions." For myself, I cannot believe in the Athanasian doctrine of the Trinity. If it were in my power to adopt this system, I should as soon as possible become a Roman Catholic. I cannot but regard our doctrinal views as more simple, true, and evangelical than theirs. But their ecclesiastical organization, rules, and polity are infinitely superior to that of any Protestant denomination in Christendom. And the more closely a sect imitates Popery in these particulars, the greater will be their usefulness and prosperity. I wish well to this ancient, venerable dispensation of Christianity. I rejoice that her churches, schools, and nunneries are multiplying on every side. I should like to see them spread from the Atlantic to the Pacific, from the Arctic Sea to the Antarctic, till the matin and vesper bells shall resound along the valleys, from hill to hill, and from mountain to mountain, throughout a republic covering the entire western continent.

A great deal has been said of late about the danger to this country in consequence of the immigration to our shores of Catholics from foreign lands. It is thought that the poor Irish, who are constantly coming among us in such crowds, will exert a most deleterious influence, putting in jeopardy our civil liberties, and sowing broadcast over the land the seeds of moral contagion and death. The poor Irish — may Heaven bless them! I want not their aid at the ballot box. Never shall I be a candidate for their suffrages. Yet I can say with entire disinterestedness that I cherish towards them the liveliest sympathies.

I have seen much of the Irish in New Orleans, in seasons of peril and disaster. I love them, however poor, for their many generous and noble traits of character. I do not fear that their influence will be injurious to us, either in a political or religious bearing. But I am reminded that they bring to our shores degraded, dangerous characters and habits. If it were really so, is it to be wondered at, when we remember what scenes of the most atrocious despotism have been grinding them to the dust for a long series of ages? They are exiles, seeking a refuge from want and oppression. They are God's children. They are our brothers. In the extremest need and destitution, should we not open our arms to receive them with a cordial welcome, and rejoice that they can find a home in this happy land of peace, freedom, and plenty? It is not in my heart to speak of them in terms of contempt and bitterness. He who applies to them vile and opprobrious epithets virtually " reproaches their Maker."

But, some say, they are stupendously ignorant. Is it their fault, if they are so? For more than seventy years, in Ireland, a Catholic schoolmaster was liable to be transported, and if he returned, to be adjudged guilty of high treason, barbarously put to death, drawn and quartered. This most iniquitous law broke up their schools. The children of necessity grew up uneducated, and must come here ignorant, if they come at all. I thank God that they do come; there is room enough for them all. I rejoice on their own account; for it is an encouraging, well-established fact that, in general, Irish immigrants, as soon as they land among us, begin to improve, and rapidly to assume a more elevated character, especially when they do not forsake their national church, and prove recreant to the faith of their forefathers. Their children can hardly be discriminated from those born of English ancestors, and lose all trace of their original descent, except in those impulses of a naturally noble and generous heart, which distinguish Irishmen in all times, in all latitudes, and under every phase of outward condition and circumstances.

Some are afraid of their religion. It is perfectly safe in a free country to tolerate all forms of religion, because the principle of reverence in man, uninfluenced by coercion, can never lead to any species of immorality. If the Roman Catholics become more numerous in this republic than any other sect, the fact will prove conclusively the superiority of their teachings and mode of worship. That they should grow, till finally to outnumber all the Protestant denominations, is hardly possible. Besides, church despotism belongs to the things forever gone by. It cannot be resuscitated. We might as easily revive a belief in knight-errantry, witchcraft, the mythologies or fabulous traditions of the old Greek and Roman states. The press, the free school, the ballot box, and universal education " have already opened to every view the palpable truths that the mass of mankind was not born with saddles on their backs, nor a favored few booted and spurred, ready to ride them legitimately by the grace of God." It is a most unfounded alarm, then, that these annually increasing immigrations of foreigners into the United States can essentially interfere with our national prosperity. The majority bring with them the means of a competent support. How could we get along without them? Deprived of their aid, what would become of our canals, railways, manufactories, rising towns and cities, and public works in general, on which depends our progress in civilization, wealth, freedom, science, morals, and religion? With the help of foreigners this republic was founded; by their help it has been preserved and advanced to its present state of glory and happiness.

The first Protestant church in New Orleans was built about forty years ago, belonging to the Episcopal denomination. The second was founded by my predecessor, the Rev. Sylvester Larned, and was first opened for public worship on the 4th day of July,

1819. On the lower floor there were one hundred and eighteen pews. The galleries were spacious, and capable of accommodating about four hundred persons. Both sides of the galleries contained free seats, which were always filled by strangers. On this account, our place of worship was often called the *Strangers' Church*. It was generally believed that its pastor was a "*setter forth of strange gods*," to use an expression of St. Paul. Hence those who regarded him as a false teacher not unfrequently came to the Presbyterian meetings to listen to the novelties of an heretical pulpit. Whatever may have been the cause, our church was honored by the attendance of the most respectable strangers during the winter season. The pews were always taken by residents of the city, and there were more applicants than could be accommodated. It was a usual saying among my orthodox friends, that the merchants and planters who came to New Orleans during the healthy months to transact business never left the city without going to "*the American theatre, the French opera, and Parson Clapp's church.*" The insinuation is obvious. But notwithstanding the slander, perhaps the friends of truth have cause to rejoice in the greater facilities which were thus afforded for its wider dissemination. Whenever and wherever I have travelled, on this or the other side of the Atlantic, I have constantly met with strangers whose first words were, "We have seen you before; we have heard you preach in New Orleans."

I dined out in London on the second day after my arrival. When I entered the drawing room, filled with a most brilliant circle, as soon as I crossed the threshold, a lady ran to greet me, saying, "Though I have never been introduced to you, I feel as if we were old acquaintances, for I visited your church several weeks in succession one winter, when sojourning in New Orleans." She then mentioned some of the subjects upon which I had preached, and the anecdotes and arguments which were employed. It affected me so deeply that I could scarcely refrain from tears. She was hardly seated before another lady claimed an acquaintance, on the same ground. One winter, it was her good fortune, she said, to be a regular attendant at our meetings in New Orleans.

In Liverpool, Edinburgh, Glasgow, Belfast, Dublin, even Paris, and Geneva, in Switzerland, I was made to feel as if I were at home, by those who recognized me at once, but had never seen me except in the pulpit, or at a funeral. Merchants, and the agents of large mercantile houses from various parts of Europe, flock to New Orleans every winter. They are, with scarcely an exception, intelligent and liberal. Among them are some of the warmest friends I have ever had. If I have spent my days in advocating sentiments essentially and fatally erroneous, perhaps no minister living has done more hurt then I have done. But if, as some believe, I have espoused the true and right, it is a pleasing reflection, that my humble efforts have perhaps contributed to the advancement of virtue and knowledge in matters of the deepest importance, both for time and eternity.

Within the last twenty years, Protestant churches

have greatly multiplied in New Orleans. At the present day, I believe they number twenty-five or thirty. The Catholic churches have increased in an equal ratio, so that Christianity has the same external means of growth and prosperity in the Crescent City as in New York or Boston. The greatest hinderance to the spread of the gospel in New Orleans is the peculiar condition of its inhabitants. Nearly half of these are what may be called a floating population. They go there only for the honorable purpose of accumulating property. No one of them, hardly, looks upon New Orleans as his home. Of course, all are anxious to gain a fortune as soon as possible. What care they for New Orleans, provided their respective personal schemes of profit and independence can be achieved? Hence the number is comparatively smaller than in places where the population is stable, who feel a deep, abiding interest in building up churches and other useful institutions. Those who do favor such objects are singularly devoted and self-sacrificing. The society is fluctuating and heterogeneous almost beyond a precedent. It is constantly changing. In a very short time, the settled pastor sees his pews emptied, and filled with new occupants. He has hardly time to form *their* acquaintance, before they vanish, to be succeeded by another set of strangers. The disadvantages necessarily attendant on such a state of things are obvious. I do not mean to intimate that the people of New Orleans are more immoral than city population in general. We do not think they are more corrupt, or depraved, or worldly, than those who live in Boston and its vicinity. It is not to be wondered at that those who go south merely to *buy, and sell, and get gain,* should say to the clergyman and his solicitations, " Go thy way for this time; when I have a convenient season I will call for thee." Upon the whole, New Orleans perhaps is rising as rapidly in the scale of moral and religious improvement as could be reasonably expected.

CHAPTER X.

SYMPTOMS OFTEN ACCOMPANYING THE LAST STAGES OF THE YELLOW FEVER, ETC.

In the epidemic of 1829, a young man of very superior character, and a member of our church, fell a victim to the yellow fever. I was called to visit him but a short time before he died. I entered his chamber precisely at noon. It was a cool, lovely day in the latter part of October. I found him dressed and walking the room with a brisk, lively step. To the inquiry, "How do you do, my friend?" he replied, "I never felt better in my life. I am free from pain, and if my attendants would allow it, I should immediately go into the streets, and take a walk. But the doctor, who has just gone out, says that if I have any unsettled business on hand, it should be arranged without delay. I have sent for you to help me." At that instant, other friends came in. His will was made, signed, sealed, and witnessed, in a few moments. The company then retired, except the nurse and myself. I was asked to read the Scriptures, and pray with him. Afterwards, he intrusted to me some messages for his widowed mother and relatives, who lived in a distant state. He then remarked, "It is possible I may be near my end, but I think that the doctor has mistaken my case. Will you tell me honestly what you think about it?" I did not undeceive him. He had made every possible preparation for his last exit, and no harm could accrue from his being buoyed up with the hope of a speedy recovery.

And I have sometimes known men apparently in the same condition that he was, get well. Nothing conduces more to promote the convalescence of a yellow fever patient than good spirits. If he makes up his mind that his case is a hopeless one, he will most certainly die. I have sometimes seen persons convalescent before they suspected what was the real nature of their malady. In two or three days more, they would have been out; but a careless servant or indiscreet visitor, contrary to the express orders of the physician, happened to disclose the secret in his hearing. He was alarmed by the intelligence, fancied that he felt worse, and in spite of all our assurances that he was out of danger, in the space of a few hours sank rapidly into the arms of death.

> "With thee, sweet Hope, resides the heavenly light
> That pours remotest rapture on the sight;
> Thine is the charm of life's bewildered way,
> That calls each slumbering passion into play."

In yellow fever, a strong, unwavering expectation of a happy issue often accomplishes more than any kind of medicine which could be administered.

In a certain epidemic, a young man of my acquaintance had the yellow fever in the severest form. As he was near me, and an intimate friend, I became one of his nurses. He had not the slightest idea of dying, and often said, "Don't be alarmed; Yellow Jack cannot kill *me*." He indulged in facetious remarks, to keep up our spirits, for he saw that we were anxious and alarmed. On the third day, about noon, he was seized with the black vomit. The doctor came in, looked at him a moment, and then taking me one side, observed, "It is all over with him; he will die before sundown; I shall give no further prescriptions; do with him now whatever you please." There was an old French nurse in the room, who had spent her days in taking care of the sick, and was familiar with the Creole mode of treating the yellow fever. She exclaimed, "If you will allow me, I think I can cure this gentleman." We of course consented that she should make the trial. By this time, the respiration of our friend was getting very difficult, and his limbs were cold. She called for ptisans, spirits, warm water, and various other remedies, intended for external application only, whose nature I do not remember. We commenced rubbing his body all over, and using every possible means to excite perspiration. In less than two hours, he began to grow warm; the *vomito* ceased; his breathing became easier; he perspired freely, and slept soundly the latter part of the night. In the morning, the doctor stopped at the door in his gig, to ask what hour the patient had died. To his great astonishment, he learned the favorable results of our experiment. In a few days after, the man entered his store, well. He is still living, and enjoys good health.

In the same epidemic, I visited a young married gentleman, not so sick as the one just mentioned, and perfectly confident that he should recover. On the third day, when the fever had reached its crisis, his wife became exceedingly alarmed. Beckoning me into an adjoining room, she said, "I am afraid my husband will die. He has never made a will. If he leaves us without making one, myself and children may be left penniless. I wish you would broach the matter to him." I replied, "Your husband is full of hope; he has no thoughts of dying; and if you will let him remain undisturbed till sundown, his danger will be passed." However, she refused to follow my advice, and declared that if I declined acceding to her wishes, she should mention the subject to him herself. I was then young, timid, and inexperienced, and consented to comply with her request. I approached the subject as delicately as possible, and remarked to the gentleman that although he was doing well, and in all probability would be abroad in a few days, yet to guard against contingencies, it might be expedient to give some directions as to his temporal affairs. "Your lady would like to have you make your will this morning." "Make a will!" he exclaimed, with a stare of astonishment; "is it possible that I am in any danger of dying?" He became exceedingly agitated in a moment, lost his hopes and courage, and in three hours was a corpse. In my judgment, if he had been let alone, he would have gone through the ordeal safely. From that day to the present, I have sought by all lawful means to inspire the sick with the most pleasing hopes, and never to intimate any thing which may tend to produce alarm, misgiving, or despair.

To return from this digression. I sat with the

young gentleman referred to on the first page of this chapter three quarters of an hour. All this time he was either walking or sitting, and engaged in cheerful and animated conversation. Suddenly, laying his hand upon his heart, he exclaimed, "I feel strangely; I feel as if I should faint; I must lie down." I immediately rose, and helped him to his bed. In one moment after his head was laid upon the pillow, a stream of warm, fresh, healthy-looking blood gushed forth from his mouth, covering his apparel, bosom, and bed clothes, as if he had been stabbed at the heart with a dirk. After that issue of blood he breathed not again. I felt of his heart, and it was still beating, and continued to pulsate for some moments after respiration had ceased. His body was quite as warm as my own. I expected with the utmost confidence that life would return; but the next morning he was buried. All these things happened in the space of one hour — between noon and one o'clock P. M.

This young man was very intelligent, and twenty minutes before he expired, conversed with more brilliancy than I had ever heard him before, when in the plenitude of health. He repeated poetry, and made profound philosophical remarks on life, death, and immortality. Among other things, he observed that nothing written by man ever impressed him more deeply than the following lines of Gray's Elegy: —

> "For who, to dumb Forgetfulness a prey,
> This pleasing, anxious being e'er resigned,
> Left the warm precincts of the cheerful day,
> Nor cast one longing, lingering look behind?

> "On some fond breast the parting soul relies;
> Some pious drops the closing eye requires;
> E'en from the tomb the voice of Nature cries;
> E'en in our ashes live their wonted fires."

He asked me a curious question but a few moments before he lay down to die. It was this: "Suppose," said he, "that I was placed in some vessel composed of the densest and hardest materials, and hermetically sealed, like the glass receivers used in chemical laboratories; would my disembodied soul find any difficulty in permeating this exterior covering? I conclude," he added, "that my spirit, if freed from mortal encumbrances, could, in an instant, pass directly through the globe, and pay a visit to our antipodean brethren, and perhaps make a journey to Orion, Pleiades, or Arcturus, in less time than it now takes to walk down to a store on Chartres Street." In this voluble and imaginative style, like a clairvoyant or mesmerized person, he poured forth words with the rapidity of a torrent, till the moment of dissolution. His whole being, both intellectual and physical, seemed to be preternaturally and powerfully excited.

"In cases of yellow fever," says Dr. Dowler, one of the most eminent physicians in New Orleans, "at the moment of death, the circulation of the blood is sometimes more active than it ever was in the zenith of life and health. In one instance, a thermometer was placed in the armpit of a corpse at the last expiration, and remained there fifty-five minutes. The first five minutes gave $105°$; the next five minutes, $106\frac{1}{2}°$; the next, $108°$; ten minutes more, $108°$; ten minutes, 108°; ten minutes, 108°; and the last ten minutes, 108¼°. The veins were greatly distended. A ligature was placed on the arm; a vein was opened; about two ounces of blood jetted out, after which a trickling took place for a considerable time, amounting to twelve ounces. The circulation was found to be very rapid about the head. The left jugular was opened, as for ordinary blood-letting, but *no bandage or pressure was used*, the head being raised, so that the orifice was on a level with the breast bone. The blood jetted out completely, without wetting the skin, forming an arch, the diameter of which continued to extend for five minutes; at the end of eight minutes, the arch had contracted, owing, apparently, to small clots on the margins of the orifice, and the skin having once become wet, the blood, without being materially diminished, ran down the neck, jetting occasionally on removing clots from the orifice.

"For about *one hour*, the flow was copious, but at the end of that time, was diminishing rapidly. I caught nearly three pounds at first; this, with what ran down the neck after the jetting ceased, I estimated to amount to five pounds, or eighty ounces, from the jugular alone. As the blood-letting progressed, the discoloration of the skin of the face diminished. There was, as already mentioned, no bandage or pressure. It would be impossible, in this way, to bleed a living man half as much, as collapse of the vein, clots, fainting, &c., would prevent it. Hence the circulation in the veins was probably more active and persistent than in health. Let it be supposed that the upper or *distal* end of the jugular contained an ounce, when opened; this being discharged, no more could replace it, only by a circulatory force. But here the tube is filled eighty times in a few minutes.

"The heat of the patient in the early stages of the yellow fever is usually very great, but it falls off towards the close of the disease, both in the convalescent and dying stages; but among the dead, in many cases, it rises higher than in life, from a quarter of an hour to six or seven hours after death, rising sometimes to one hundred and thirteen degrees, and falling in the very same and in different regions both internally and externally."

The cases just enumerated are phenomena not, indeed, ordinarily witnessed in yellow fever epidemics. In this as in all the works of God, amidst a general uniformity, individual instances are greatly diversified. Is the yellow fever one of God's dispensations? Undoubtedly. It is a deduction of reason, — may I not say of common sense? — that there is but one efficient Cause of all the phenomena, both physical and moral, which take place in our world. The Bible affirms repeatedly, and in the strongest terms, that no evil can befall man without the knowledge, permission, and appointment of our heavenly Father. God does not love men less because they are writhing in pain, and "stretched in Disease's shapes abhorred." These calamities are just as necessary for man's development and highest good as the charms and advantages of ease, health, youth, bloom, and beauty.

In New Orleans, the instances have been numerous of patients rising from their beds, putting on their apparel, and engaging in conversation about their business, and plans for the future, but a few hours, or even only a few minutes, before death. Dr. Cartwright, in his account of the epidemic yellow fever which occurred at Natchez, in 1823, says that " in the last stage, in which *fever*, in the etymological sense of the term, disappeared, and all severe pain with it, the patient, before debilitated, often regained his strength so as to be able to walk about the room, and converse cheerfully with his friends. When there was no evident cause for this apparent recuperation, it invariably portended a fatal termination.

" A shoemaker, the day before death, got out of bed, went to work, and nearly finished making a shoe." He also says that " in the hospital, four or five patients, in the last stage of the disease, acquired great strength, left their beds, got brooms and the like, and after parading through the rooms for a time, died almost instantaneously." A man has been known to arise, shave, make his toilet with unusual care, sit down and write a letter to his distant relatives, informing them of his convalescence. It was folded, sealed, put into the hands of a servant to be conveyed to the post office, and before he could return to his master he had expired. In another instance a man arose, dressed himself, and walked the streets the length of several squares, and fell lifeless on the banquette. Monsieur Robin, in his Travels in Louisiana, mentions the case of a physician attacked with yellow fever, who, unconscious of any sickness, continued to attend his patients until just before his death. When interrogated, he declared that he was in good health. Others died reading, apparently in the greatest joy, and sometimes in raptures of delight. A young man indited a beautiful epistle to his betrothed as the world was receding forever from his view. Going to see a sick man one morning, I found him sitting at a small table, with his usual costume on, and reading a newspaper. He was in the greatest flow of spirits, full of wit, laughter, merriment, and jesting. I was requested to take a chair directly opposite to him, and the table was so narrow, that our faces almost touched each other. He was very fond of talking on phrenological subjects. There was an acquaintance, whom he did not prize very highly, who had just before left the room. He was describing his craniology in terms so irresistibly facetious that we both burst into a peal of laughter, when, in an instant, — in the twinkling of an eye, — he dropped his head upon his arms, which were laid upon the table before him, and breathed not again. We immediately placed him upon the bed, to see if he could not be resuscitated. But life had fled to return no more.

CHAPTER XI.

ON THE CONNECTION BETWEEN MY RELIGIOUS TEACHINGS AND THE PREVAILING CHARACTER OF THE PECULIAR EXPERIENCES THROUGH WHICH I HAVE PASSED IN NEW ORLEANS.

FENELON, in a work which he wrote on preaching and the composition of sermons, says that " no book is more important to a clergyman than the volume of human life. He should read it by day, and meditate thereon by night. Such a study will enable him to accommodate directions and exhortations to persons of all ages, conditions, and circumstances. And whenever a preacher advances what touches a man's character, or is applicable to his peculiar state and deficiencies, he is sure of being heard. To discover a person to himself, in a light in which he never saw his portrait before, produces a wonderful effect."

Since my settlement in New Orleans, I have tried to adopt the platform recommended by this venerable prelate of the Roman Catholic church. Setting aside the Bible, I have learned more about religion from reading the phenomena of the human heart and human life, than could be acquired from all the uninspired books in the world. The topics to which I allude in this remark are the following: What is man? Why have we been created capable even of angelic virtue, in a world where unavoidable circumstances render us so vile and grovelling, so frail, unwise, and unworthy? Whence these longings for exquisite, uninterrupted, ever-increasing happiness, where existence is made up of such adverse fates, hardships, and sufferings? We feel desires, aspirations, that soar upwards to the illimitable heavens, yet, in fact, are as destitute as the worm under our feet. Whence these strange extremes of joy and sorrow, light and darkness, good and evil, earth and heaven, which are mingled in our nature and allotments? These questions weigh heavily upon every reflecting mind.

With the exception of man, we see all things around and above us moving on in obedience to laws, wise, orderly, and harmonious. How magnificent is yon firmament! How bright and blessed are the beams of the sun! Mountains, hills, plains, valleys, and lakes are formed into scenes of indescribable loveliness, as if earth was intended to be a paradise. The groves are full of melody. Happy beings range every walk and department of the brute creation; but man groans under the crushing burdens of existence. He struggles and wears himself out in efforts to obtain that food, and other accommodations, which the brute enjoys in absolute exemption from labor and anxiety. Finally, at an unexpected moment, death steps in to close this short, eventful career. The curtain falls; the actor takes his final exit for regions hidden from mortal sight by clouds and shadows utterly impervious to the light of human reason.

How inexplicable do these things appear! I have

been surrounded with honest and inquiring sceptics. Often have they addressed me thus: "Why were we not made like the brutes, to run a constant round of gratification only? Why were we not so created as to be capable of accomplishing all the purposes of our existence, and attaining the highest happiness, by the indulgences merely of our natural desires and appetites? How different is our condition from this! At every step we encounter various forms of opposition. Obstacles and obstructions come from without and from within. Every day we feel the pressure of wants which earth cannot supply; every week, in spite of ourselves, is more or less a week of trials, sorrow, temptation, and bereavement. Now, reason looks upon this state of things, not with wonder only, but also with utter amazement. Reason inquires, If God is good, why is not man a larger recipient of his goodness? Why do not conscience and pleasure, desire and duty, always speak the same language? Why are they *ever* clashing, opposite, and contradictory, the one clamorously demanding what the other forbids? Why have not things on earth been so arranged that our state here might correspond with the picture suggested by these lines of the poet: —

> 'To virtue in the paths of pleasure trod,
> And owned a Father when they owned a God;
> No ill could fear in Him, but understood
> A sovereign being, but a sovereign good'?

Yet in the sublime depths of Nature above, around, beneath, and within us, we see no traces of a

Father's hand. As if in contempt of our weakness and misery, she rolls on in her course — dark, stern, silent, resistless, and appalling as the grave."

To such objections I have usually replied in the following terms: It is obvious that if we had nothing to guide us but animal appetites and passions, we could not occupy the rank of moral and accountable beings. We should in that case, like the bird, reptile, or fish, belong to the brute creation merely. What, then, would become of glory, wisdom and worth, indomitable energy and resolution, the trampling upon the mean and base, the triumphing over the vile — all those beauties and sublimities of virtue which shed eternal lustre on the character and history of man, that proclaim his alliance to the Divinity, and the everlasting expansion of his destiny? If our passions were not so constituted as to rebel often against our sense of the true, good, and proper, we should be as incapable of performing noble actions as the oak of the forest or a buffalo on the prairies.

I am compelled, then, to regard the world in which we are placed as perfectly adapted to our wants and the sublime purposes of our creation. There is no other spot in the universe where we could be as well off for the time being as we are here. God has placed us in this school of difficulties for benevolent purposes only, that by resisting, struggling against, and overcoming them, we might develop our powers, rise to a more intimate union with himself, and form the habits required for our exaltation and blessedness, as we shall travel onward upon the line of an existence that can never terminate.

The peculiar life which I was called to pass through in New Orleans enforced upon me the conclusion of Scripture that there is no absolute, eternal evil in the boundless universe of God. Nothing that we call evil is final. It is only the necessary means of a greater and ever-expanding good.

> "Presumptuous man, wouldst thou the reason find
> Why made so weak, so little, and so blind?
> First, if thou canst, the harder reason guess,
> Why made no weaker, blinder, and no less;
> Ask of thy mother earth why oaks are made
> Taller and stronger than the weeds they shade;
> Or ask of yonder argent fields above
> Why Jove's satellites are less than Jove;
> Say not, then, man's imperfect, Heaven in fault;
> Say, rather, man's as perfect as he ought,
> His knowledge measured to his state and place,
> His time a moment, and a point his space."

Again, by living in New Orleans I have been deeply impressed with the vanity of human ambition, and the worthlessness of what men usually most covet — the possession of wealth. Cases of the following description have been constantly passing before my eyes, like the successive pictures of a panorama. A young man settles in New Orleans. He is noble and highly gifted, the delight and hope of his friends, relatives, and acquaintances. After the ordeal of the yellow fever, he becomes established in a profitable course of business. With a most commendable perseverance he carries forward his various enterprises, till he believes himself independently rich. Happening to be in the counting room of one of these fortunate persons, on a certain morning in the month of November, he spoke to me thus: —

"I pity you, when I think of the hard, cheerless, and unprofitable labors of your professional life. You are just emerging from the toils and horrors of another epidemic. Poor you are to-day, and probably always will be. Nor is your destitution to be regarded in any other light than a misfortune beyond your control. The sufferings which you are compelled to relieve will always keep your purse empty. It will be impossible for you, as long as you live here, to lay up any thing against sickness or old age. My own fortune I consider as a fixed fact. This coming winter I intend to wind up my affairs, and retire to some healthy part of the world, to enjoy the remainder of my days in leisure, in the tranquil pursuits of an independent country life. What is the use of clerical labors in such a place as this, where Mammon and Bacchus reign supreme? If you were a lawyer, merchant, or politician, you might succeed here. And if you are determined to pursue your present vocation, would it not be better to repair to a more propitious latitude — to Boston, or some northern city, where the institutions of religion are settled, and where your labors and talents would be better understood and appreciated?"

This advice emanated from a noble and sincere mind, but it was a mind which had never been lifted above the low plane of a merely physical and sensual world. At that time I was upon the vestibule of my clerical career, young, and inexperienced as to the vicissitudes of a temporal life. Walking from this interview to my study, the reflection was deeply impressed on my heart that the counsel of

my friend was deserving of serious consideration.
It might be that he was right. It might be that I
was making a foolish and visionary sacrifice, by
occupying such a forbidding and unpromising field
of labor as New Orleans. The subject weighed
heavily on my mind. I never for a moment harbored the idea of engaging in any secular profession.
But the thought occurred to me that it would perhaps be expedient to accept the invitation of my
friend to accompany him the next summer on a tour
through the Northern and Western States, with a
view, among other things, of selecting a more eligible theatre for my professional pursuits.

Here the matter rested for a while. In the inscrutable scheme of divine Providence, this person
was not permitted to realize the beautiful plan which
he had marked out for future consummation. It
was otherwise decreed in the counsels of Heaven.
Within a few weeks after the conversation just mentioned, and before he had enjoyed an opportunity to
call in his means, and invest them in permanent
securities, a great, sudden, and most unexpected
revulsion in the commercial world swept over our
city. His darling fortune, which he had looked upon
to be as stable as the everlasting hills, was swallowed
up forever. All his possessions and glories vanished
in a day. He never recovered from the blow. A
few years afterwards I saw him laid in the grave, a
bankrupt not only as to property, but also in regard
to moral worth and spiritual excellence.

This and similar incidents put an utter end to all
thoughts of taking any steps to better my outward

circumstances in life. I felt the surpassing wisdom of those words of the Psalmist, "Verily, every man in his firmest state is but a vapor. Surely every man walketh as a shadow. Surely he disquieteth himself in vain. He heapeth up treasures, and knoweth not who will enjoy them." The heathen poet Horace somewhere says, "What is less durable than flowers in spring? What is more changeable than the moon? Yet these are the best images of human life. Why, then, should creatures, by nature formed to mortality, fatigue themselves with endless and uncertain projects?" The anecdote to which I have adverted presents a point of instruction, although not, indeed, novel, nor extraordinary; yet I look back upon it as an epoch in my moral history, and as such, it is, perhaps, deserving a place in these very humble records. I could multiply instances of the kind, in my subsequent experiences, whose recital would fill volumes.

About that time my mind was first opened to realize the truth and beauty of the following description, which, though familiar to me from a child, I had never before appreciated: —

> "Know then this truth, (enough for man to know,)
> Virtue alone is happiness below;
> The only point where human bliss stands still,
> And tastes the good, unmingled with the ill;
> Where only merit constant pay receives,
> Is blessed in what it takes and what it gives;
> The joy unequalled, if its end is gain,
> And if it lose, attended with no pain;
> Without satiety, though e'er so blessed,
> And but more relished as the more distressed;
> The broadest mirth unfeeling folly wears
> Less pleasing far than virtue's very tears;

> Good, from each object, from each place acquired,
> Forever exercised, yet never tired;
> Never elated while one man's oppressed,
> Never dejected while another's blessed;
> And where no wants, no wishes can remain,
> Since but to wish more virtue is to gain."

This is a poetic paraphrase of those memorable words of Scripture, " Great peace have they who love thy law. They have a happiness which the world can neither give nor destroy." For years I have been in the habit of repeating this quotation, many times in a day — I might almost say continually. Its beauties have pervaded my soul, and dictated the predominant thoughts, feelings, and actions of my life. They have afforded me not only a purer but an infinitely higher degree of happiness than I could have derived from all the merely temporal possessions and glories of earth. That hour I became richer than gold could make me, when God was pleased to reveal to my heart the sublime sentiment, that human happiness does not consist in the pleasures of a physical and sensual world, in whatever profusion or variety they be enjoyed.

Jesus Christ began his first discourse by declaring to his hearers that it was not in wealth, fame, office, power, or pleasure, to confer the bliss they sighed for. Blessed, he said, are they only who are enamoured of the charms of wisdom, integrity, and moral excellence; who admire a gentle, meek, forgiving, pure, social, loving spirit; who have the *living* God for their help, and whose only hope is in his infinite life, light, truth, love, wisdom, power, and beneficence.

Of the whole number of young men who have immigrated to New Orleans since my first acquaintance with that place, very few have succeeded in acquiring an independence. One of the fortunate few retired to his native place, and built a charming villa, where he and his family might be happy for the rest of their days. But in one year after their removal, the father, mother, and two children were laid in their graves, and left their wealth to others. Now, this gentleman was wise in accumulating property by all the honorable means in his power. I think, too, that he was wise in leaving New Orleans when he did, and fixing his residence in a more salubrious and beautiful place. But he was not wise in abjuring religion, and going upon the ground that his happiness depended upon outward condition and circumstances only. There is no delusion by which mankind are greater sufferers than this.

It is hard for them to believe that virtue and happiness are coincident. The doctrine of the New Testament is that all living, whether high or low, learned or ignorant, rich or poor, would be happy to-day, if they were sincerely actuated by the principles of the gospel. It is hard to admit this truth. We struggle against it to the last. Tell a young man that he may live and die poor, and yet be a noble being, obtain the highest honors of life, and enjoy its purest pleasures, your words will sound to him like the very essence of folly and fanaticism. He thinks that his mission in this world is to get riches, to amass gold, to scrape together the dust of earth, and that without these he will sink into utter wretchedness and insignificance.

Imagine the external condition of mankind to be represented by a scale resembling that of a thermometer. Place a rude, illiterate, inexperienced, wicked young man, say of the age of twenty, at the lowest degree in this scale. Now, suppose that, without the slightest intellectual or moral improvement, he were to ascend from one stage to another of success, till he became invested with the splendors and advantages of a millionnaire. During all this progression of outward good, he would suffer a regular diminution of enjoyment, and in his final state would be more wretched than he was at the beginning. This may seem incredible to some, but I feel certain of its truth, because in several instances I have witnessed the identical experiment, and carefully noted the result.

I once heard a merchant, now in his grave, who began life with nothing, and had acquired a large estate, confess that no successes which attended him in the accumulation of property had added a particle to his happiness. "So far as circumstances of fortune are concerned," he remarked, "I was far happier when a poor boy fifteen years old, in a country store, and earning a few dollars only per month, than I have been at any subsequent period of my life." Yet this man had never failed in his business, had never met with any considerable reverses of fortune. The course of his affairs had been remarkably smooth and prosperous. At the same time he was surrounded with the endearments of a refined, happy family, and not a member of his domestic circle had ever died.

This gentleman took a pew in our church. He had occupied it but one Sunday previous to the visit, during which the conversation just referred to took place. Monday morning I called on him, and was conducted into a private apartment, a recess to his counting room. Alone and undisturbed we had a long conversation on the subject of religion. He led off by saying that "yesterday was the first time he had ever attended church in New Orleans, and that he had never in his life before had any conversation with a clergyman on religious matters." It was evident that he had read and thought much. But from a youth he had cherished the idea that Christianity was but a delusion, and that death was an eternal sleep. When I asked why he came to hear me preach, he replied " that Judge C. had told him that our pulpit advocated some new views of the Bible and a future state, which he thought would be interesting to me." Then he made the remark already quoted, that he had not found happiness in temporal prosperity. "Can you explain," said he, "the reasons of my failure?"

I answered him by making a quotation which seemed to me relevant. In my efforts to enlighten and convince honest inquirers after truth, it has long been my habit to use, as far as possible, the arguments and words of distinguished writers in preference to my own suggestions. In this manner I have given to the ideas which I wished to communicate the power and authority of a great name, that to many minds is quite irresistible. I said Dr. Paley somewhere remarks, " It is a well-established fact in the science of human happiness, that no plenitude of outward gratifications can make their possessors happy, unless he have something in reserve, something to look forward to, and hope for, beyond the the grave. The merely worldly man feels himself confined; he sees the limits on every side, there is no room for an adequate expansion of his soul. The human mind is so organized that it can never be filled, sufficiently interested by the realities of to-day. It is constantly looking beyond the scenes of the present tense, to find refreshment and support in the anticipated glories of some distant event or attainment. Condition, external circumstances, have so little connection with our true welfare as to render it probable that the means of happiness are equally distributed among mankind, and that in this respect one person has no advantage over another. Throughout society, every external blessing that one possesses, not enjoyed by his neighbor, has some offset or counterbalancing drawback, every peculiar evil to which he is subjected some peculiar compensation."

He replied, " Dr. Paley was a great man, but I cannot receive, even on his authority, what seems unreasonable, repugnant to common sense. That poor mechanic, whom you see there laying brick, is obliged to work hard every day to support himself and family. Do you intend to say that his means of felicity, so far as external matters are concerned, are equal to those which I possess? Does not my fortune enable me to taste of a multitude of enjoyments absolutely inaccessible to this workman?"

I replied, "You may not estimate correctly the connection between mere wealth and inward peace. What do you actually gain by your superior abundance? Can it purchase for you mental acquisitions — the joys, hopes, treasures of wisdom, knowledge, and piety? Is there any golden key wherewith one can unlock the gates of paradise? Can silver buy exemption from weakness, sin, error, pain, disease, bereavement, death, or any other evil? O, how little can it add to our real satisfaction! Juvenal, a heathen poet, says, 'In your prayers do not ask the gods for silver, gold, houses, lands, fame, power, and other gifts of an outward fortune, but rather beseech them to bestow on you the blessings of good sense, a generous heart, moral excellence, a pure and virtuous life.' These constitute the only source of substantial happiness. And the means of enjoying these, like the light and air, are universally diffused.

"I repeat it, that poor operative has essentially the same means of satisfaction which you enjoy. He has the same body, with its wondrous mechanism, and power of action and enjoyment; the same attributes of mind — reason, conscience, love, joy, hope, and immortal aspirations; the same access to the pleasures which are derived from the pursuits of business, society, books, the intercourse of friendship, and the domestic circle. He has the same sun, air, earth, water, food, nightly repose. He has the same Bible, the same God, the same Saviour, and the same prospect of final, ever-progressive bliss in the kingdom of heaven.

"Contrasted with these sublime possessions, how utterly insignificant are those accidents which flatter pride and vanity! That man may, this instant, as he is adjusting that brick, cherish a single thought which, on the score of happiness, is worth more than all your perishable treasures."

Not long after the conversation above narrated, this gentleman, who had become a regular attendant on our preaching, was called to taste the bitter cup of grief. Two of his children died, not far from the same time; then his wife expired, very suddenly. His own health soon failed, and he was numbered with the dead. In the last conversation which I had with him, he said, "I no longer doubt the reality of a future state of existence. Could I have been so made as to remember and love my wife and children after their decease, if we were destined never to meet again? It seems to me impossible. In that case, I am deceived, trifled with, and cheated, by the inevitable laws and operations of my own mind. Besides, if there be no future state, human life is not worth having. We exist here only to be broken with toil and years; to be racked with pain; to be wasted with sickness; to be desolated with one surge of sorrow and disappointment after another, till we sink, to be seen no more on earth. If I thought that this was the last of us, I should be an atheist." He died a firm believer in God, revelation, virtue, and immortality.

Is there a greater delusion among men than the false estimate, which is almost universal, concerning the external advantages of life, as a means of happiness? Cowper somewhere says, "I have no doubt, if we saw the whole truth, we should behold more of divine love in what is called the evil, than the good, of human existence, and should rather encounter every day the greatest difficulties and sufferings, than to float smoothly and quietly down the current of a being, calm and untroubled, but self-regarding only."

My experiences have taught me another lesson — that, in every instance, persons are happy just in proportion as they are earnest, self-sacrificing, and unwearied in endeavoring to discharge the offices of mercy. Cold, narrow, unsympathizing, self-indulgent people are always miserable. In the epidemic of 1853, a wealthy family of my acquaintance left New Orleans before the sickly season set in, to spend the summer in travelling. They crossed the Atlantic to gaze upon the wonders of the old world — its scenery, its palaces, parks, and galleries of art. It was wise and commendable in them, no doubt, to employ their time and means in this way. I allude to the fact simply for the purpose of illustration.

Near my residence was another family, in moderate circumstances, who never went out of the city during that awful visitation. They spent the summer in the labors of philanthropy, visiting the poor and sick, devoting their days and nights to the relief of destitute and deserted strangers, for several months in succession. Now, if these people were animated by the beautiful sentiments of love, by sympathy, heroism, and the soul-exalting spirit of self-sacrifice, — to say nothing of duty, — were they not happier in performing those noble works of philanthropy than their neighbors, who passed the same time in journeying through foreign lands? I answer this question affirmatively; for true happiness comes not from the perishable glories of earth, from luxury, the accumulation of wealth, from ease, vanity, or pride, but from conflicts with and triumph over selfish desires, the subjugation of dishonorable appetites and passions, the devotion of our lives, and all our resources, in the service of God and humanity.

Happy is he who feels the nobility of a humble and benevolent spirit. We read that Jesus Christ lived to deny and sacrifice himself for the salvation of a world. A child knows that "for the joy that was set before him, he endured the agonies of the cross." He tells us that we must follow his example, tread in his footsteps, and daily take up the cross. This is, of course, figurative language. It means that we must be ready at all times to sacrifice our feelings, taste, convenience, and emolument to promote the well-being of those around us. We are bound to goodness by the laws of an everlasting necessity. He who feels not the impulses of Christian love, though in possession of the amplest means, excludes himself even from temporal enjoyment. He can derive no real bliss from heaven above or earth beneath — from nature, business, amusements, art, society, science, or literature.

24*

There is an ordinance appointed by heaven for the government of the planets, sun, moon, and stars. Fire, earth, sea, air, times and seasons, trees and animals, are in harmony with the laws prescribed for them by the Creator. Now, God has so fashioned and attuned our intellectual and moral faculties, that as the thrusting of the hand into a flame of fire awakens acute pain, so a merely self-indulgent life narrows, darkens, and agonizes the soul, and by a law as fixed as that which carries the heavenly bodies through the fields of space.

If, then, we thoroughly understood the soul, and consulted its essential wants, we should be lovers of God and duty more than lovers of self and selfish pleasure. We should realize the impossibility of getting along happily without rejoicing with those that rejoice and weeping with those that weep. We should esteem it of more importance to be actuated by a strong sensibility to the wants and sorrows of our fellow-beings, than to gain wealth, ease, or aggrandizement. If we understood ourselves, we should realize that our own welfare and advancement were indissolubly connected with the interests of our neighbors.

O, there is no bliss for man on earth but that which flows from noble and divine thoughts, a soul alive to God, energetic, spotless, unwearied, zealous in doing good, a heart warmed with the sunshine of a heavenly world, enriched with a godlike, calm, unwavering hope, through Jesus, of that immortal blessedness which awaits the children of God. The man who lives only for himself, and cares not for others, is always restless and dissatisfied. Preaching, arguments, the impressive appeals of human experience, affect him no more than if he were " a brother to the insensible rock, or sluggish clod, which the rude swain turns with his share, and treads upon."

I have studied the Bible every day for the last forty years. This devotedness to the volume of revealed truth has given to my theological views and preaching those peculiarities which have been so extensively regarded as erroneous and unscriptural. But the particular subjects of my sermons in New Orleans were generally suggested by things which parochial visiting enforced upon my attention. Events, incidents, casual remarks, hints given in some hasty discussion of a supposed fallacy in my customary teachings, or something else which happened in my usual rounds each Monday morning, led me into trains of thought and reasonings which were embodied in my next Sunday's discourse. I have never advocated in the pulpit what is technically called the *faith* or *creed* of any particular denomination, but have endeavored to accommodate instructions to those individual cases and exigencies which at the time seemed to demand especial and immediate attention. My daily out-door experiences and sermons on the Sabbath sustained to each other the relation of cause and effect. Hence my preaching had some novelties, and a great many imperfections; but they were unavoidable, and grew out of circumstances and influences which were above and beyond my control.

CHAPTER XV.

DANGEROUS ILLNESS. — CONVALESCENCE. — JOURNEY TO EUROPE.

The first week of November, 1846, disease, in one of its most painful and incurable forms, made me a prisoner in my chamber for the space of ten weeks. Some years previous to this date, I had suffered at times severely from a morbid state of the liver, one of the most prevalent complaints among those residents of Louisiana who were born in the latitude of snow and ice. An internal abscess was formed, which, fortunately for my preservation, matured and came away (to use a phrase current in the medical profession) spontaneously.

During the whole month of November, my strength gradually but constantly declined, till I was prostrated to infantine weakness. It was a great effort to raise my hand, and respiration was so difficult, I felt as if every breath would be my last. That point of my disease termed the crisis continued two or three days. During this time I was unable to close my eyes, and had abandoned even the hope of recovery. One night I said to Mrs. Clapp, "I am dying." She thought so too. An icy coldness had nearly reached the citadel of life. We were alone. I was in perfect possession of my consciousness. From some cause or other, my mental powers were much more active than when in health. My memory was so excited, vigorous, and grasping, that I recalled easily the whole of my life, and could repeat to myself passages in the Hebrew, Greek, and Latin languages without an effort. All the literature that I had acquired came up before me with supernatural freshness and charms. A true record of my thoughts and feelings that memorable night would fill a volume — and a volume infinitely more interesting than any other exercises that I have ever enjoyed.

Strange as the declaration may sound to some, that was probably the happiest night of my life. My soul was filled with delightful imaginations. I fancied that I saw angels playing on their golden harps, in the most exquisite and enrapturing airs. A kind of profound curiosity, mixed with the highest delight, dwelt on my mind. For at that period I was not afraid to die. I kept looking to catch a glimpse of the spirit land, whose scenes I expected every moment would burst upon me, when I should close my eyes on earth and open them upon the light of a day whose sun will never go down. Nothing which I had ever read seemed so sweet to me as the following words of the Psalmist: "Yet am I ever under thy care; by my right hand thou dost hold me up. Thou wilt guide me with thy counsel, and at last receive me to glory. Whom have I in heaven but thee, and whom on earth do I love in comparison with thee? Though my flesh and my heart fail, GOD is the strength of my heart, and my portion forever." Had my death occurred that night, I should have expired with the lines of Dr. Watts upon my lips: —

> "Jesus can make a dying bed,
> Feel soft as downy pillows are,
> Whilst on his breast I lean my head,
> And breathe my life out sweetly there."

As to the sins or the virtues of my past life, the thought of the former gave me no pain, and that of the latter afforded me no joy, hope, or consolation, with respect to my future destiny. I could think of nothing but the infinite, everlasting, unchangeable mercy of God in Christ. I felt certain that he would go with me through the valley of death, and beyond the dark, dying struggle, introduce me to the inheritance incorruptible, undefiled, and unfading. I rejoiced in the thought, that before another rising sun, I should be permitted to lay down the burdens of this "worn being, so full of pain." A feeling not unlike regret accompanied my first impression that I was returning back to mingle again in the trials, duties, and vicissitudes of earth.

About one o'clock in the morning I began to lose my sight, and was for some time almost blind. Now I said, "'This is the last of earth.' *Father, into thy hands I commend my spirit.*" After the lapse of an hour or two, during which consciousness never forsook me an instant, my vision began to return. The vital powers rallied, the chill of death abated into a genial warmth and gentle perspiration. Before the dawn of day the physicians were in the room, and announced that a favorable change had taken place in my symptoms. Yet, they said, my debility was so extreme, that nothing but the most careful nursing could raise me again. There was

but one person on earth able and willing to afford
me the attention which my case required. That
was my wife, who scarcely left my bedside for two
months. She watched over me day and night,
and administered with her own hands the various
restoratives prescribed by the physicians. Her extraordinary and unintermitted efforts saved my life.
And were I in possession of the whole earth, I could
not make adequate returns and acknowledgments
for her unparalleled self-sacrifice in my behalf.

I have not mentioned my feelings in the immediate prospect of death as furnishing any evidence
of personal piety, or the correctness of my religious
faith at the time. No test of character is more
vague, indefinite, and unsatisfactory, than the experiences of a dying hour. I once saw a man, who
had led what is called an immoral life, walk down
that valley of mystery with a sustained demeanor, with
a calm aspect, with a firm step, with expressions of
the gentlest sympathy towards surrounding relatives
and friends, and with a hope triumphant and transporting. On the contrary, I have seen the timid,
pure, conscientious Christian die in despair, though
professing to believe in One who has destroyed the
power of death, who came to deliver us from its fear,
and unfold to a suffering world the bright and exalting hopes of a future, endless, and blessed existence.
Why? Because he had imbibed the erroneous sentiment, that future happiness will be awarded to
those only who die in the possession of a peculiar
faith. Eternal bliss is bestowed upon the principle
of grace irrespective of our character and conduct

this side the grave. The New Testament makes it certain that a disembodied spirit cannot commit sin, nor suffer pain.

The beginning of the year 1847 was blessed with mild, balmy weather, precisely like that which prevails in what is termed the Indian summer. The thermometer for a fortnight ranged, on an average, from sixty to seventy degrees with a clear, bracing atmosphere, and a lovely Italian sky, "which does not seem to bound your thought, scarcely your vision, but carries them away to the serene, ever-opening depths of the illimitable heavens." Every one, who, after suffering severe illness, has, from the extreme of emaciation and weakness, recovered a new existence, has probably been conscious of the same delightful sensations of convalescence which I experienced. When I became strong enough to walk across my room, though in such a state of debility that two minutes' exercise fatigued me so much that I was obliged to sit down and rest, my bosom was filled with calm, placid, and serene sensations, not unlike those which are supposed to be the portion of the perfect and sinless in the land of immortality.

Often during the day my feelings became buoyant, elastic, bounding with thrills of happiness which I do not remember to have experienced before or since. The recollection of the manner in which the world had affected me in former years, its ten thousand hopes, desires, and passions, seemed like a dream. I felt sure that those vanities would never return upon me; that they had departed forever from my bosom and embrace. But alas! when health returned, life and earth regained their wonted charms, and feelings and passions revived which I had hoped would never again knock at the door of my heart for admission. But they did knock with a fiendish impatience, and a legion of demons at their back, ready to commence dread havoc upon that beautiful structure, which I fancied sickness and renewed promises of faithfulness to God had reared to be the everlasting dwelling place of my soul. This illustrates the meaning and truthfulness of that portion of Scripture in which the apostle affirms that God has placed us here, under the dominion of laws which make all men more or less foolish, weak, erring, sinful, and unhappy, in spite of their utmost wisdom, prayerfulness, resolution, and self-denial.

I shall never forget, until memory has lost her seat, the first time I rode out after being shut up in my chamber more than two months. It was on a pleasant morning, about eleven o'clock. Every object had a new aspect and a new coloring. I looked with fresh and admiring views upon the heavens and earth, the gardens and fields, as if I had never before beheld the beautiful face of nature. I thought of the words of the dying Rousseau. When he apprehended that his final exit drew near, he desired the windows of his apartment to be opened, that he might have the pleasure, as he said, of beholding nature once more. "How lovely she is!" he exclaimed; "how pure and serene thy countenance!" Were not those feelings natural and becoming a Christian? Who knows but they sprang from the workings of a heart touched at that solemn crisis by divine grace, and prepared to be ushered into the higher scenes, wonders, and glories of a spiritual existence? I had a quantity of happiness that morning more than enough to counterbalance the pains of my whole life.

I think the greatest sin of which we are guilty is ingratitude. Life here, properly viewed, is crowned with glory and honor, with loving kindness and tender mercy. "It is a great and ineffable good. God saw and pronounced that it was good. It is good in the unnumbered sources of happiness around it. It is good in the ten thousand buoyant and happy affections within it. It is good in its connection with infinite goodness, and in its hope of infinite glory hereafter. True, our life is frail in its earthly state, and it is often bowed down with heavy burdens; but still it endures, and revives, and flourishes; still it is redeemed from destruction, and crowned with superabounding mercies. Frail, indeed, and yet strong is it in its heavenly nature. Here the immortal is clothed with mortality, and the incorruptible with corruption. It is like an instrument formed for celestial melody, whose materials, like those of an organ, were taken from things that moulder and go back to dust; but lo, the hand of the divine Artificer has been upon it! It is curiously wrought; it is fearfully and wonderfully made; it is fashioned for every tone of gladness, hope, and triumph. It may be relaxed, but it can be strung again. It may send forth a mournful strain, but it is formed also for the music of heavenly joy. Even its sadness is pleasing and mournful to the soul. Even suffering is hallowed and dear. Life has that value, that even misery cannot destroy it. It neutralizes grief, and makes it a source of deep and sacred interest. Ah, holy hours of sorrow and suffering! hours of communion with the great and triumphant Sufferer! Who that has passed through your silent moments of trust, prayer, and resignation, would give you up for all the brightness and beatitude of earth's temporal prosperity?"*

The third Sabbath of January, 1847, though still too feeble to study or preach, I insisted upon being carried to the church, that I might once more sit in the pulpit a few moments only, and look out upon a congregation that I had never expected to meet again on earth. Notice of my intention was inserted in the papers of the previous day — Saturday. The morning was fair, and the house was filled to overflowing. When the carriage was at the door, my friends advanced the strongest motives to dissuade me from fulfilling the appointment. But my family physician overruled their objections, on the ground that it would probably do me good to gratify the intense longing which I had to revisit the sanctuary of God. It was agreed that I should not attempt to speak at all, but sit quietly in the pulpit whilst the choir sang an anthem, accompanied with the organ. I fully intended to keep my promise. My friends helped me up the pulpit stairs. The ascent exhausted me, and I sank into the chair in a fainting condition. I could not see the faces of the hearers. Cordials were applied freely, and in a few moments I felt better. The organ struck up its heavenly tones.

* Dr. Dewey.

Soon I could see the audience distinctly, and recognized many countenances of dear and beloved ones, to whom I had in my mind bidden an eternal adieu. The effect was overwhelming. I felt as if I had returned from the dead, to afford ocular demonstration that our life will not be lost in the dark, silent tomb.

When the music ceased, prompted by an irresistible impulse, I rose to speak. One of the trustees, who sat in a chair near me, in a whisper said, " You must not attempt to address the audience. Pronounce the benediction and retire." But I could not help repeating a few verses of the 103d Psalm: " Bless the Lord, O my soul, and all that is within me, bless his holy name," &c. This excited me so much, I felt such an excess of joy, that I was compelled to relieve my mind by giving it utterance in something like the following words: —

" My brethren, I have been raised from the borders of the grave by that ever-present Friend who giveth us life, breath, and all things. One night during my late confinement, I expected every moment to breathe my last. My mind was never more calm or composed. What made me so? An unfaltering faith in God, Jesus, and immortality; the thought that I belonged to God, not only by creation, an upholding providence, and a solemn accountability, but by a love vast as infinitude — a love that no amount of iniquity on my part could change into coldness, indifference, or hatred — a love that can never, even for a moment, intermit its depth, fervor, strength, tenderness; can never waver or fail; which makes it certain that we cannot be finally and forever lost, because our own glory and happiness are identified with those of the Creator himself. The atoning, reconciling sacrifice made by Christ is simply a clear, unambiguous revelation of God's love for man.

"The moment that a person understands and appreciates the doctrine of the gospel, — that the works of nature, the events of time, and the destinies of a coming eternity, are but the counsels and unfoldings of a perfect, boundless beneficence; that the Power which called us into existence, and has ordained all the changes of health, sickness, joy, sorrow, prosperity, and gloom, which we experience, is infinite, unchanging, eternal, and almighty love, — that very instant he becomes an enlightened, rejoicing disciple of the Son of God. As the light of this revelation dawns upon his soul, he exclaims, ' All is good, all is well, all is right, and shall be forever.' His religion is not a cold, barren speculation, but a profound sentiment; a deep, intense, all-subduing, and sanctifying faith; a faith that every thing which befalls him, from the cradle to the grave, will issue in results great and glorious beyond the reach of thought or imagination. Through the telescope of the Bible, he looks out upon the enrapturing scenes of a future state, rising in all the effulgence of an ever-progressive glory, beyond the sad ruins of earth and time. Hope in an inheritance so exalted lifts the mind above all the reverses, sorrows, and convulsions of earth. What can reach or disturb the profound peace awakened by a principle so divine?

"My friends, when you come to die, if blessed

with an unimpaired consciousness, how utterly worthless will then appear to you the wealth, fame, and aggrandizement for which so many strive and struggle, weary and wear themselves out, regardless of their higher interests! Then, too, you will find no satisfaction in the memory of your good deeds — deeds of faith, repentance, devotion, holiness, or charity. Though ever so eminent in Christian attainments, you will feel that you have no more claim, on the score of justice, to the divine mercy than the greatest reprobate that ever died. Your only prayer will be that of the publican, 'God be merciful to me a sinner.' Your only hope, then, will be that it is the free, undeserved, omnipotent *purpose* of the Father, in spite of your sins and follies, to raise you finally to that higher existence where wisdom, virtue, and holiness will reign unclouded and immeasurable.

"I do not believe that it is in our power to love God at all without a firm, full, and immovable expectation of living forever in a world to come. Suppose that at this very moment, by irresistible arguments, or any other means, each of us should become inspired with a deep, intense, undoubting conviction that we had no souls; that the Bible, church, pulpit, and philosophy are themselves deluded, and are deluding the world, touching this subject; that what we call the mind, is destined to pass away with the body, bend before the same resistless law of change, decline, die, and go back to dust; imagine, I mean, that we were compelled to feel, with absolute certainty, that as beast, bird, fish, and insect retire at last from every blade of grass, flower, shrub, tree, plain, and valley, hill and mountain, from every region of water and air, to exist no more, so we, also, at the expiration of this feverish, transitory life, will be doomed to close our eyes on a glorious universe, and be swallowed up in the dark gulf of eternal forgetfulness. Now, I ask, with such a gloomy, revolting creed, could we possibly cherish the emotions of piety, offer adoration to the Supreme, rehearse even the Lord's prayer with sincerity, present upon the altar of this or any other church the sacrifice of a calm, contented, grateful, and rejoicing heart? This question requires no answer. We must be able to look away with buoyant hope beyond the grave, before the thought of an almighty Creator can inspire us with wonder and delight — before we can become enamoured of the charms of virtue, cease to indulge and obey the bodily appetites, or exult in the manifestations of infinity, omnipotence, and boundless love displayed in the beautiful, but shadowy, evanescent scenes of the present world. When a person fully believes that a nobler, immortal destiny awaits, not himself, relatives, and friends only, but all the race of Adam, he must of necessity become pious; his heart is instantly replenished with holy, divine affections, and goes forth to engage spontaneously in the love, worship, and service of the great Father.

"In my late sickness, I was made unspeakably happy by the assurance, resting on the revelation of Jesus, that my heavenly Father can never allow a real *hurt or injury* to be inflicted upon me here or hereafter; can never permit me to be *hurt or injured* by myself or others, (punishment is not hurt, but healing;) can never allow my intellectual, moral being to be crushed out by the mysterious forces of time, nature, change, sin, or death. All the inhabitants of New Orleans would become Christians to-day, if they could be made to realize the true character of God — if they could be brought to see the wonders of that higher existence which Jesus has unfolded; an existence where, instead of sin, sickness, broken, bereaved hearts, and bitter tears, will reign unmingled purity, ever-advancing knowledge, and constantly increasing joy in the realms of a life which can never terminate."

I was occupied twenty minutes in delivering the above address. My friends remarked that at the commencement my face was as pallid as that of a corpse; but as I warmed with the subject, it was flushed with a glow rarely exhibited even in my days of health. Words flowed from me with the ease and freedom of one speaking under the influence of mesmerism. The perspiration flowed in streams. I was carried home and laid upon the bed, where I slept profoundly till the next morning. No alarming consequences followed the effort, as my friends anticipated. On the contrary, I felt much better for it, and went to the church every succeeding Sabbath morning the next two months. On the first Sunday in April, 1847, I preached a farewell discourse preparatory to my leaving for Europe. It was the wish of my physicians that I should select a mode of crossing the Atlantic which would protract the period of my voyage as long as possible. I therefore embarked in a merchant vessel for Liverpool, which left New Orleans the beginning of May.

It took us fifty-five days to make the passage. For one week we advanced scarcely a mile, being obliged to lie to in order to repair damages received from a tornado. Dr. Dewey, in his Journal of a Tour to Europe, says, " I defy any body, not thoroughly accustomed to the sea, to enjoy its grandeur, after having been rocked into that indescribable state of ennui, disquiet, discomfort, and inertness which the sea often produces. I do not mean seasickness, but a sickness of the sea, which has never, that I know, been described. It is a tremendous ennui, a complete inaptitude to all enjoyment, a total inability to be pleased with any thing. Nothing is agreeable — neither eating, nor drinking, nor walking, nor talking, nor reading, nor writing ; nor even is going to sleep an agreeable process, and waking is perfect misery."

My experience was directly the reverse of this description. Every thing was agreeable to me. I never passed as many happy days in succession on land as I did during my voyage from New Orleans to Liverpool. I will speak of the delightful sensations which I experienced under two heads, to adopt the sermon style — those which came from an *external* source, and those derived from an *internal* origin. I will begin with the external, premising that, like Dr. Dewey, I was never seasick for a moment in my whole life. On the contrary, when at sea I have a more voracious appetite, and a keener gusto for the indulgences of the table, than I ever feel on shore. I could sit all day and gaze with rapture on the great sea, that majestic and lovely emblem of the all-wise, all-perfect, all-beautiful, and eternal One. The mighty deep mirrors his amazing, illimitable perfections. Its wonderful extent, of which we can form no adequate conception, — its unexplored abysses, lower than plummet ever sounded, — are appealed to by inspired writers as the most striking revelations of infinitude and omnipotence which our globe presents. The continual motion and irresistible force of that mass of waters compel us to feel our nothingness — how entirely dependent and insignificant we are. I cannot imagine how it is possible for even an unreflecting person to look on this theatre of a Creator's manifestations without a sublime, thrilling sense of his presence and attributes.

> "Thou glorious mirror, where the Almighty's form
> Glasses itself in tempests; in all time,
> Calm or convulsed, in breeze, or gale, or storm,
> Icing the pole, or in the torrid clime
> Dark-heaving, boundless, endless, and sublime —
> The image of eternity — the throne
> Of the Invisible."

The ocean does not, as some suppose, exhibit always to our view the same unvaried and monotonous scene. Far from it. Its aspects are endlessly diversified. No genius of poet, painter, or scholar can adequately delineate them. I remember one morning, when in the middle of the Atlantic, that, as far as my eye extended, there was an expanse which looked smooth, unruffled, and shining like a surface of polished glass. Not a breath of air disturbed the deep serene. All was still — silent as the tomb. I fancied, almost, that I had entered some new, strange world, some boundless solitude of waters, that were incapable of motion. But all at once a change came over the scene; from the point where I was sitting on the deck to the utmost verge of the horizon, the surface of the sea began to crisp or quiver; it was roughened as if fanned " by the invisible wings of elves and fairies on some maritime expedition." This was followed by a slight, delicate, graceful undulation of the waters, of surpassing and ineffable beauty. If we beheld the ocean only in this state, we should not suspect that it was an element made for this dark, stormy planet, " but to kiss and lave with blessedness the beautiful shores of some sunny emerald isle of unfading flowers, eternal spring, and cloudless skies."

But in a few moments, all this loveliness disappeared. I was struck with a sublime, awful sound, like the mighty roar of Niagara. It was the precursor of a storm. Soon the main was lashed into terrific fury. I thought of that magnificent description of a tempest in the first book of Virgil's Æneid. On every side, white-crested billows were seen rising up in the shape of pyramids; hills and mountains, alternated by corresponding depressions; eddying, boiling, maddened whirlpools of foam. For some reason or other, the waves all seemed rushing towards the vessel. But this appearance, as the captain informed me, was a mere ocular deception. When a mountainous mass of waters fell upon the deck of the ship, it trembled in every plank and timber, like a leaf in the wind. Sometimes her course was checked by the crushing weight, so that for a moment she would seem to stand still. The force of a downward billow often breaks in pieces the bows of a vessel in an instant, consigning all on board to a watery grave. The wind continued to blow harder and harder through the day.

The night came on, terrible with blackness, thunder and lightning. All nature seemed to be in commotion. My berth was a hammock, suspended in the centre of the main cabin, on which I hardly felt the motion of the vessel. And although to my inexperienced eye our condition was very perilous, I laid myself down, and slept as soundly as I ever did on shore, in my own chamber, in the full quietness and peace of a happy home. Every thing that human power could effect was done to secure our safety. With perfect composure, I was enabled to leave the issue in the hands of God, under whose providence we are just as safe in one situation as another. I thought of the following eloquent passage in the writings of an old divine: "We are all travellers, prosecuting the voyage of time; launched upon an ocean where storms and tempests often prevail; where the elements are agitated, and the waves boisterous; where clouds frequently gather upon our prospects, dark and fearful, and the winds blow bleak and wild. Thus endangered, nobody can be happy without the firm faith that some arm mightier than that of man or nature holds the helm of affairs, and some wisdom more far-reaching than mortal ken is our guide, guard, and panoply, amid the rocks, shoals, and whirlpools that beset our perilous way."

A clear, placid, summer evening at sea is a scene

resplendent with beauty. The last red hues of expiring day are fading in the twilight; seated on the deck, you are charmed with the evanescent loveliness of the setting sun, and think, "Even thus transitory is all of earth, which we so much admire." As the heavens seem to be sinking into utter night, a solitary light shines out; it is in the direction of your home; you think of those relatives and friends whom no distance can remove from your affections; in a few moments, hundreds more make their appearance. Then comes the galaxy, — the milky way, which the ancient poets called the high road or pathway of the gods, — having a boldness and brilliancy never seen on land. With what grandeur does a sight of the firmament strike the imagination, when beheld in a clear night at sea, filled with stars scattered in such infinite numbers, and in such splendid profusion! The ship runs so smoothly that you are almost unconscious of motion. All her sails are filled; and seen at a distance, she resembles " some snow-white, beauteous bird, afloat in the heavens on her airy pinions."

But a change comes over the prospect. The moon unveils her peerless light; the stars hide their diminished heads; a silvered radiance sparkles over all the waters; you witness the same phenomenon which Homer described three thousand years ago, at the close of the eighth book of the Iliad: —

> "At length the moon, refulgent lamp of night,
> O'er heaven's clear azure spreads her sacred light;
> When not a breath disturbs the deep serene,
> And not a cloud o'ercasts the solemn scene,
> A flood of glory bursts from all the skies."

As you dwell on the scene, your imagination is overpowered, and you wander in a world of fancy and enchantment; your bosom is filled with those pure, ennobling, and refined sentiments that recognize the infinite — which open to the inward eye glimpses of the calm, bright, unbroken peace of that happier and immortal state of being to which death will introduce us.

One's enjoyment at sea depends materially upon his daily habits. He should arouse himself in the morning at the first peep of dawn. Whilst the decks are being washed, let him attend to his toilet, and with as much care and particularity as when on land; then let him read his Bible, and say his prayers; by this time, breakfast will be ready; when finished, he should walk on deck an hour at least; the rest of the morning may be spent in study, reading, and conversation. These remarks refer to one who does not suffer from seasickness. If such a person is miserable at sea, it is because he eats too much, sleeps too much, or gives way to sensations of indolence.

How glorious a morning on the ocean! "Yonder comes the powerful king of day." At first you see only a small portion of his disk — not more than a hair's breadth above the ocean's bed. Bright rays, like long lines of gold, are sent out over the trembling waters, that seem rejoicing to welcome the new-born day. Soon the whole orb appears, bathed in a flood of light, brilliant in all the orange, azure, and purple glories of the rainbow. Presently light, fleecy clouds collect around the sun. These are constantly changing their tints, from a deep yellow, then a straw color, then a willow green, and finally perhaps the dark, beautiful gray of autumn. Beneath all this glory, the boundless field of waters reflects, with unspeakable beauty, the splendor of the clouds and sky, leaving the impression that you are in some fairy regions, infinitely removed from the dull realities of earth. The same wonders are often repeated at the close of the day. Is it strange that the poor Indian, when gazing upon the sublimities of the sunset, should realize the presence of the Great Spirit, and cherish the hope of a humble heaven "behind the cloud-topped hill," where he will some day repose under the shade of the tree of life, and bathe in the waters of perennial bliss? O the surpassing freshness and beauty of an early dawn at sea! Its glowing radiance, its crimson splendors, its rich, variegated drapery of clouds, present to the eye the most glorious assemblage of beautiful objects ever beheld.

Nothing to me is more mysterious than the idiosyncrasy of an educated gentleman who is miserable on the ocean, although not seasick. For myself, I should like to make a voyage once a year, if I had the means and time. I can say with Byron, —

> "And I have loved thee, Ocean, and my joy
> Of youthful sports was on thy breast to be
> Borne, like thy bubbles, onward; from a boy
> I wantoned with thy breakers; they to me
> Were a delight, and if the freshening sea
> Made them a terror, 'twas a pleasing fear."

To me it seems an enviable end to be submerged or lost at sea. All is soon over; there is no trouble about a shroud, coffin, funeral, or tomb. "Old ocean's gray and melancholy waste" is a magnificent sepulchre. Who would not like to sleep in it? Perhaps it may be my own destiny to be buried there. I have no objection, if such be the will of Heaven. I ought to have been a sailor. My natural taste and feelings fit me for such a mode of life; and a good sailor is quite as useful and respectable a being as a good clergyman. Some may wonder at the taste above expressed.

> "Let him who crawls, enamoured of decay,
> Cling to his couch, and sicken years away,
> Heave his thick breath, and shake his palsied head,
> While gasp by gasp he falters forth his soul;
> Ours with one pang, one bound, escapes control."

Now I will look at a few of those pleasures which a thinking man may enjoy at sea, derived from internal sources. To illustrate this topic, I will state an item of my own experience. When I crossed the Atlantic, I carried in my pocket a small edition of the New Testament in Greek, with the Polymicrian Lexicon, in the same language. Along with them, I kept by me constantly the Psalms of David, in the Hebrew. They were three little books of the duodecimo size, with paper very thin, and distinctly printed. They occupied such a small compass, and were so handy, that I was never without them for a moment. For the last forty years it has been my habit to abjure desultory reading. I never think of perusing a book through in course. I use it just as an advocate does his law books, to find arguments, facts, or beauties, with reference to some particular subject. Before reaching the Balize, I adopted the following platform: First, to examine what the New Testament says about Jesus Christ; secondly, what it teaches on the subject of rewards and punishments; thirdly, the revelations it contains in regard to a future state; fourthly, I resolved to collect and to compare all the representations in the gospel, as to the nature of true holiness. I determined to devote every morning to these biblical investigations, and every evening to other reading, conversation, and exercise.

During the whole voyage to Liverpool, which occupied nearly eight weeks, I followed faithfully this programme, with the exception of three or four days, when, the vessel being sorely tempest-tossed, there was no opportunity for reading. I will barely state the result of my scriptural researches on the topics which have just been specified. First, it cannot be denied that there is a mystery in Christ's nature, mission, and saving influences, not solved in the New Testament. But there is a mystery in every thing. "Science," says Lord Bacon, "is built upon, and encompassed on every side by, problems which the human mind never has, and never will be able to solve this side the grave. So Christianity may be compared to a monument, lifting its head to heaven upon the very boundaries between the known and unknown. Still, we are taught that Jesus Christ is not, strictly speaking, an infinite being, a being whose nature is coëxtensive with God's, and covering the whole immeasurable area of the universe, physical and spiritual, created and uncreated. As we are so organized that we cannot help feeling that five is less than twenty, so we know that the same being cannot be at once finite and infinite, dependent and almighty, bounded and at the same moment unbounded. The mind of Jesus is a human mind, perfectly immaculate, and endowed with the highest possible gifts and graces." For it pleased the Father that in Him all fulness should dwell — the fulness of the Godhead bodily. Hence he is called our elder brother, which he could not be, unless his intrinsic, inherent, essential nature was precisely the same as ours, sin excepted. In addition, he was sent forth into the world and commissioned by the Father to teach, enlighten, sanctify, and immortalize the children of men.

Secondly. It cannot be proved by the teachings of Christ and his apostles, that punishments dispensed for the bad actions which men do in the present world will continue forever. On the contrary, we are told that death, the *last* enemy of man, shall be destroyed; and also that he who is dead has lost even the power of sinning. Consequently the future world is a very different one from this. Where there are no bodies, no earthly appetites or passions, there can be neither sin nor suffering. In the disembodied state individuals will doubtless enjoy a higher or lower degree of happiness in proportion to their previous attainments; but none can be miserable. Yet the consequences of our conduct in time will flow on forever, sin and pain excepted.

Thirdly. The happiness of man in the future state is based by the New Testament writers altogether upon the resurrection from the dead. It affirms repeatedly that all mankind, both just and unjust, will be brought to enjoy a state of immortality beyond the grave. It affirms also that in the immortal world there will be no death, no sin, no suffering, because all there, being the children of the resurrection, will be the sons of God, and equal unto the angels. A person has no more power to fit himself for a happy immortality than he has to create a world. Our only ground of hope as to the future is the promise of Jesus that all mankind, irrespective of their character or conduct here, in a future state will be endued with a nature spiritual and incorruptible.

Fourthly. Paul and his coadjutors represent the hope of a blessed existence after death, as a most efficient principle of sanctification. He who has this hope will no longer " be foolish, deceived, disobedient, serving divers lusts and pleasures, living in envy and malice, hateful, and hating others." No longer will he be irreverent and unthankful towards God. No longer will he prevaricate or falsify, or stain his conscience for profit or pleasure. No longer will he steep his soul in the gross and debasing indulgences of sense. The charms of rectitude, humility, and other moral qualities, that constitute Christian excellence, will so captivate his heart as to render him insensible to the inferior attractions of an outward, worldly life. Holiness, as defined in the gospel, is a deep, intense, supreme, absorbing love of spiritual beauty, self-government, the joy of a benevolent spirit, the smiles of an approving conscience, the calm, gentle, soul-satisfying affections of hope, gratitude, and trust in God.

I am well aware that there is no originality in these views. But during this voyage they came to my mind with a freshness, power, and plenitude that I had never before experienced. I kept them before me morning, noon, and night. By them I was enabled to commune with God and feel the inspiration of his Spirit, as I gazed upon the amazing manifestations of divine majesty in the mighty deep. I felt that Christianity was from God, that mere men were no more competent to originate it than to create the Atlantic Ocean. When I sat on deck in a pleasant night, admiring the diffuse light of the galaxy, that astronomers tell us is composed of the mingled effulgence of innumerable stars, each of which is probably the centre of a system, like our own sun, — when I thought of the immensity of the physical universe, those worlds upon worlds, and systems upon systems, stretching onward and onward to infinitude, and all revolving in the course of inconceivable ages around some common centre, — all these external glories did not appear to me more striking and magnificent than that spiritual world which Jesus has unfolded, and of which the material creation is but a type, symbol, or representation. Nay, the moral character of Jesus struck me as more grand than the outward universe, with all its sensible laws and phenomena. As I look upon the Son of God, in that last trying scene, when the storm of a world's scorn and hatred was beating over him, — calm, gentle, forgiving, intrepid, resting solely upon the eternal truth of God, — superior to vulgar passions and fear, to pain, peril, and death in its most appalling form, — I am impressed with a sense of the sublime, in comparison with which, heaven, earth, and sea, and all that is therein, seem poor and insignificant.

Akenside, author of the Pleasures of Imagination, in the following beautiful passage, describes the vast superiority of moral sublimity, when contrasted with that of the natural world: —

> "Look, then, abroad through nature to the range
> Of planets, suns, and adamantine spheres,
> Wheeling unshaken through the void immense;
> And speak, O man! does this capacious scene
> With half that kindling majesty dilate
> Thy strong conception, as when Brutus rose
> Refulgent from the stroke of Cæsar's fate,
> Amid the crowd of patriots, and his arm
> Aloft extending, like eternal Jove,
> When guilt brings down the thunder, called aloud
> On Tully's name, and shook his crimson steel,
> And bade the father of his country hail!
> For lo! the tyrant prostrate on the dust;
> And Rome again is free."

But who was Brutus, (conceding the purity of his motives,) who was Socrates, or Plato, compared with Jesus? And yet, if Jesus has taught truly, there is not a child of Adam who will not become, ultimately, as wise, as immaculate, as great, as divine as he himself was on the day of his crucifixion. The mind of Jesus was essentially a human mind filled with the fulness of God. Nothing loftier, nothing less. He could not be higher without becoming God himself — very God. He came to save all men. Hence it is certain that the lowest and weakest person of our race will make an everlasting advancement in wisdom and goodness. His faculties will go on unfolding and ripening forever; his acquisitions more extended, his range of thought wider, his perceptions more clear, his character more beautiful; and thus he will ascend from height to height, from glory to glory, without ever reaching an acme — the final summit of intellectual and moral attainments; for that summit is the infinite Jehovah.

Yes, it was when sailing

> "O'er the glad waters of the dark-blue sea,
> My thoughts as boundless, and my soul as free,"

that grace was given me to realize, with new, fresh, ecstatic delight, my relation to Jesus Christ, the Author and Finisher of our faith. I used to be continually saying to myself, as I looked out upon this vast creation, "I am indeed a child of its infinite Author — bound to his throne by the indissoluble ties of a common nature; a child ennobled and redeemed by the mission of Jesus, standing in the centre of this magnificent panorama of worlds, with the glorious certainty that they are all my own inheritance, that I shall live to enjoy them forever. For all things are mine, whether the present world, or life, or death, or things present, or things to come; all are mine, because I am Christ's, and Christ is God's." Such were the thoughts that made those fifty-five days an epoch in my life — an epoch brighter than any of its predecessors. I felt all the time as if I could see God, as if I were a partaker of his spirit and perfections, and through them was destined to triumph over nature, frailty, change, sin, corruption, and the grave. And even in the worst weather, I laid myself down and slept as sweetly, with a heart as calm, and light, and joyous, as if, like the sea bird, I could weather the fierce storm, and float unhurt on the tossing billows.

In the afternoons my reading was more easy, miscellaneous, and discursive, interspersed with the pleasures of social intercourse. Yet there were but two persons on board with whom I held much conversation — the captain and the only passenger except myself. The former was a native of Salem, Massachusetts, a gentleman of extensive reading, who had spent forty-three years of his life at sea, and seen the whole globe. His memory was most retentive, and he had a fund of information and anecdote absolutely inexhaustible. He was a pious man, and had prayers in his state room every morning and evening. A love stronger than death grew up between us during this voyage. He was blessed with the taste of a finished scholar, a knowledge both of books and mankind, which I have rarely met with, and freedom from bigotry more perfect than I ever saw before or since. He died two years ago, and is now beyond the praise or censure of mortals.

My fellow-passenger was a resident of New Orleans. Although a most intelligent, agreeable, and worthy gentleman, and most excellent company, he was at that time inclined to be sceptical on the subject of religion. But when I met him last winter, I found that he had become an ardent, zealous spiritualist, and of course a firm believer in God, inspiration, and immortality. The change was to me the more extraordinary, because he has a mind remarkably cool, clear, and philosophical. I have never known a person less liable to be led astray by sophistries and enthusiasm of any kind. Who dares say that there is nothing true, divine, or beautiful in modern spiritualism?

CHAPTER XIII.

INCIDENTS OF TRAVEL IN EUROPE. — REFLECTIONS WHICH A SUPERFICIAL VIEW OF THE OLD WORLD AWAKENED IN MY MIND.

I HAD read with deep interest and close attention, for many years, the most celebrated works concerning Europe, published by the tourists and literary men of the United States, before I saw the old world with my own eyes. I carried with me across the Atlantic Dr. Dewey's Journal of a Tour in Europe. From what I knew of this great and good man, I was able to rely on the fidelity of his pen with a full, unlimited confidence. By a universally acknowledged superiority of culture, imagination, and capacity of observing, he was eminently qualified to give a vivid and beautiful description of the various scenes and objects which attracted his notice.

A careful perusal of what he had written, I vainly imagined, would present ideas and pictures to my mental eye essentially resembling those derived from actual observation. Before landing at Liverpool, I thought myself pretty well acquainted with that city and the objects of interest which it contained, because my reading about them had been so minute and thorough. When we were sailing up St. George's Channel, I observed to the captain that I did not expect to be much smitten with the external appearance of any thing which I might see in Wales,

England, or Scotland; for long familiarity with the best descriptions of the various objects which they exhibit would probably make them seem to me like old acquaintances. He replied, smiling at my stupidity, (I suppose,) "You may have acquired from books a rich fund of information concerning the geography, statistics, and history of these regions, but the impressions which the seeing of them makes on the minds of beholders cannot be expressed by words. Words can bear no natural resemblance, like a picture or statue, to the external objects which they signify."

This is a fact of which many writers, as well as readers, do not seem to be aware. One who has always been deaf cannot enjoy the pleasures of melody and harmony; the blind cannot be initiated into the charms of color by words. Equally impossible is it for a stranger to acquire, by reading, the ideas and feelings which would be poured into his mind by the sight of any particular scenes of nature or art, such as Mont Blanc, Jungfrau, Lake Geneva, the wonders of Rome, Paris, London, or Edinburgh. A writer, after having been admitted to these striking spectacles, may amuse and entertain the minds of readers by his glowing and eloquent delineations; but no power of mere words could inspire their souls with one of the thoughts or sentiments which the actual beholding of them would produce.

To illustrate my meaning, I will give an instance. "On the 24th of September, we had such a sky as I have not before seen in Europe — as I never saw surpassed in America. Nor do I look for any thing more glorious in Italy. Such splendid transparency, such serenity, such unfathomable depths of ether, such heavens indescribable, seem to me the fit element in which Mont Blanc, fourteen thousand seven hundred and fifty feet above the sea, should appear, to give the fullest and fittest impression. The evening, too, spread the light of a full moon upon the mountains; and here were all objects, — snowy peak, bare, sharp pinnacle, rising, a single cone, from its base three thousand feet; the deep gorge; the dark fir grove; the bristling glacier; the embosomed valley, — every thing of majestic scenery that could make such a night an appropriate close to such a day. Surely no fire from heaven, no altars built with hands, could be needed by him who came to worship here. It was one of those seasons of life when you are silent all the day long, and can scarcely sleep at night, from the burden and pressure of thoughts that can find neither utterance nor repose. The next morning we began our return to Geneva. Perhaps it would not be possible that any contrasts in light and shade should surpass those which were presented in the panorama of mountains that we left behind us. In the distance lay the snowy range of Mont Blanc, beneath the dazzling splendors of the morning, and there was brightness; nearer, and on the left, lay mountains covered with fir, which the morning ray had not touched, and there was darkness; on the right were hills, partly cultivated, partly wooded, on which streamed the rich light of early day, and there was beauty."

To me — for I have seen all the objects here mentioned — the above description, though as good as words could make it, is ineffably flat, feeble, frigid, and inadequate, it falls so much below the glorious reality. To one unacquainted with them it can no more convey a true image of the original, than a single brick or stone could represent the accurate symmetry, the beautiful and sublime proportions, of St. Peter's Church at Rome. Whilst in Europe, I made notes enough, as to outward and visible things, to fill a volume or two. When I reached home, my intention was to have them arranged and published. But a single incident changed my resolution. I prepared as good an account as I could make of some of the most interesting objects which I saw in crossing the Alps, accompanied, as it seemed to me, with fit and impressive moralizings. I delivered it from the pulpit, in my own church. Walking home with one of my warmest friends, a plain, uneducated, but sensible and strong-minded mechanic, who had never travelled, I asked him how he liked my discourse. He said, "that it impressed him as something very splendid and well-sounding, but really he could gather no definite instruction from it." I felt that the criticism was just, and followed its suggestions. My descriptions of St. Peter's, St. Paul's, Mont Blanc, Snowdon, Arthur's Seat, Menai Bridge, Abbotsford, Oxford, Cambridge, Hampton Court, Windsor Castle, Shakspeare's birthplace, &c., will never be laid before the public, though in my best judgment they are not vastly inferior to the common run of American literature touching these and similar objects of interest which travellers in Europe so much admire.

I reached London on the last Thursday of June. I had numerous letters of introduction to distinguished persons, and among them, one to a Unitarian clergyman, who, at the time of my arrival, was out of the city. It was left at his residence on Friday morning; in the course of the same day, I received a note from his wife, giving me an urgent invitation to preach for her husband the next Sunday at eleven o'clock A. M. She observed that Mr. T. was not expected home till a late hour on Saturday night, and would be most glad to hear, on his arrival, that a brother, fresh from the United States, had consented to preach for him. Although I had not a single manuscript sermon with me, nor any memoranda adapted to aid memory in the delivery of a discourse, I felt it to be a duty to accept the invitation. My time was divided between company and sight-seeing the whole of Saturday. After dinner, a gentleman of my acquaintance, and formerly of New Orleans, walked with me to see Westminster Abbey. By this time, I began to feel no little anxiety about the engagement I had made for Sunday morning. My mind was, to be sure, not inert; but so excited and absorbed by the objects and novelties on every side, about which I had read and dreamed so often from my childhood, that I could think of nothing else. As we were about entering the Poets' Corner, I remarked to my friend that I had very foolishly promised to speak for a clerical brother to-morrow. "I have no sermon in my pocket or head, and it is impossible, at this late hour, to prepare one suitable to the place, hearers, and occasion." He replied, "I should think that the inspiration of this memorable spot, these monuments of distinguished statesmen, warriors, scholars, and artists of renown, would suggest to your mind materials enough for a dozen homilies." At this moment, we reached the place where stands the statue of Shakspeare, the arm of which, extended, seems to point the spectator to the following lines: —

> "The cloud-capped towers, the gorgeous palaces,
> The solemn temples, the great globe itself,
> Yea, all which it inherit, shall dissolve,
> And, like this insubstantial pageant faded,
> Leave not a rack behind."

"Here is a text for you," remarked my friend. The hint struck my mind forcibly, and awakened trains of thought, which in the course of a few hours were moulded into what seemed to me might possibly answer for a sermon, if delivered even with moderate graces of style and elocution. Forgetting the extreme shortness of the nights in that latitude, the morning dawn found me walking my room in deep study. I did not leave it till the bells rang for church. I was conducted to the vestry, where I saw for the first time the gentleman whose pulpit I was to occupy. After a moment's conversation, he inquired, "Have you forgotten your gown?" "I have none," was the answer. No clergyman of any denomination ever preaches in England without a robe. Several were suspended in a recess of the room, of different sizes. One was selected which I could wear. This difficulty being obviated, my clerical friend asked, "Where is your sermon?" "I have brought none with me," was the reply. " Good God," he instantly exclaimed, " are you going before a London audience without a written discourse?" "Sir," said I, "for the last twenty-five years it has been my duty to preach regularly to a Unitarian congregation in New Orleans, and I have never taken a manuscript, nor even a note, into the pulpit with me. During all this time, I have not written out fully more than two or three sermons; and were they this moment in my hands, it would be of no avail as to the present emergency. But if you have any misgivings as to my competency, I beg you to allow me to be disrobed, and excused from preaching on this occasion. It would be much more agreeable to me to take a seat among your hearers." This proposition he politely declined, and led my way to the pulpit. I was forty-five minutes in delivering my message. The subject selected was from these words: "Who hath abolished death, and hath brought life and immortality to light through the gospel."

I preached exactly as if I had been addressing my own people at home. The thoughts which were advanced on the subject of immortality had been essentially familiar to my mind for years, and were therefore uttered with more ease and fluency than if they had been read from a manuscript. Most preachers are not aware of the great difference between written and oral language. The latter mode of communicating ideas is vastly more effective than the former. To be sure, in a set, carefully-composed, manuscript sermon, a minister may be more correct in his expressions, avoid redundancies and repetitions, and use words that are perfectly appropriate. Still, though he may be admired as learned and eloquent, he cannot be so agreeable and persuasive as those who in preaching adopt the easy and natural manner of an unaffected speaker.

After the services were finished, my friend was pleased to say that he was delighted with my performances, and that, if it were in his power, he would adopt a similar style of preaching. It was the first time, he added, that his congregation had ever listened to extemporaneous preaching, and " they were interested, raised up, and carried along with you." One gentleman from New Orleans was present, who had often heard me; he said this sermon was one of my happiest efforts. I was, indeed, much excited. I thought of the antecedent generations who had acted their parts in that great metropolis, and were that moment in a higher, nobler, and deathless existence; and I asked my hearers to look out upon the perspective of that better land, and tell me whether, in their estimation, the evanescent advantages of wealth, rank, and fashion, were the brightest things within our reach; whether there was not something in our horizon more sublime than the attainments of ease, profit, pleasure, or aggrandizement, which could be enjoyed only for a moment. And, with what seemed to me affecting views of the vanity of human ambition, and the utter worthlessness of merely mortal possessions, when I summed up, at the conclusion, all that is sublime and tremendous in the prospect of a future destiny, lost in the fathomless abysses of an immortal being, and contrasted it with the shadows, the dreams of earth and time, my feelings bore me away, and tears started from the eyes of many persons, whose faces had looked to me previously as cold and immovable as marble statues. My hearers appeared to be deeply stirred, and most of them, as I learned afterwards, were highly cultivated, educated gentlemen — *savans*, artists, and authors.

Travelling through Europe, I met with many intelligent men, who said they had no faith in Christianity. On conversing more freely with them, I ascertained that it was not the absolute truth taught by Jesus which they denied, but only some of those numerous follies, which, through a long course of ages, have been assumed, by the benighted and superstitious, as so many doctrines of Christ and his apostles. If the New Testament were properly explained and understood, there would hardly be an unbeliever in it throughout all Christendom.

The next day I was invited to dine, with a select company, at the house of the clergyman whose pulpit I had occupied Sunday morning. I had hardly crossed the threshold of the drawing room before a lady rushed forward and grasped me by the hand, saying, "I do not wonder that you look astonished at what may seem to you an act of rudeness; but I heard you preach in New Orleans some years ago, and am most happy to greet you in my native city." She had hardly finished her address, before another lady came forward and claimed to be an acquaintance on the same ground. Then a gentleman, whom

I had never seen before, called me by name, saying that he was acquainted with scores of my relations who resided in the county of Devonshire, where he was born and lived till he came to London. At this time I was standing on the vestibule of the room, and had not yet had an introduction to the company within. This unceremonious, warm, and friendly treatment, where I had expected to pass as one unknown, moved me even to tears, and I passed through that scene with more freedom, cordiality, and happiness, than I ever before experienced in any social circle to which I had been admitted in the United States. I love the English. I love their manners, character, and society. What an illustrious nation! One fact astonished me, because it was so contrary to all my preconceived ideas. A learned, well-bred Englishman, blessed with a knowledge both of books and the world, is quite as candid, liberal, and unprejudiced, as any gentleman belonging to the higher and best informed classes of France or the United States.

While travelling through Great Britain, I heard a considerable number of her most celebrated preachers of different denominations. It was my good fortune to have an opportunity to attend worship one Sabbath in the chapel of Cambridge University, that ancient and venerable seat of learning. In the course of the day, two sermons were delivered by divines of the highest reputation for piety, learning, and eloquence. A gentleman who accompanied me, a native of England, and a graduate of one of her universities, remarked, at the close of the day, " that in all his life he had never listened to abler discourses." Supposing his judgment to be correct, I think it no injustice to say that the ordinary style of sermonizing in the United States is not at all inferior to that of the church of England, either as it regards delivery, sound doctrine, literary merit, or the power of making efficient and salutary impressions on the conscience. I admit that my expectations were raised to the highest pitch, and nothing but superior performances could have fully answered their demands.

I will give a sample of the reasoning that characterized the morning's discourse, which was pronounced by a distinguished doctor of divinity, and a man of extensive scientific acquirements. This sermon had two separate heads, or general divisions. The first undertook to specify the cardinal or leading doctrines of the Christian religion. It began with the Trinity. The speaker said that one of the strongest proof texts in support of the supreme, absolute divinity of Jesus was the 27th verse of Luke, 11th chapter: "And it came to pass, as he spake these things, a certain woman of the company lifted up her voice, and said unto him, *Blessed is the womb that bare thee, and the paps which thou hast sucked.*" The gist of his argument ran thus: At the time these words were uttered, it was a settled, universal belief of the Jews, that God was about to appear among them in a human form. This form, of course, must be born of a woman. Under all the circumstances of the case, in this instance, the calling Mary "*Blessed,*" &c., was the same precisely as to say,

"All hail, mother of our God." Therefore the Son of Mary is the second person in the ever-blessed and adorable Trinity. This may be sound logic in Cambridge University; it would not satisfy Trinitarians on this side of the Atlantic.

Next to the trinity of persons in the Godhead, the orator expatiated on the time-hallowed doctrine of original sin. Under this head the audience was regaled with the richest fragrance of Calvinism. He solemnly reminded us that the first sin of Adam and Eve, which blasted the immortal bloom and beauty of an earthly paradise, was the source of all the ills to which man is liable, either here or hereafter. Upon this doctrine, he said, rests the superstructure of revealed religion. Then were quoted the following beautiful lines of Milton : —

> "So saying, her rash hand, in evil hour,
> Forth reaching to the fruit, she plucked, she ate;
> Earth felt the wound, and Nature, from her seat,
> Sighing through all her works, gave signs of woe
> That all was lost."

Without the chimerical creations of Dante and Milton, what would become of that system of theology which accepts the Calvinistic idea of the fall of man? I was surprised to hear the bishop assert that the physical evils of every description, which now afflict mankind, are the necessary, legitimate consequences of the original transgression in the garden of Eden. He specified sickness, want, pain, the dissolution of the body, inclemency of weather, the fading of flowers, the suffering and death of brutes, earthquakes and volcanoes, the boisterous ocean, the tempestuous wind, thunder and lightning, all violent, destructive elements, sterility of soil, briers, thorns, and poisonous reptiles, and laid down the doctrine that all these have proceeded *from the eating of the forbidden fruit.* "If our first parents had not sinned," said he, " earth would have been entirely beautiful — an Elysian scene, free from all imperfections, inhabited by beings pure and deathless as the angels of heaven." Alas! alas! that such tempting and deleterious fruit should have been placed within the reach of the first man and woman, whose conduct was to decide for eternity the fates and fortunes of countless millions then unborn! He summed up this topic by saying " that the fall of man was not unforeseen nor unprovided for in the arrangements of Infinite Wisdom; and that without it Jesus and the glories of his mediation for a ruined world would have had no place in the universe of God."

When giving his views concerning the Holy Spirit, this doctor of theology, with particular emphasis, cautioned his hearers against the use of reason in interpreting Scripture. " Reason," he told them, " is so dreadfully darkened by the fall, that we cannot be safely guided by its judgments on the subject of religion." What is the use, then, of preaching? What is the use of the Bible itself? Is it not addressed to the reason of mankind — " the divinity that stirs within us "? Scepticism and bigotry are not always distinguished by very distant boundaries, but in many instances seem to sustain to each other the relation of intimate, congenial friends. Both concur in assuring us that we have no natural faculties which qualify us for the successful investigation of religious truth. Both affirm that revelation is the antagonist of reason, and cannot be believed without renouncing the noblest and highest powers which God has bestowed upon us.

Under the second head of his discourse, the position was maintained in the most unqualified terms, that the only true church in the world is the ecclesiastical establishment of Great Britain. He said that God had smiled upon England, and had raised her to her present pinnacle of prosperity, because she adhered so faithfully to the only immaculate, genuine form of Christianity on earth. "The same age," he remarked, "that beholds the downfall of our national church will also witness the obsequies of our secular empire and glory. Our civilization and church are inseparably associated." A powerful argument, indeed, for the annual disbursement of forty millions of dollars from the public treasury, to feed, clothe, and enrich the only true successors of the apostles! I was sorry to hear all other denominations (even the Roman Catholics were not excepted) expressly named only to be denounced and stigmatized as beyond the pale of the Christian church, with nothing to depend upon but what was styled by the orator "*the uncovenanted mercies of our heavenly Father.*" The Unitarians came in for the most vehement and especial vituperation. They were called infidels, who, with ineffable audacity, had assumed the Christian name and paraphernalia.

The above synopsis is a fair representation of the staple thoughts contained in the ablest orthodox ser-

mon which I heard during my rambles in Europe.
The style as to clearness, purity, and precision of
language, and the structure of sentences, was fault-
less; not needlessly overcharged with technical
phrases, nor squeamishly avoiding them when the
subject required their introduction. The manner of
this eminent prelate was calm, quiet, dignified, and
polished, but cold as ice. The true church would
be shocked by a sermon, however superior in intrinsic merits, delivered in the ardent, impassioned tones
and manner suited to the eloquence of nature. Of
the sincerity of this distinguished preacher I did not
entertain a doubt; but he exhibited a sample of bigotry which it is painful to think of. He said there
was no power under heaven that could authorize a
person to become a teacher of Christianity, and an
administrator of its sacraments, but the hierarchy of
the Episcopal church; that if a man should appear
in England as wise and holy as the Son of God himself, he would have no right to preach, baptize, or administer the communion, unless he were ordained by
some bishop belonging to the national establishment.

In the English preaching which I heard, there
were two capital defects. First, it was overshadowed
and encumbered with the dismal, chilling, unintelligible dogmas of an obsolete, antiquated, scholastic
theology. What interest can this active, enlightened
generation feel in the metaphysics of St. Augustine
and Athanasius, touching the mysteries of the Godhead, original sin, the fall of Adam, supernatural
conversion, and the unimaginable glories or terrors
of the world eternal. It is time that clergymen

should every where abjure the folly of wasting their days and talents in worse than useless efforts to fathom the unsearchable, and reconcile contradictions. What is wanted in Great Britain is a more simple, popular, earnest, practical style of pulpit communications, showing the important relations of the Christian code to the every-day affairs of life — to commerce, trade, government, pauperism, literature, amusements, ancient usages and customs, and all the nameless diversified scenes, pursuits, and interests of mankind this side the grave. In England the Christian minister should have the disinterestedness and moral independence requisite to enable him to set his face resolutely against all those principles and practices which he considers, in his inmost soul, contrary to sound morals and undefiled religion, however popular, prevailing, or fashionable they may happen to be.

Again, the English pulpit is lamentably deficient in fervor and pathos, in all those qualities necessary to arouse and kindle the passions. The sacred desk should every where, like that of England, possess large and various knowledge, correctness of taste, fertility of illustration, a clear and copious flow of words; but these will be of no avail, unless it deeply sympathize with all those natural forms of beauty, truth, and goodness, which strike, charm, and captivate the great heart of humanity. The business of a preacher is not so much to convince the understanding of his hearers, as to persuade their wills — to communicate to their hearts rapture at the morally beautiful, joy in the true, exultation in the pure and good — those far-reaching sympathies and sublime sentiments which proclaim our origin divine, and our destination immortal.

During the last week of June, 1847, I enjoyed several fine opportunities of listening to the best speakers in the Parliament of Great Britain. I heard Lord Brougham, Sir George Bentinck, Lord John Russell, Lord Morpeth, Mr. Disraeli, Mr. Hume, and many others. I will here record a few paragraphs from a note book containing an account of my daily experiences at that time.

When I first cast my eyes on this far-famed assembly, the personal appearance of its members made a deep and quite agreeable impression. Their mien in general is imposing, and highly expressive of the wisdom and refinement which should adorn the representatives of an ancient, powerful, and splendid nation. English gentlemen present the most perfect model extant, as it regards the proprieties of manner, costume, and external bearing. Horace somewhere remarks, that a man of great intellectual abilities, but of forbidding, uncultivated manners, may be compared to a field possessing a rich soil, yet untilled, its surface rough with weeds, briers, and thorns. True it is, that a legislator of clownish appearance, slovenly in dress, who mixes the spirting of tobacco juice with the finest sentences which fall from his lips, may be a man of great worth and genuine patriotism.

The most distinguished talents may be concealed beneath his unpolished exterior. But a moderate share of gentility would not only render him more agreeable to our perceptions, but also make an important addition to his weight and influence in the scale of usefulness. I regret that my countrymen, when travelling in foreign lands, sometimes act as if they thought it would involve a sacrifice of personal freedom and independence to observe the decorum of time, place, and circumstance, in their intercourse with others. To avoid the least approach to servility on some occasions, they rush into the opposite extreme of rudeness, and gross disregard of conventional rules and customs, which have an imperative claim to our notice, when they do not conflict with the requirements of morality. For reasons which I cannot now examine, the people in the southern parts of our Union are more mild, gentle, refined, and obliging in their manners, not only at home, but abroad, as a general fact, than the inhabitants of the free states, Boston and our other large cities excepted.

The members of Parliament, as far as I could judge, possess the advantage of a finished education. At any rate, those who spoke when I was present appeared to be perfectly acquainted with the business that was going on, never wandered from the main point, and advanced only the most appropriate facts and arguments tending to elucidate the subject upon which they were deliberating. Long-winded, rambling orators are never tolerated in the English legislature. They are put down by concerted noises, such as coughing, stamping with the feet, &c. Hence no one attempts to speak on a subject of which he is ignorant; but only when he is provided with an ample stock of materials, that have been thoroughly digested and lucidly arranged. Indeed, the condensation of the speakers in Parliament, their close, rigid attention to the business before them, and the beautiful appropriateness of their language were so striking, that on one occasion I listened, with an almost unvaried interest, to a series of speeches on different topics, but mostly of a local character, which were protracted from seven o'clock P. M. till near two the next morning. And I remarked that in those replies, which must have been strictly extemporaneous, the prominent characteristics were relevance, distinctness, brevity, and wit. Their coruscations of wit were often vivid and irresistible, but always polished and good natured. In a legislator, knowledge is power; and the more copious the fund of his intelligence, the more efficient will be his oratory. When a speaker is full of important, connected facts and arguments touching a given subject, his address may be forcible and persuasive, without the graces of a pleasing voice and elocution. Good sense is the foundation of every species of eloquence, and it cannot be compressed into too small a compass. I have heard a fluent speaker in our Congress, for an hour or two, pouring forth his loose, vague, indistinct, cloudy abstractions, when the most attentive and enlightened listener could gain no clear, definite conceptions from his pompous, frothy declamation. Such a phenomenon is unknown in the legislature I am speaking of.

In Parliament, as I saw it, there was one characteristic to me alike surprising and inexplicable. I allude to the invariable deficiency of feeling, the apparent apathy which distinguished their greatest orators, even when expatiating on topics fitted to arouse the strongest emotions. I should have inferred from their style of speaking that the predominant trait of their minds was stoicism — a calmness of soul as incapable of pain, pleasure, or passion of any kind, as a block of marble. In both houses of the English legislature there is the finest scope for the most animated species of eloquence; for that ardor of speech, that vehemence and nobleness of sentiment, which can proceed only from a mind enriched by the elements of science and learning and inspired by some great and magnificent theme. One night, almost every word that was uttered related to the passage of a bill that had been introduced primarily to afford relief to the starving poor of Ireland. In the House of Commons the matter underwent a thorough and lengthened discussion. And all the time, to the eye of a spectator, that assembly was still as the Dead Sea. Not a ripple disturbed its glassy, polished surface. Yes, living, breathing men, in the attitude of communicating their ideas on a theme of all others, perhaps, most likely to excite the human mind, were, to appearance, as passionless as those portraits which transmit to us the forms and features of orators that are now no more. I could not but feel the striking difference between the scene before me and the meeting which was held the winter previous in the Commercial Exchange, New Orleans, to devise measures for the relief of suffering Ireland. At that meeting the two most prominent orators were the late Hon. Henry Clay and

S. S. Prentiss, Esq. In the course of their remarks they were so deeply affected as to shed tears, and there was a mutual sympathy between the orators and the audience. We who listened were stirred and carried along with them. Our hearts wept in view of the miseries which they painted. It was enough for us to know that thousands on the other side of the Atlantic, united to us by the ties of a common nature, were perishing for want of food. Prompted by those generous sentiments which make the wants and sorrows of others, however distant, our own, we loaded vessels with the requisite supplies, and sent them relief with all possible despatch.

But let me not do injustice to the distinguished men of whom I have been speaking. I most fully believe that the apathy to which I have alluded was not real, but only apparent. They cherished in their *bosoms* the appropriate emotions, but fashion, or something else, forbade the manifestation of them. I was told that they would have exposed themselves to ridicule by speaking in that pathetic, vehement tone which is suited to the American taste. It gives me pleasure to testify that the orators, on the evening before mentioned, with one or two exceptions, admitted the sacred claims of Ireland to English philanthropy. "Ireland," said they, "is not only visited by the judgments of Heaven, (alluding to the famine,) but it is also crushed by the misrule and oppression inflicted by the English government for centuries past. We must help her; we will not allow her to perish." One of the members stated, that during that session of Parliament, (1847,) eight millions of pounds sterling had been already appropriated to the relief of the neighboring island, and "now this bill," said he, "calls on us to give for the same object nearly another million. I shall vote for it." Neither the American heart, nor the French heart, nor any other human heart, is in reality more noble, more humane, more generous, or philanthropic, than that of those very orators whose imperturbable calmness of countenance and manners might lead a stranger to suppose that they were given over to the insensibility of utter, obdurate, invincible selfishness, and indifference to the misery of their fellow-beings. Indeed, the almost boundless charities of the English to relieve every species of want and suffering among them, demonstrate the vitality of their religious principles, and that they are quite equal, if not superior, to any other nation in recognition of the claims of our common humanity.

The opinion prevails in the United States, that piety is at a very low ebb in the church of England. This is an error. That church is not inferior to any other on earth in fulfilling God's command to do good to all men, without distinction; in toiling and suffering for the cause of human progress; in diffusing freedom, virtue, and intelligence; in relieving the poor; in succoring the fallen, the orphan, and the widow; in breaking the yoke of the enslaved and down-trodden; in sending the Bible all over the globe; and in redeeming our misguided, unhappy race from the countless forms of sin and woe. The church of Oxford, and Rome too, are not below their neighbors in genuine holiness; they comprehend within their limits millions, who, according to the measure of their knowledge and means, are sincerely striving to be conformed to the will of the common Father of us all, and obey the precepts of his Son. Some seem to think that when an assembly worships with harmonies of splendid music, fumes of incense, ancient liturgies, and a gorgeous ceremonial, it cannot be pure and holy in the sight of God. But they who look below the surface which the church militant presents to a superficial eye, and who are not bewildered by the din and confusion of conflicting sects, creeds, and diversities of forms, know that men who differ ever so much in opinions and rites may nevertheless feel in their hearts as becomes Christians, and gaze with admiration, gratitude, and hope, on the divine and benignant image of that Redeemer who has tasted death for every member of Adam's race.

Some one has said, our minds are steeped in imagery, and where the visible form is not, the impalpable spirit escapes the notice of an ignorant, unreflecting multitude. Cuvier could trace the sublime unity, the universal type, the central idea, existing in the creative intelligence, which connects as one the mammoth and the snail. So profound Catholic observers can perceive the holy unity that pervades all those of every name and denomination, who "confess with their lips the Lord Jesus, and believe in their hearts that God hath raised him from the dead." As to church organization and forms, to be sure I have my preferences, and indulge them; but I should be chargeable with one of the most debasing forms of bigotry, if I thought that one denomination was any more acceptable to God than another. Whoever worships the Father with sincerity of intention will be blessed, though he kneel before the altar with a mind darkened with vulgar superstitions, unfounded fears, narrow prejudices, and vain imaginings. The different sects in Christendom have no just reason to look upon one another with unfriendliness, antipathy, and discord. " I admire," says Dr. Channing, " the venerable names of Thomas à Kempis, Fenelon, and Cheverus, of the Romish church; I admire the names of Latimer, Hooker, Barrow, Heber, Milton, Newton, John Locke, and Samuel Clark. They breathe a fragrance through the common air; they lift up the whole race to which they belonged towards the illimitable heavens. With the churches of which they were pillars and chief ornaments I have the warmest sympathies. To confine God's love, or his good spirit, to any sect, party, or particular church, is to sin against the fundamental law of the kingdom of God, to break that living bond with Christ's universal church, which is one of our most important helps to perfection."

When I was in St. Peter's Church, Rome, on a beautiful Sunday morning in July, 1847, the Lord's Prayer, in Latin, was repeated by the priest who was officiating at one of the altars. Nothing which I ever heard uttered in a church affected me more deeply. " Our Father," &c., — that is the Father of all. These words inspired me with the thought that mankind are indeed one, — one in origin, in birth, in life, in love, in suffering, in death, — one, too, in hope of that inheritance incorruptible, undefiled, and unfading, through Christ, reserved in heaven for all the countless millions of woman born. The love of which the cross is the emblem is as uncircumscribed as that of the Lord's prayer. It enables us to look beyond the shadows and sorrows of mortality, to a future existence of endless and ever-progressive glory, in which all mankind will eventually participate. "Uniformity of creeds, of discipline, of ritual, and of ceremonies, in such a world as ours! a world where no two men are not as distinguishable in their mental as in their physical aspect; where all that meets the eye, and all that arrests the ear, has the stamp of boundless and infinite variety! What are the harmonies of tone, of color, and of form, but the results of contrasts — contrasts held in subordination to one pervading principle, which reconciles, without confounding, the component elements of the music, the painting, or the structure? Just so in the spiritual works of God: beauty could have no existence without endless diversities." The human constitution is so organized, that honest men, however enlightened, are compelled to form dissimilar views of divine truth as long as they live in the body. Honest men can no more think alike than they can look alike. Truth is God's law, indeed; but if all will profess to think exactly alike about it, all must be hypocrites, and live a life of habitual falsehood. How cold, dull, deformed, uninteresting, even hateful, would be a community in which there was no difference of opinion on moral and religious themes! There are no more nor other forms of Christianity among men than are wanted. Their existence demonstrates their necessity. Nor has any particular form a right to arrogate to itself precedence or superiority over their neighbors.

I can enjoy the communion of any church where the Lord's Prayer is understood and sincerely adopted; where the worshippers are taught to believe that God is not almighty wrath, but an infinite Parent, who introduced them into this world without their consent, and has watched over them in all their past vicissitudes of sickness and health, joy and sorrow, and who will continue to take care of them — be the friend, strength, and portion of their spirits through the serene, unclouded, eternal processions of a heavenly state. I feel at home in any church where I see a banner floating aloft above its dome, on which is inscribed the motto, GOD OUR FATHER, MAN OUR BROTHER, JESUS CHRIST OUR REDEEMER.

I went into churches of every denomination when travelling in Europe, from the Roman Catholic to the Unitarian, was permitted to commune in all, and felt that the "Holy of Holies" was in each of those communions; that in each were humble, sincere, thankful Christians, bearing faithfully the trials of their lot, forgiving their bitterest enemies, shedding the tear of sympathy at the sight of a neighbor's suffering, toiling with disinterestedness to relieve it, and transported by a hope in Christ triumphant over time, nature, death, and the grave. Religion is flourishing all over Europe, not excepting Germany. Things may appear the reverse to superficial observers. Since Christ expired on the cross, his cause has been progressing every hour.

We sometimes feel inclined to despondency, when we see scepticism in the pulpit, or the professor's chair, or in the circulating literature of our times. But we forget that by these very means the glorious cause of revealed religion is carried forward. Look through the annals and eras of the past, and behold when the church seemed to human view to be delivered completely into the hands of its enemies, it was only undergoing a transition to a higher and more brilliant state. When Jesus was laid in the tomb, to mortal eye annihilated, *then* was the most signal triumph of the cross. No events can retard or retrograde the advancement of God's truth. If the Bible is divine, no real adversity can befall the church. The church can no more fail, nor be retarded, than the eternal Cause that breathed it into existence. All storms, all waves that beat upon it, all the wrath and opposition of men, are the instrumentalities which Providence uses to promote its development and prosperity.

I was very anxious not only to see, but to converse with some of the most celebrated scholars and authors of Great Britain. Mr. Bancroft, the historian, who was then our ambassador at the court of St. James, afforded me all the attention and civilities in his power. I was especially desirous to become personally acquainted with Thomas Carlyle. Mr. Bancroft told me that it would be impossible for me to obtain an introduction to him except at one of his evening levees, because he spent every morning in his study, and received no visitors until after dinner. "But these levees are always crowded," said he, "and allow no opportunities for extended conversation." As he had called my countrymen a nation of *bores*, I concluded to assume the character and impudence which the term designates. Mr. Carlyle resided two miles from Morley's Hotel, where I had lodgings. I was told that his breakfast hour was eight o'clock. I found my way to his dwelling one morning, when the clock was striking nine, with letters from distinguished men on both sides of the Atlantic. A lady, with a very intelligent appearance, met me at the door. I said to her, " I have called this morning to see Mr. Carlyle : is he at home ? " She replied, " Mr. Carlyle has just entered his study, and no *gentleman* can see him this morning. If the Queen of England should now call here and request an interview with him, it would not be granted." I then asked her if she could oblige me by carrying a written message to his study. " With pleasure," said she. I sat down and wrote with a pencil the following words. " Dear sir : No *gentleman*, but a *man*, is at your door, — a Unitarian, a Yankee, a democrat, and a radical, all the way from the banks of the Mississippi ; a careful reader and great admirer of Mr. Carlyle, — and begs the favor of a short interview, which must be granted *now*, or never this side the grave." I sent my letters along with this scrawl. Directly the invitation came : " Walk up, sir ; I shall be happy to see you."

I was received in the most kind and unceremonious manner. The topics on which we conversed were so numerous that I have not room even to mention them. The colloquial style of this gentleman is plain, easy, natural, and unaffected, and bears no resemblance to that of his later writings; has none of those qualities commonly called transcendental. Our conversation was protracted till afternoon. Though I rose several times to depart, he insisted upon my staying longer so earnestly, that I acceded to his wishes. Much of the time was spent in answering his inquiries concerning the statistics of the United States, the peculiarities of our government, laws, manners, schools, churches, literature, &c. He professed to be much gratified with the information which I gave him in regard to these subjects. He was very particular in his questions about slavery, and the narratives of the terrible sufferings to which African bondmen are habitually subjected in our country. The real facts appertaining to the case, as I stated them, were in direct antagonism to all the representations of anti-slavery writers and orators which he had seen. He was rejoiced to hear that the slaves in our Southern States were well fed and clothed, not over-worked, and mercifully treated in all respects. I told him that they were quite as well off, both as to their temporal and spiritual interests, as any class of operatives, either in the field or shop, that existed in Great Britain or any part of continental Europe.

He then uttered words nearly as follows: "From what you say, — and I cannot doubt the correctness of your statements, — it seems that slavery, as it exists in your republic, is a subject enveloped in the thick mists of ignorance, prejudice, and misrepresentation. It is indeed true that not more than fifty years ago our own merchants were employed in transporting native Africans to your shores for sale. It is true that Great Britain originated the system when you were colonies, under her influence and jurisdiction. At the same time the ships of New England were devoted to the odious traffic. The Southern States were never engaged in the slave trade. To be sure, they purchased the captives whom we sent to them, because they were exactly fitted by nature for the climate, and because they believed, as every body then did, in the entire rectitude of such exchanges. I understand what you say — that southern planters cannot possibly manumit their slaves immediately without involving them in utter perdition. It is their duty to keep them in bondage for the present, till it please Providence to open a way for their exaltation to a higher state. The blame of African bondage in your land, if blame there be, belongs chiefly to us. We set up the institution among you by the force of law, even against your desire and earnest remonstrances. And we are doing all in our power to foster and perpetuate it. We live by slave labor. What feeds our immense cotton manufactories? Destroy them, and we should be ruined. All those communities that use the cotton, rice, sugar, coffee, &c., produced by slave labor, are just as much implicated in the wrong as slaveholders themselves, and just as criminal in the sight of God. In the guilt of slavery, as things are, the whole civilized world participates. How unjust, then, the reproaches and vituperation poured out upon you, for a state of things which was forced upon you by an inevitable providence, and the cancelling of which is out of your power! The principle, I admit, is wrong; 'but let him who is without sin cast the first stone.' It is idle, it is worse than idle, for one to indulge in acrimonious declamation against African slavery in the United States, who is unable to specify any feasible method of abolishing it."

Such was the strain in which this far-seeing, just, and noble man expressed ideas touching slavery, which must appear true and beautiful, I should think, to every candid, impartial, and enlightened mind. And all the anti-slavery men with whom I conversed in England, spoke on the same subject in the accents of a calm, gentle, humane, profound, and considerate philosophy. They are free from that spirit of harshness, invective, and denunciation, which characterize, almost invariably, the effusions of American abolitionists.

We have few literary men, who, in depth, compass, and variety of learning, can be compared with such scholars as Macaulay, Martineau, Beard, Carlyle, and many others of the same description. In my judgment, Ralph Waldo Emerson has as much acquaintance with literature, and is as great a thinker, as any person in Europe. The Hon. Edward Everett, and Mr. Bancroft, the historian, belong to the same category. Outside of the circle of my acquaintance are scores, perhaps, of educated Americans, who are entitled to be placed upon the same platform with the distinguished men just named. But as a general fact, our scholars and professional men are sadly deficient in culture. The clergymen whom I saw in England do not confine themselves to the study of theology, but are conversant in every department of learning. They are not so showy as a certain class of ministers in the United States. They have not the same knack of dressing up trite and commonplace thoughts with those ornaments of style which are most fitted to attract the gaze of an ignorant, unreflecting crowd. But they are more solid, lay more stress upon their matter than manner, and prefer the plain, simple, manly, and strong, to the empty, foppish, gaudy, and superficial. American literature is too often diluted, unoriginal, adapted to secure the ephemeral applause of the day, rather than to command lasting and universal admiration.

CHAPTER XIV.

SOME FURTHER PARTICULARS WITH REGARD TO MY INTERVIEW WITH MR. CARLYLE. — ERRONEOUS IMPRESSIONS PREVALENT AMONG THE WISE MEN OF EUROPE CONCERNING THE UNITED STATES. — THE ALPS.

THE news of Dr. Chalmers's death, the great divine of Scotland, had just been received. Reference was made to the opinion expressed in his Bridgewater Treatise, that all which we call evil is phenomenal only — the necessary means of something in itself good; or, as R. W. Emerson has expressed it, " Evil is good in the process of formation — good in embryo, in incubation." " Dr. Chalmers," said Mr. Carlyle, " was as good as he was great. His heart was expanded, and in conversation he often uttered sentiments which are directly at variance with the dogmas of the church to which he belonged. I enjoy an extended personal acquaintance with ministers of various denominations in England and Scotland. Neither in nor out of the pulpit have I ever heard one argue in favor of the doctrine of endless evil. I am satisfied that no intelligent clergyman among us embraces it. It is a melancholy fact, that until the present century, a great majority of professedly Christian teachers represented the Almighty Being as decreeing and delighting in human misery. How inexplicable that educated men, closing their eyes against the irresistible evidence of unbounded goodness and power in the natural world around and within them, should make themselves believe that final, hopeless, remediless misery is the grand, sublime consummation of the Creator's moral achievements! The horrid doctrine is not to be found in the New Testament. There is no intimation given, in any part of the Scriptures, of a doom so inscrutable, and so repugnant to those inevitable ideas which we all entertain of the divine perfections. It is certain that the Greek word *aionios*, which is sometimes applied to punishment in the gospel, does not prove its eternity. For throughout Greek literature, sacred and profane, it is often employed to signify a limited duration."

When speaking about the Athanasian creed, he remarked, "The doctrine of three persons in the Godhead had no existence in the primitive church till after the Council of Nice. The question of debate at that meeting did not relate to the equality of the Son with the Father. This idea was not then advocated by any divine in Christendom. It was universally admitted that Jesus was inferior to God himself. The subject of discussion in that far-famed assembly amounted to this: Was the Son formed out of the very substance of the supreme Jehovah, or was his spiritual nature essentially the same as that of angels, or that of Adam before he had sinned? This was a thesis sufficiently subtile and absurd, to be sure, but it was infinitely removed from the Athanasian theory concerning the Godhead."

The last thing published by Dr. Chalmers, but a

few days before his decease, was a letter in which he expressed his opinion, that the Christian religion cannot be permanently prosperous in any country, without the support of legislative enactment. "Conversing on this subject," he said, "it was remarked by an intelligent American whom he had met in London, that more persons, in proportion, resort to some place for religious worship every Sabbath, in our republic, than in any other civilized land on the face of the globe. A little band of pioneers go into the wilderness to subdue it — to spread around them green pastures, cultivated fields, blooming gardens and orchards, with all the charms and luxuries that follow in their train. They build their cabins, and begin to fell the trees. Almost at the same instant the log school house and church spring into existence." He subjoined these words: "It would, no doubt, be best that church and state should every where be completely divorced. Men in all grades and conditions of life, barbarous and civilized, have their gods to whom they flee for help in their hours of weakness, peril, or suffering. If unacquainted with the God of the Bible, they will carve out an idol, an image of brass, marble, or some other substance, and repair to its altar for protection. Some repose their confidence in the sun, the moon, or stars; in beast, bird, tree, reptile, or insect. Thus, through every land, from every temple and altar, from every bleeding victim, and from every prayer, a voice proclaims that every man, however vague or erring his notions of spiritual truth may be, must betake himself to some real or imaginary divinity in scenes of weakness, change, sorrow, disease, and death. Worship, then, is enforced upon the children of men by inevitable laws.

"It is the dictate of our nature. The principles of of piety are deeply founded in the human mind. It is no less essential to us than to possess the attributes of speech and reason. The most sceptical and misanthropic person must trust in something superior to himself; and that object of trust is to him divine. The influences best calculated to refine and moralize mankind are education, domestic training, parental example, literature, the customs and fashions of society, and the Sabbath, with all its beautiful, hallowed ceremonies. Mere arbitrary law is an odious thing in the sight of all the world. The mass of any people will therefore look with suspicion and dislike upon a church which is identified with the civil government. The voluntary system is vastly preferable to any of those that recognize the rectitude and expediency of coercion in matters of faith. It is just as absurd to vote that men shall be religious at all, or in any particular way, as to vote that they shall be initiated into the science of fluxions, mathematics, or natural philosophy."

Mr. Carlyle, speaking of modern poetry, said that, "although Wordsworth was not so popular, so generally read and admired as many of his contemporaries, yet he ascended to the highest grounds ever occupied by poetic genius. In his writings are sounded some of the noblest strains of poetry recorded in ancient or modern literature. No author is more original, happy, and delicate in the use of metaphors and comparisons." Several instances were quoted, one of which seemed to me so transcendently noble, that I will give it a place here. Wordsworth describes the tendency of human life to beautify man's nature in the following lines: —

> " As the ample moon,
> In the deep stillness of a summer even
> Rising behind a thick and lofty grove,
> Burns, like an unconsuming fire of light,
> In the green trees; and kindling on all sides
> Their leafy umbrage, turns the dusky veil
> Into a substance glorious as her own;
> Yea, with her own incorporate, by power
> Capacious and serene, — like power abides
> In man's celestial spirit; Virtue thus
> Sets forth and magnifies herself; thus feeds
> A calm, a beautiful, and silent fire,
> From the encumbrances of mortal life,
> From even disappointment — nay, from guilt;
> And sometimes, so relenting Justice wills,
> From palpable oppressions of despair."

The philosophy contained in these words came from the Bible. It is the great, immutable truth often expatiated upon by the sacred writers, that all events are made to subserve the march of knowledge and happiness; that by all which happens through the years, ages, centuries, and cycles of time, that by all the ordinances, appointments, fates, vicissitudes, sins, and sufferings of our earthly allotments, only great, everlasting, and beneficent results are accomplished.

> " Respecting man, whatever wrong we call
> May, must be right, as relative to all."

Or, to use the ideas of Emerson, in his profound work, " *Representative Men*," " That pure malignity can exist, is the extreme proposition of unbelief. It is not to be entertained by a rational agent; it is atheism; it is the last profanation.

> 'Goodness and being in the gods are one;
> He who imputes ill to them makes them none.'

To what a painful perversion has that theology arrived which admits no conversion for evil men hereafter! But the influence of the Holy Spirit is never relaxed; the power of the sun will convert carrion itself into grass and flowers; and man, though now in dungeons, or jails, or on gibbets, is in a state of preparation for all the beauty and bliss of which he is capable. Atheism is not so dreadful as that vindictive theology which peoples an Inferno with devils utterly depraved and incorrigible. Every thing is superficial, and perishes, but love and truth only. The largest is always the truest sentiment. Every man can exclaim, —

> 'Immortality o'ersweeps
> All pains, all tears, all sins, all fears,
> And peals like the eternal thunders of the deep
> Into my ears this truth — Thou liv'st forever.'"

The most painful sight which I saw in England was the great inequalities which mark the different classes of society. The established church is proverbially rich. Wealth in itself should never be regarded as an evil, either as it respects individuals or communities. The ministers of religion cannot be too opulent, provided they make a beneficent use of their means. In this instance the evil arises from a most unrighteous distribution of the funds appropriated for the support of religion. The bishops have princely incomes. The inferior clergy, who do all the preaching and parochial labor, are in the main very poor, and sometimes straitened for the necessaries of life. If the annual disbursements of the English government on behalf of Christianity were divided equally among its ministers, each man would receive only about five hundred dollars a year, which is not larger than the average salary paid to clergymen in the United States. It appears hard that the dissenters should be compelled to contribute towards the maintenance of the establishment, besides supporting their own institutions. It seems to be the most flagrant injustice and iniquity that six or seven thousand persons — the younger sons of noblemen — should receive their livings from the church funds, who never perform clerical duties. They hold their stations as benefices, or sinecures. Besides, they are often openly, desperately depraved and dissolute.

Here I would remark that the opinion most prevalent in this country concerning the character of the English bishops is altogether erroneous. When will men learn to do justice to their fellow-beings? Although these prelates have large revenues, and are surrounded with a temporal splendor, which, in the eyes of a plain democrat from this western world, may appear utterly irreconcilable with the character of a gospel minister, as described by Paul in his Epistles to Timothy and Titus, yet for the most part they are humble, self-denying, noble men, worthy to be considered as the successors of the apostles. To be sure, some melancholy exceptions might be mentioned; but bad men are found in every hierarchy under heaven. I admire and honor the English church, that during the seventeenth and eighteenth centuries, and that portion of the nineteenth already elapsed, has stood forth like an impregnable fortress against the assaults of infidelity, a spiritual promontory, on which the storms and waves of opposition have expended their fury in vain. Ever since we ceased to be colonies, some dissenters among us have cherished the most bitter and unfounded prejudices against Episcopacy. No church in this republic is more useful or glorious. It is a haven of repose, whither the calm, intelligent, and refined of all the dissenting denominations may repair, and find a refuge, after having been tossed, perhaps for years, on the boisterous sea of theological strife. Not a minister of this denomination has ever been known to pervert the gospel by making his pulpit the arena of political huckstering, forgetting the fundamental precepts of Christ — the merciful designs and charitable spirit of his mission — to deal out falsehoods, bitterness, and vituperation, instead of the gospel, to subserve the vilest purposes of unscrupulous ambition and depravity.

The American traveller in England, I have before said, is continually pained with those disparities of condition and marked contrasts which arise from an aristocracy established by law from entailed estates and hereditary titles to honor and power. The whole west end of London shows like a city of the gods; St. Giles, Wapping, and other sections are filled with squalor and the extremest wretchedness, whose inhabitants seem more like devils than human beings. In these districts, I was told that children grow up not only crushed and blighted by destitution, but taught to believe that lying, theft, licentiousness, and kindred vices are right and honorable. Are they to blame, then, if they put on terrific attributes, bid defiance to morality, or even imbrue their hands in blood? They know no better. They are not to blame, but the society is which tolerates such a state of pauperism and ignorance. In London there are thirty thousand persons, perhaps, or more, who live in all the luxuries and magnificence which their imagination can devise, and there are quite as many who know not when they rise in the morning where they shall lay their heads at night.

When in Liverpool, I went one morning to visit an extensive park, more than twenty miles in circumference. In it were lawns smoothly shaven, avenues of majestic trees, and gardens presenting every variety of vegetable beauty. It was a perfect paradise. The stately mansion of its owner, through long ranges of splendid apartments, is filled with the works of art and the creations of luxury, with paintings and statues, with silken couches, gorgeous furniture, and costly libraries, exhibiting a scene of magnificence hardly surpassed by the grandeurs represented in the pages of Arabian romance. Throughout England, travelling in any direction, every few miles you come across these magnificent domains belonging to the aristocracy. Indeed, they own nearly all the land in Great Britain. Consequently the surface of England presents scenes of splendor, which makes the stranger feel as if he were journeying through some fairy land.

In England, about thirty-two thousand persons out of a population of thirty-two millions, possess aristocratic wealth and honors. Eight or ten millions own the entire property of Great Britain, both real and personal. The remaining twenty-four millions are paupers, doomed to severe, unintermitted, crushing toil through life, in order to obtain a bare subsistence. From infancy their food is of the poorest kind, and insufficient in quantity. Millions of them feel the pain of unsatisfied hunger perhaps every moment during their waking hours. They are half clothed; and cold, wet weather is to them a scene of constant suffering. They cannot read or write, and are cut off from the endearments, joys, and blessings of domestic life. Their domicile is a hedge or a hovel. In mind they are inert, stupid, and mean beyond any specimens of humanity that have fallen under my observation elsewhere, either in the old or new world, either white or black. Strolling one day along the banks of the Avon, I accosted a peasant who was engaged in haying. Among other questions, I asked him the name of the stream on whose bank we stood. He replied that he did not know. On further inquiry, I found that he was born in that neighborhood, and had been a laborer in those fields for more than forty years. When sickness, age, infirmity, and decrepitude overtake them, they are conducted to the poorhouse, and breathe their last with no one to shed the tear of sympathy. They are followed by others who run the same round of wretchedness and almost brutal degradation. So it has been for a long series of ages — from time immemorial. This description is applicable to eight or ten millions of persons.

Now, such a state of things, as all admit, — such a depression of the many to exalt the few, — is the result of feudal aristocracy, the transmission of hereditary honor, entailed estates, &c., factitious distinctions, created and upheld by the theory of the English government. "If any one can doubt about the essential injustice of this system, let him go back in his thoughts to the origin of society. Let me ask him to suppose that he, with a thousand other persons, all standing upon terms of equality, were about to reconstruct society, or to establish a colony on some distant shore. Suppose this company assembled, at the commencement of their enterprise, to form a civil constitution; at this meeting, they all stand upon the same level. Now, imagine ten of these colonists to propose that they should be made earls or lords; that they should be made an hereditary branch of the legislature, with a negative upon the wishes and interests of all the rest; and that, in order to secure their permanent respectability, they should be permitted to hold their estates in entail — a proposition very pleasant and palatable to the ten, doubtless; but could the rest of the company listen to it? I put it to the veriest tory in the world, whether, as one of that company, he would listen to it; I put it to him to say, whether he would consent that lots should be cast to determine on whom the mantle of nobility should fall." *

* Dr. Dewey.

Attending a dinner party at the residence of a wealthy banker of London, I had a good deal of conversation with a very learned man, who was a graduate of Cambridge University, but had never travelled the distance of one hundred miles from the metropolis. To him England was of course the cynosure of nations, a perfect model as to civil government, laws, literature, manners, church, and all else that belong to civilized life. He was saturated with knowledge of books and theories, and so purely English in his tastes and prepossessions, that his conversation was rich, lively, and entertaining. His prejudices against republican forms of government were so strong, that I did not venture to utter a syllable by way of their defence or explanation. He said " it was a Utopian dream that any nation could enjoy permanent order and prosperity without a throne, an established church, and a privileged, hereditary class of nobles. The people are the base of the social superstructure; the lords, temporal and spiritual, are the pillars which support this edifice, the columns and Corinthian capitals by which it is adorned.

"Where are the republics of former times? Where is Athens of old, the birthplace of democracy, the spot first consecrated to freedom, where the arts and graces danced around man in his cradle, bound his head with laurel wreaths, built for him cities, temples, theatres, statues, and tombs, and irradiated the pages of literature with the light of genius? A monarchy, an establishment, and an aristocracy like ours would have made Greece eternal. But now she is a mere vision, existing only in the fanciful schemes of political dreamers, and flashing upon the pages of history —

> 'Like the rainbow's lovely form,
> Evanishing amid the storm.'

Your republic has lasted a little more than half a century, because you have a widely-extended territory and a sparse population. But when you shall have as many inhabitants on a square mile as England contains, what will prevent the ignorant, vulgar, reckless, unprincipled, and impoverished rabble from laying violent hands on the possessions of their neighbors, and subverting the sacred rights of property? Indeed, upon the principle of universal suffrage, they can appropriate to themselves the estates and chattels of the wealthy without open violence. It may be done under the ægis of your laws and constitution. The majority, if it pleases, every five years, will be able to enforce an agrarian division of property by the ballot-box; and where property is insecure, civilization will soon die out."

It is almost impossible for an untravelled Englishman to realize that property is nowhere perfectly safe but under a government like ours, which enables the poorest man, if healthy, to become a landholder, to live in his own house, and to possess in fee simple whatever is essential to his subsistence and comfort. The great body of the people here — nine out of ten — have a spirit of contentment and independence, because in possession of a reasonable competence. When I hear men talk about the danger of their rising, in fury and madness, to destroy that very tenure, that very security, upon which their own possessions rest, their words seem to me dreamy and chimerical. It supposes that will happen which the laws of human nature render impossible; that men may enter into a conspiracy to sweep into the pit of ruin themselves, their wives, their children, their houses, their lands, and all that is dear to them on earth. To pass an agrarian law in such a country as this, would be striking a blow that must so certainly and instantly react upon its authors, that no civilized and reading people, no people capable of even the foresight of a child, could possibly be guilty of such folly; it would be an act so plainly and perfectly suicidal. Besides, if we turn over the histories of the past, we shall find invariably that the rich, oligarchical few, and not the poor plebeians, have been the assailants of the rights of property. If any one will take the trouble to examine the annals of former ages, he will see that mobs, conspiracies, and insurrections have always originated in the mutual dissensions and persecutions of the loftiest and most privileged classes of society. The mass of the people are always sound, and if allowed to take their own way, unseduced and unterrified, would seldom choose the wrong path; and when led into error, they would soon find it out, and promptly and cheerfully retrace their steps. The state of things with us, touching this topic, is happily described in the following lines: —

——— "Self-love in each becomes the cause
Of what restrains him — government and laws.
For what one likes, if others like as well,
What serves one will, when many wills rebel?

> How shall he keep what, sleeping or awake,
> A weaker may surprise, a stronger take?
> His safety must his liberty restrain;
> All join to guard what each desires to gain.
> Forced into order thus by self-defence,
> The worst learn justice and benevolence;
> Self-love forsook the path it first pursued,
> And found the private in the public good."

Our conversation next turned upon the bill before Parliament for the establishment of free schools — to extend to all children born into the kingdom the knowledge of reading, writing, and numbers. He said, "To me it is plain that the common people ought not to be educated. Popular education is one of the delusions which, in my day, have taken possession of the public mind. Lord Brougham has exerted his utmost abilities and eloquence to give it currency. He talks about raising the body of the people to intelligence, self-respect, and self-dependence. They know enough already to fulfil aright their missions in life; more knowledge would tend to destroy their habits of subordination and submission to their superiors; it would render them rebellious to lawful authority, and discontented with the condition which Providence has allotted them." Referring to Cousin's Report to the French Government on the Prussian School System of Education, for authority, he added, "It contains this extraordinary and astounding statement, viz., *that in the best educated departments, the greatest amount of crime has been found to exist.* This is a matter of statistics. Cousin says, that in France, education, where it has been tried, has made the common people worse. The knowledge of reading and writing, com-

municated to the lower orders, would qualify them
to run more successfully the career of crime. He
who writes a good hand can easily become an adept
forger or counterfeiter; he who is skilful in arithmetic may carry on those stupendous schemes of
fraud which would be forever beyond his reach, were
he ignorant of numbers. A reading people, who
through the newspapers form an acquaintance with
those measures of government, or conduct of individuals whom they dislike, may easily be inspired
with ambition, envy, discontent, and unhappiness, and
by these means be urged on to excesses, vice, and
extravagance; to treason, rebellion, mobs, tumults,
and massacres."

Such sentiments are almost universally expressed
by the aristocrats of England. I heard them advanced by a bishop in the House of Lords; but in
justice I must add, that he expressed the opinion
that it would do to teach all children to read, if they
could be taught by ministers of the established
church, who would subject them to a wholesome
spiritual influence, and train them up to religion by
the facile and insensible degrees of a pious and virtuous education. He asserted that the doctrine
which considers intelligence in itself favorable to
virtue an "utter folly," a most "dangerous mistake." Even in the United States, I have often
heard gentlemen urge arguments against the cause
of popular education; yet these men, at the same
time, were employing teachers, books, travel, and
every other means, to make their own children wise
and learned. There is no gulf into which we are

liable to fall but the dark gulf of popular ignorance. Into it the nation will inevitably descend, unless it be closed up in time. "No single sacrifice, like the fabled sacrifice of the Roman Curtius, can avert the danger. A representative government represents the character of the people. And that government which represents prevailing ignorance, degradation, brutality, and passion, has its fate as certainly sealed, as if, from the cloud that envelops the future, a hand came forth, and wrote upon its mountain walls the doom of utter perdition."

But the majority in this land are not a blind, ignorant, reckless, unprincipled rabble. The blessings of a free press, free schools, a free church, and universal suffrage, pour upon the minds of our people the effulgence of knowledge and refinement. As returning spring covers the earth with verdure and beauty, so these divine principles shed upon the moral landscape the light and loveliness of order, peace, and intelligence. The fundamental error of all our moral, religious, and political systems is the hateful doctrine that men are naturally depraved — incapable of goodness and self-government. This error pervades the very spirit of civilized society, all its maxims and institutions, and the general tone of education. How much of all literature has been prostituted to the unholy work of traducing and depreciating human nature — the noblest creation of infinite love with which we are acquainted! The popular and prevailing idea, that sin is an essential, inherent part of man, is so wide spread, radical, comprehensive, fearful, and fatal in its bearings, as to overshadow almost with despair the moral prospects of an enslaved and benighted world.

That portion of the English who possess cultivated minds, wealth, and all its advantages, are to me less than nothing, and vanity, compared with the millions of wretched, impoverished beings there, that for a long series of ages have been the unpitied victims of injustice and oppression. Yes, my sympathies are with that *rabble* — as I often heard them called — whose rights and interests are crushed down to earth by the banded tyrannies of church and state. And with sorrow I asked wise men the reason of all this. The only answer was, " They must be kept in this depressed condition to prevent them from rising to carry on a war of extermination against property — against the government, the throne, the church, and the nobility. It is necessary to our preservation that they should be excluded from the higher advantages of literature, art, science, freedom, and civilization."

This undervaluing of human nature, this blindness to its original worth and capabilities, is a leading defect in the preaching and measures of many clergymen in the United States. The pulpit here is often exceedingly troubled with apprehensions lest the mass of the people, through ignorance and depravity, should imperil and subvert their civil rights and prosperity. They show a great want of confidence in the good sense and rectitude of their fellow-beings. Hence hundreds of ministers in the Northern States have been engaged, the past summer, in preaching politics. They tell their hearers that they must look to them for guidance and information in all these things, as well as in matters appertaining to the salvation of their souls. Though the people are trained to investigate political affairs for themselves; though books and newspapers abound which treat of these subjects, and are in the hands of every one; and although they are ably and constantly discussed every week day, in legislatures, mass meetings, the family, the shop, the field, the store, the rail car, and the steamboat, yet these clergymen think it necessary, for the enlightenment of the people, to address them from the pulpit on the slavery question, and other topics, which should be left to the exclusive management of *statesmen and professed politicians*.

As a class, the laity are much better informed on these subjects, and more competent to their discussion than ministers. Besides, by this practice the church is entirely desecrated. People go there on the Sabbath to have their thoughts lifted up towards God, heaven, and the life immortal. And what do they hear? A mere political harangue, bitter denunciations of a large class of their fellow-citizens, and inflammatory appeals calculated to inspire them with hatred, prejudices, and all the worst passions of which our nature is capable. Such ministers do more to destroy respect for Christianity than all the infidel writings and preaching in the world. If these ministers are right, then professors should be appointed in all our theological seminaries, to initiate the pupils into the elements of political science. I thank God that the people of the United States are capable of managing their own affairs, and that if every clergyman in the Union were this day to breathe his last, laymen in sufficient numbers, and well qualified, would immediately step forward to fill their places.

I went through England, Scotland, Wales, and Ireland, and examined the most interesting objects which they present to the notice of travellers. A description of my experiences would fill volumes. I had read the history of those lands from a child. England was endeared to me as the birthplace of my ancestors, as adorned with all the embellishments which art, science, learning, and religion can bestow. I hardly saw a town, city, castle, river, lake, a hill covered with shrubbery and heather, a plain, valley, or mountain, which did not awaken in my mind long trains of historical associations. So that the glories of my fatherland for centuries past, as I moved along, rose and stood before me, with all the vividness of real life — a panorama of the grand, beautiful, good, and picturesque of former ages. Every step of my way was on classic ground. For instance, at Holyrood Palace, near Edinburgh, I saw the bedroom and dressing room of Queen Mary, and the apartment in which Rizzio was murdered before her face by Darnley, Ruthven, and others. I lingered on that spot for hours. For a time I was a spiritualist. I beheld and conversed with the beautiful, accomplished, but unfortunate Mary. Perhaps, were it not for her beauty and sufferings, her name would not have been embalmed in the memory of everlasting ages. With Mary, thoughts of the persons and scenes that determined her extraordinary fates and fortunes, the events of the age in which she lived, the distinguished men and women who were her contemporaries, rushed into my soul with the fulness and rapidity of a torrent. Overborne, carried away with the images and emotions inspired by the place, I staid there till it was nearly dark, and then went to my room to write notes and pass a sleepless night. This I did more than half the time whilst I was in Europe.

The next day, taking leave of the Scotch metropolis, I went round through the Highlands to Glasgow. I saw the beautiful windings of the Forth, the Grampian Hills, the wild, magnificent Trossachs, Ben Nevis, and Ben Venue, the haunted waters of Loch Katrine, and the bold, majestic shores of Loch Lomond. From Glasgow I directed my course to Belfast, Ireland, and the Giant's Causeway. I had previously become acquainted with the scenery of Wales and the northern counties of England, Cumberland and Westmoreland, which present a most indescribable assemblage of sublime and beautiful objects: lofty craggy mountains, precipitous cliffs, looking down upon the sweetest valleys; small, secluded, verdant farms, in the highest state of cultivation; crystal lakes of the most romantic forms — sparkling gems in the landscape; streams of pure, living, transparent water; trees and flowers of the most elegant hues and shapes; animals grazing; gardens; cottages with their sheltering bowers; and other things innumerable, whose expressiveness, delicacy of coloring, gracefulness of figure, and boldness of outline, can be understood by those only who have seen them with their own eyes.

But I must confess that the scenery of Switzerland, the Alps, and Italy far surpasses the noblest exhibitions of nature in British landscapes. It is on a larger scale, and has peculiar features of grandeur and beauty, which adorn no other part of the world that I have seen. What is there in Great Britain, which her poets have sung so much about, comparable with Lake Como and its enchanting shores? I entered Switzerland from the southern or Italian side, through one of the beautiful valleys of Piedmont, which commences near Lake Maggiore, about dark. There was no passenger in the diligence but myself. The sky was clouded and lowering. In a few moments it began to rain violently, accompanied with vivid flashes of lightning and tremendous peals of thunder. This was the only thunder storm which I witnessed in Europe. By the help of the lightning I could see the towering mountains on each side of me. By the echoes from the surrounding summits the claps of thunder were intensified, and made awfully grand. I felt and enjoyed the truth of the lines from Byron:—

> "The sky is changed! and such a change! O night!
> And storm, and darkness, ye are wondrous strong,
> Yet lovely in your strength, as is the light
> Of a dark eye in woman! Far along,
> From peak to peak, the rattling crags among,
> Leaps the live thunder! Not from one lone cloud,
> But every mountain now hath found a tongue;
> And Jura answers through her misty shroud
> Back to the joyous Alps, who call to her aloud!"

In the midst of wind, rain, night, clouds, lightning, and thunder, we stopped at a small hotel to change horses. Here I was joined by two English gentlemen, who were on their way to Geneva. They proved to be quite intelligent, agreeable companions, and in the space of ten minutes the most cordial and friendly relations were established between us. I had been alone not more than two hours before they entered the diligence. At the beginning of the valley above named, a Scotchman, who accompanied me all the way from Milan, was stopped by the police, in consequence of some alleged informality in his passport. Being pressed with want of time, I was compelled, with much regret, to part with him. This short period was the only occasion in which I was left absolutely solitary during the whole of my wanderings on the continent of Europe.

The morning came " with breath all incense, and with cheek all bloom," glowing with life, radiance, and beauty. After breakfast we crossed the bridge of Crevola, and began to ascend what is called the Simplon road, which was constructed by the Emperor Napoleon, and is generally called Bonaparte's road. The highest part of this road is six or eight thousand feet above the level of the sea. It is forty or fifty miles in length, and passes on the extreme declivity of ridges, over awful gulfs, that seem to be thousands of feet deep, and roaring torrents, and through tremendous precipices, which, as you approach them, appear like perpendicular barriers of impassable rock, reaching to the heavens. Yet over these ravines, gorges, and cascades, and down tremendous cliffs, you are carried as easily as if you were riding in a pleasure carriage along a smooth, level turnpike. The ascent is so gradual that it nowhere exceeds two inches and a half in six feet, and carriages can descend without locking the wheels at any place. I am speaking now of the Italian side of the Alps, which to me was much more striking in scenery than that of Switzerland. The road sometimes is terminated in one direction by a perpendicular precipice, towering from unfathomed depths below, absolutely precluding farther progress, except by making a tunnel through the solid rock. Of these galleries, the largest, if I do not mistake, is six hundred feet long, twenty-seven wide, and thirty high, with three wide openings through its side to admit light. On the lower side of the road there is a wall laid with stone and mortar, whose solid masonry resembles the sublime works described in ancient story as the creation of giants. The road passes over nearly three hundred bridges. At certain intervals, stone houses are built across the mountains, the occupants of which are bound to keep their stoves heated night and day, in cold weather, and a room ready for travellers. The Catholics have small oratories on the route, where the faithful may pause and perform their devotions. Near the summit is a hospice, in which strangers may find good entertainment.

No work of art ever made so strong an impression on my mind as this road. Its features are in keeping with the sublime and awful scenery through which it passes. As the traveller makes his way to the top of the Alps, panoramas of mountains are presented to his view one after another, each of which has a type of wildness and grandeur peculiar to itself. No two are precisely alike. Some are snowy peaks; others rise in the shape of a cone formed of bare, naked rocks, utterly devoid of every kind of vegetation. One summit, whose altitude is perhaps thousands of feet, is clothed with dark fir groves. Another, separated from this only by a deep gorge, and to the eye not much more lofty, has on its sides the mingled phenomena of summer and winter. In point of fact they may be miles apart, but to the eye of the traveller they appear to be neighbors. Here is every form of majestic scenery, within the circumference of fifty miles, which our globe exhibits. Travelling through the Alps, you may see masses of snow descend to a certain point on the sides of the mountains; and at that very point vegetation commences; the cattle feed; and even up to the very fields of snow, within twenty feet thereof, are grass, shrubbery, trees, gardens, herbage, and cottages. But there is no space, had I the power to describe these things. No words can picture the charming valley of the Rhone, the beautiful Lake of Geneva, Mont Blanc, as seen from the surrounding mountains, Chamouni, Mer de Glace, or the Glacier de Boisson, with their stupendous masses of ice, crowding down into the verdant valleys, or shooting up in the figures of pyramids and pinnacles, stupendous, unequalled, and ineffably sublime.

Northern Italy, about Lakes Como and Maggiore, has made indelible impressions on my memory.

That and Switzerland awakened in my soul higher ideas of natural beauty and sublimity than I had ever before entertained. There is nothing in the United States comparable to them as it regards interesting scenery. I was struck with the singular blending and contrasts which they present of all that is most magnificent and lovely in nature. There is hardly a spot in those regions where the traveller's horizon does not at the same moment embrace in its sweep mountain tops, ragged cliffs, fertile valleys, rich plains, verdant meadows, vineyards, gardens, embowered cottages, hills moulded into exquisite forms of elegance, crystal streams sparkling in their purity, and clear, placid lakes, — so clear that, like a mirror, they reflect the blue depths of azure above, — the surrounding shores, with their terraces rising one above another, and lessening towards the top, the clouds and mountains, and the variegated hues and tints of the sky. These objects, innumerable and indescribable, set up in the galleries of my soul pictures of loveliness and grandeur which can never fade away — which enable me to commune with God, to feel the inspirations of his Spirit, and to catch partial glimpses and revelations of the wonders and glories of that higher world, destined for our immortal inheritance. Yes, the seeing of Italy and Switzerland filled my soul with treasures, — perceptions, feelings, glorious images, worth more than all the material wealth of Europe, — treasures that will last long as the throne of heaven, which are the dispensers of all the true happiness that lies within the sweep of time, or the boundless walks of futurity.

For myself, I am accustomed to see God in every thing which awakens my love and admiration. Whenever I behold any object, new, fair, orderly, proportioned, grand, or harmonious, in the physical world; whenever I witness a high display of moral excellence, honor, faithfulness, and truth; whenever heaven from its majestic heights, or earth from its lowly vales, sends one sweet, delightful, or elevating thought into my mind, — that thought is to me but a revelation of the ever-present, ever-beautiful, ever-blessed Creator. The outward universe of majesty and beauty, as much as the Bible, is an unfolding of our Father's infinite perfections. And if we could think thus habitually and constantly, we should soar upward above these dark vales of time, their sorrows and gloom, and realize that no joy, no rapture on earth, can be likened to the ecstasies of a soul whose supreme affections centre on God. The holiest prayer which I am capable of offering is the thoughts and feelings which seize upon me when thinking of the character of Jesus, and the wonders of Calvary. Scarcely less profound and absorbing are my emotions when I hold deep communion with nature — nature, that possesses not an item of glory but what radiates far more brightly from the person, truth, and history of the Son of God.

I cannot but repeat it, I thank God that I have been enabled to see Switzerland, — its endlessly-diversified mountains, cragged pinnacles, deep defiles, wild and romantic scenery, the varieties of hue and shade, the images of purity and repose, the flitting shadows and changing colors, which at the rising and setting of the sun pass in rapid succession, like fairy forms, across the gently rippled, tremulous waters of her lakes. When gloomy or melancholy thoughts come over me, I recall to memory some of these charming scenes, and sadness flees away. The clouds are dispersed. All around is like a bright, balmy, fragrant morn of spring. I listen to a sweet concord of melodious sounds. I look through "golden vistas, into a serener, happier world," and exclaim, —

> "Thou art, O God, the life and light
> Of all this wondrous world we see;
> Its glow by day, its smile by night,
> Are but reflections caught from thee;
> Where'er we turn thy glories shine,
> And all things fair and bright are thine."

CHAPTER XV.

INTERIOR OF FRANCE. — THE MONOTONOUS ASPECT OF ITS SCENERY. — MANNER OF KEEPING THE SABBATH ON THE CONTINENT OF EUROPE, ETC.

AFTER sojourning in Paris a few days, I engaged a seat in the *coupé*, or front apartment of a diligence, for Chalons, a town situated on the Saone. When I ascended to my place, I found that my companions for the tour were two gentlemen, one on my right hand and one on my left, with an air, mien, and expression completely French. Not a word was uttered by either of us while the carriage was rattling along the paved streets of the city. When we entered the country, the road became as level and smooth as a parlor floor. Then I ventured to break the disagreeable silence by addressing some questions in French, (which I supposed was their vernacular,) first to one and then to the other of my fellow-travellers. They pretended not to understand my *patois*, shook their heads, and continued dumb. I then tried the English, but was equally unsuccessful. The man on my left had the looks of one belonging to some learned profession. I ventured to speak to him in Latin, a language with which all scholars on the continent of Europe are familiar; but even this attempt elicited no response. They were as still as marble statues. I was about giving up the case as utterly hopeless, when the thought occurred that perhaps they mistook me for an Englishman; for my friends in London had remarked that I looked much more like John Bull than Brother Jonathan. Immediately I remarked that I was a stranger from the United States, and this was my first visit to Europe. At this announcement their faces no longer wore a forbidding frown, but were lightened up with joy and kind expression. They apologized for the incivility with which I had been treated, by confirming what I had before suspected. One was a merchant of Paris, who spoke the English with ease, and had visited Boston, New York, and Philadelphia. The other resided in Lyons, and was a lawyer of the largest information and the most agreeable powers of conversation. He knew every rod of ground we travelled over, and pointed out the localities of some of the most interesting scenes recorded in the history of France.

From Belgium to Marseilles almost every acre of land is under the highest state of cultivation. Immense open fields, separated by no hedges or enclosures of any kind, stretch along in almost unbroken succession for hundreds of miles. Through unknown centuries past, they have poured forth their annual crops of fruits and vegetables. The stock in the pastures are kept from wandering, not by fences, but by shepherds, with the aid of dogs, which manifest a degree of intelligence almost equal to that of man. I scarcely saw a piece of woodland or swamp; but through my entire route I remarked long avenues of trees, — elm, poplar, beech, — all trimmed up so as to be very lofty, without any under branches.

For many miles together the road is lined on both sides with them; and ranges of trees, forming squares, triangles, and groves of parallel rows, are seen every where. But the scenery was so monotonous that I soon grew tired of looking at it. In travelling more than five hundred miles by land, from the north of France to the Mediterranean, we did not meet a single pleasure carriage, or any other vehicle, except mail coaches and the carts of the peasantry going to or returning from their daily labors. All whom I saw had a melancholy air, were poorly clad, and apparently broken down with excessive toil.

When I passed through these regions it was the season of harvesting. A great majority of the laborers in the fields were women, and they performed the hardest kind of work, for the men mixed with them seemed in general to be aged, infirm, and feeble. All over England, Scotland, and Wales, I beheld the same spectacle — women in companies of ten, twenty, &c., digging, drudging, and delving in the fields, doing precisely that kind of work which slaves perform with us in the Southern States. By the help of my intelligent companions I learned much of the statistics that regard the peasantry of France. Millions in that country do not live as well as our slaves, work harder, are a great deal poorer, and incomparably less happy and less free.

Yet, in conversation with enlightened Frenchmen, I was often reminded that the glory of our republic was impaired by the shocking evil of slavery. In reply, my invariable practice was to ask for a clear and precise idea of the term slavery. A talented, disingenuous man may conceal truth, and build up error by the use of equivocal and uncertain combinations of speech. Vague and indefinite terms and statements have filled the moral world with doubts, misapprehension, and falsehood. All whom I met on this subject were willing to subscribe to these words, found in the treatise of Dr. Paley on Moral Philosophy : " Slavery is an obligation to labor for a master without one's own consent." " But our peasants and operatives," said one of my fellow-travellers, " are free ; no master can compel them to work."

In answer to this assertion, I remarked, " You have just told me that the multitudes whom we see (most of whom are women) going to the fields with hoe and shovel in hand, or to the markets with heavily-laden baskets on their heads, are so poor that they cannot obtain the most scanty fare without this wearing toil and exposure, which deprives them of all the charms and advantages of civilized life. According to your own statement, these women would starve if they did not regularly hire themselves out to work in the field, at the price of eighteen sous (less than eighteen cents) per day. At the same time, they, in part, support themselves, take their breakfast, which consists of nothing but a plate of thin, mean, sometimes rancid soup, at home ; their employer providing some bread and a pint of sour wine for their dinner, and not a particle of meat of any description.

" They have no holidays but the Sabbath and the festivals of the church. They have never had, at one time, money enough to travel twenty miles from the spot where they were born. And as to their not being compelled to toil, they can no more help it, — they can no more emancipate themselves from the fetters and manacles which bind them down with an adamantine necessity, — than they could create the vegetables and fruits that they grow and carry to market. More, this hopeless indigence and depression, which have been handed down from time immemorial, are the result of your laws. It has been ordained by your civil constitution in the same sense that the government of America has legalized African bondage. It is one of the sad remains of ancient feudalism. Besides, your slaves are 'bone of your bone, and flesh of your flesh.' They are as noble and capable by nature as their masters. But with us the slaves are black, belong to an inferior race, and are just as incapable of enjoying equal rights and freedom with their masters, as the horse, the ox, or the mule. It is an empty boast that you have no slaves in France. Within your territories are millions enslaved by the hand of law, and beyond all comparison more destitute, helpless, and wretched, than African bondmen in our republic."

I noticed the prevalence of the same delusion in England. The morning on which I reached Manchester, the newspapers stated that fifty thousand persons in that city were suffering from starvation, and eloquent appeals were made to the community on their behalf. In a few moments after reading this notice, I called on a distinguished scholar and philanthropist, with whom I had held some correspondence, through the introduction of a brother who resided in New Orleans. I was scarcely seated before he introduced the subject of American slavery, remarking that he was president of the Abolition Society in Manchester, and that the day before a handsome collection was taken up to further their objects. " Though far off," said he, " our hearts bleed for and sympathize with those among you, whom, in defiance of the sacred principles of the Declaration of American Independence, you are subjecting to a cruel and most merciless bondage. We learned from a speech delivered here a few days ago by one of your own countrymen, that the poor slaves in the south are habitually scourged and tortured by inhuman masters, to make them work harder; that they have insufficient clothing and inadequate food. He showed us pictures exhibiting the dreadful form of punishment practised, as he alleged, on the cotton and sugar plantations in general." In my reply, it was attempted to prove that the impressions which this gentleman had imbibed in regard to American slavery were entirely erroneous. He listened to the statistics which were given him with the greatest joy. He used no invectives, no harsh, unchristian language, such as constantly fall from the lips of anti-slavery apostles in this country, who generally meet the mildest arguments of their opponents by foaming out their anger, malevolence, and shame. Indeed, he went so far as to say that if my statements were true, (and he fully believed in their correctness,) the condition of our slaves, all things considered, would not be bettered by emancipation, were the experiment actually tried, and that the funds raised by British philanthropists for their relief should be expended in feeding the starving millions at their own doors. " 'Tis distance lends enchantment to the view." Constantly, when conversing with the wise and good of the old world about the American republic, I was asked how it was possible that a people so enlightened and generous could deliberately unite in disfranchising a large class of their fellow-beings, and withholding from them all the blessings which freemen most highly prize. But I found no difficulty in convincing them that we were not guilty of conduct so immoral and inconsistent with our political principles; that we allowed the negroes among us as much liberty as they were capable of, and that they had a much larger share of temporal means and happiness than any class of operatives that I had met on the continent of Europe.

Paris and the other cities of France far surpassed my expectations. But I was sadly disappointed with the country, though it is so old, so rich, and so highly cultivated. About forty years ago, I took a journey, with two friends, through the State of Illinois. It was in the summer, and in several instances we travelled for a whole day without meeting a human habitation, directing our course entirely by a pocket compass. Although the widely-extended prairies, of which the eye could find no limits, covered with grass and wild flowers of every form and hue, filled with deer, grouse, and other game unterrified by the approach and presence of man, presented a rare combination of sublime and beautiful scenery, yet the journeying across them inspired me with strange feelings of desolateness and melancholy. No loveliness of natural scenery can render an immense solitude agreeable, so strong and predominant are the social propensities which God has given us. In travelling through the interior of France, amid all its rich fields and vine-clad hills, I saw no beautiful country seats, no cottages embowered with trees, no fine houses, no bright and happy faces, no children going to school with book in hand, no equipages, no persons apparently walking or riding for pleasure; but a dreadful solitariness and seclusion seemed to reign every where. There may be people in those rural districts who possess the advantages of wealth, learning, leisure, and taste. None of this description are seen along the roads. Almost the entire population that meets the eye of the traveller belongs to the toiling multitude — miserable-looking people, tramping about in wooden shoes, heavy in their movements, their faces weather-beaten and unintelligent, living in low, filthy stone houses, destitute of comfortable furniture, whose large, projecting roofs embrace not only domicile, but also barn, stable, wood house, sty, &c., where the accommodations for man and beast are almost equally mean, dirty, and disagreeable.

But on the Sabbath, the country differs very much in appearance from the aspect which it wears on the other days of the week. One Sunday I chanced to be in a lovely district on the banks of the Saone. The people, dressed in their best apparel, through the morning repaired in crowds to the churches. The Sabbath, all over the continent of Europe, in the afternoon is kept as a holiday. I saw small parties, families, kindred, and friends, when their religious services were over, engaged in conversation and appropriate amusements. They seem cheerful, refreshed, elastic, and happy. I could hardly realize that they were the same beings whom I had gazed on the evening before with sad emotions, as, exhausted, haggard, and care-worn in their looks, they were lifting off from their necks the iron yoke of toil. I was struck with the quietness and decorum which marked these laborers during the hours devoted to relaxation. Though the population was all abroad after the season of divine service, in the streets, gardens, and public places, there was an entire, remarkable abstinence among the multitudes from all boisterous mirth, loud talking, and laughter, frolicking, profaneness, intemperance, and excesses of every kind. Indeed, they were as quiet, orderly, and restrained as the collections around our church doors, when assembled for public worship. I noticed the same peculiarity all over France, Italy, and Switzerland. May not this extraordinary decorum be ascribed to the fact that the whole Sabbath is not, as with us, devoted to religious services, but a part of it is employed in innocent and useful recreations?

At any rate, I could not help feeling, with respect to these poor people, that the Sabbath was the most glorious portion of their earthly allotments; that it far outweighed in value all their other temporal blessings and possessions. No words can describe the importance to the humbler classes of that regular return of hallowed rest, which secures to them a weekly day of release from injustice and servility, from ignoble toil and wearing drudgeries. By this divine appointment, the poorest peasant has one day in seven for the ennobling pursuits of knowledge and virtue, for the enjoyment of freedom and independence, and for the concentration of his thoughts upon God, Jesus, and immortality. The Sabbath tells the meanest slave that, however sad and forsaken on earth, he has an ever-present, almighty Father in heaven, who will one day admit him to " the glorious liberty of the children of God." To a poor family, the Christian Sabbath is more important than all the external wealth and magnificence of an evanescent world. The observance of this sacred day is not to be traced to the selfish, arbitrary enactment of a cunning, interested priesthood, but is enforced upon us by a law as eternal, omnipotent, and unvaried, as that which causes our globe to revolve in its annual circuit around the sun. If death were an eternal sleep, the Sabbath would still be indispensably necessary to secure the highest enjoyment of health, bodily vigor, temporal peace, and prosperity. To destroy the sabbatical institution, then, you must take human nature to pieces, and reconstruct it upon another far different and sublimer economy — an economy assimilating us to the inhabitants of that celestial world where toil, pain, fatigue, sleep, and mortality are never known.

A distinguished American divine, writing home from France, says, " There is no Sabbath here; for the Catholic custom prevails of spending the afternoon of the first day of the week abroad in the gardens, promenades, streets, &c. The most pious parents may be seen desecrating holy time by walking or riding out with their households for amusement. Nor is the practice regarded by the most scrupulous as inconsistent with the Christian character." I should like to ask this eminent man if any law of God contained in the New Testament forbids the walking or riding out with children and friends on the Sabbath. On the contrary, the law of reason, of common sense, and Jesus Christ, proclaims that both practices are highly becoming and salutary. I can scarcely imagine a more improving exercise of the head and the heart, than that of taking one's children, and leading them abroad, in a sweet afternoon, to inhale the balmy air, to gaze on the flowers and herbage of the fields, to look on Nature, and "through Nature up to Nature's God," till, rapt above this sublunary sphere, they break forth, perhaps, in the glorious words of Thomson, —

> "These, as they change, Almighty Father, these
> Are but the varied God; the rolling year
> Is full of thee."

From the bottom of my heart I commiserate the narrow soul who can look upon such forms of relaxation as tending to dishonor God or his ordinances; who conceives the Creator as capable of frowning a parent down to hell, and following his children from one generation to another with his wrath and curse, for the crime of an hour's innocent recreation on a Sabbath afternoon. Such absurd views have invested the Christian Sunday with forbidding gloom and melancholy, darkness and mourning, made it revolting to the glad spirit of childhood, and surrounded it with associations to young minds inexpressibly odious and terrific.

At Marseilles, I went on board a steamer which plies as a regular packet between that city and Naples, touching on its way at Genoa, Leghorn, and Civita Vecchia. I visited the principal objects of interest around the Bay of Naples, the delightful environs of Naples itself, Vesuvius, Herculaneum, Pompeii, the tomb of Virgil, the grotto of Pausilippo, Capri Baiæ, and the mouldering remains of villas, gardens, palaces, baths, and museums, which were the ornament and boast of the civilized world two thousand years ago. From this interesting spot I went to the Eternal City, crossed the Apennines to Milan, thence over the mountains to the Rhine, to Holland and Belgium. Soon as I entered London on my return from the continent, I ceased to feel as if I was in a foreign country. The accents of my native language, and all the objects which greeted my senses, bore such a striking resemblance to those of an American city, as to render it impossible to realize that the broad expanse of the Atlantic intervened between me and the land of my fathers. I could not help fancying that I was already on the banks of the Mississippi, in the presence of wife, children, and friends.

When I commenced this writing, it was a part of my plan to include in it a more extended account of my experiences in journeying through the regions above named. Such a narrative would present many curious and interesting details, but there is no room for their admission into these pages, which have been already multiplied beyond my original intention.

CHAPTER XVI.

CONCLUSION.

BORN on the 29th of March, 1792, I am now well advanced in my sixty-fifth year. I contemplate the end of my earthly existence full of gratitude and delightful hope. I thank Heaven that my lot has been cast in this wonderful age, and in this glorious land. This age has advantages which were not possessed by any of its predecessors. The beautiful thoughts and brilliant deeds of the antecedent generations of time constitute a portion of our inheritance. The earliest period of which history gives an account has contributed its quota to the resources of wisdom and happiness enjoyed by those who are now actors on the stage of human life. To us belong the poems of Homer, the writings of Plato and Virgil, the eloquence of Demosthenes, and other luminaries which irradiated former days. To us belong the lofty examples of heroism given by all the great and good whose names are inscribed on the annals of time. The reformation commenced by Luther, is now lavishing its benefits on every part of the civilized world. "For us the sailor at the mast head, on the evening of the 11th of October, 1492, cried out, Land! land ahead! and Columbus with his followers kissed the dust of a new continent." For us the Puritan Fathers, amid the horrors of winter and a rock-bound, savage, inhospitable coast, reared their altars and sang their hymns to the God of civil and religious freedom, imploring his blessing upon their efforts to found " a church without a bishop, and a state without a king." From those who have gone before us have been derived most of the arts, science, learning, institutes, comforts, and blessings of the present civilization.

But the good, true, and useful accumulate as time rolls on, and this age is richer in the beautiful than any which has preceded it. Does the correctness of this position appear doubtful to any one, I would say to him, let us look back only as far as our own memory reaches. During that time, what progress has been made in the means of personal, domestic, and social peace! What advances have we ourselves witnessed, running through the whole circles of education, art, government, and literature! Improvement has taken wings and visited the remotest lands, every where asserting her claims, and emancipating millions from the dominion of ignorance, injustice, and oppression. And this spirit of improvement, which has done so much in our time, is instinct with the principle of self-preservation and everlasting growth. Education, freedom, and the sublime, ennobling principles of Christianity are the recuperative means which must one day overspread the earth, and roll the mighty burden of man's bondage and sorrow into the gulf of annihilation. The human mind can never stand still. Its faculties continually grow more vigorous and expansive — become fitted for wider excursions and higher views of truth and duty. The world never stands still, nor takes a step backward. To do the one or the other is not within the limits of possibility. It cannot be doubted but that in time to come civilization will increase more rapidly than it has done during the last half century. No mortal can foresee its progress. But judging its future triumphs from the past, we may conclude that the day will certainly come when all mankind will be completely delivered from evil, and the kingdoms of this world become the triumphant kingdoms of the Prince of Peace.

We are intimately and forever allied to all who have lived in former ages. "We should consider ourselves as links in that vast chain of being which commences with our race, and runs onward through its successive generations, binding together the past, the present, and the future, and terminating with the consummation of all things earthly at the throne of God."* The revelation of Jesus Christ enables us to look back through the dim and misty shadows of by-gone times, with all their vicissitudes of honor and shame, tears and rejoicings, crimes and virtues, and discern the divine, mysterious web of that sublime destiny by which God is weaving for each and all of Adam's race the issues of everlasting life, brightness, and beatitude. The Creator has never been disappointed. He sees the end from the beginning. Mankind, in each of the antecedent epochs and eras of earth's history, have been in exact accordance with that plan of creation which has existed eternally in the unsearchable counsels of the Father. The question is often asked, Why did not

* Webster.

the advent of our Saviour take place at an earlier date? The true answer is suggested by the apostle — "The fulness of time had not yet come." The world was not ready to receive him sooner.

Mankind have always been rising in the scale of perfection, and as soon as they were sufficiently elevated to justify the dispensation, Jesus Christ appeared among them. Far be it from me to utter any sophistries calculated to lower the ideas which Christians generally entertain concerning the enormity of sin. But I have long thought, that as water cannot run up stream, so the moral characters of individuals and nations cannot range in general above the level of their allotments. By allotments I mean place of birth, parentage, succeeding years, with all their surroundings. Reflect on the almost inevitable fate of one born in China; on the banks of the Ganges, Missouri, or Niger; in Constantinople, Boston, New Haven, or Mexico. The most dark, disgraceful pages of civil or ecclesiastical history do not prove that former generations were more corrupt in the sight of God than we are, but simply that their means of exaltation and happiness were inferior to those which we enjoy. All things considered, they did as well as they could. Their capabilities and aspirations could not have been more elevated than the plane of their allotments.

I have said that this age is more glorious than any of its predecessors. Why? First, because the humbler, poorer, dependent, and industrial classes possess a much larger share of physical comforts than they ever did in former times. When Egypt was in the zenith of prosperity, serfs, poor, broken, and crushed to the dust, built cities, pyramids, and tombs, tilled the ground, and gathered harvests, not for themselves and children, but for others — a proud aristocracy, who looked upon the condition of a laborer as base and dishonorable. What a change has taken place since! I am satisfied from the best data, that the wealthiest person living in Great Britain six hundred years ago did not enjoy more extended means of physical happiness, than the poorest man in possession of good health and good character now has throughout the United States. Nor is it improbable that in the year 2500 of the Christian era, the humblest operative will be better off in a temporal point of view than the wealthiest inhabitant of London, New York, or Boston at the present day. The prediction of Dr. Franklin is not absurd, that the time will arrive when the burden of immoderate and oppressive labor will be taken off from all classes, and the most impoverished will have leisure enough, every day, to cultivate their minds, acquire mental wealth, enjoy society, and prepare themselves for the destinies of a higher existence.

Again, I thank God that I have been permitted to live under the best civil government which the world has ever seen. I rejoice that my birth was in the land which WASHINGTON, FRANKLIN, ADAMS, JEFFERSON, and their illustrious compatriots, rescued from the severest of all the curses which have afflicted our race — the curse of tyranny and superstition combined. Above all other parts of the world, I love the soil where repose the ashes of those noble and magnanimous fathers, who, in the spirit of the blessed Jesus, gave up their all — wealth, ease, sacred honor, and life itself, for the benefit of after ages, for the political and moral regeneration of a world. I love the soil in which my mortal remains must shortly be laid, but not without the transporting hope that it will be trodden, to the last verge of time, by innumerable millions, free, enlightened, and happy.

That God, who was a Friend, Benefactor, and Saviour in the eventful and perilous exigencies which marked our progress during the protracted war of the revolution, till we had attained a place and name among the nations of the earth, has been our shield and protection ever since, and is this day enriching the inhabitants of the United States with a greater variety and amount of the means of happiness than were ever bestowed upon any other people, either of ancient or modern times. Within a little more than two centuries, large tracts of the vast continent on which we are placed have been changed from an unbroken, unsightly wilderness, into a succession of rich plains, fertile valleys, green meadows, waving wheat fields, gardens, orchards, peaceful hamlets, smiling villages, splendid cities, with all the diversified laws, institutes, manufactures, charities, and public works that are requisite to raise a community to the highest enjoyment of art, science, social refinement, and the countless blessings of Christianity. Our territory reaches from the regions of eternal ice to the unfading verdure and flowers of the tropics. On the one hand it touches the shores of the **Atlantic**, on the other those of the Pacific. We have every variety of climate and soil, and inexhaustible resources of mineral wealth. If all our natural riches were developed, we could easily feed and clothe the present population of the globe. Our commerce spreads its white pinions to the winds of every zone, ploughs the bosom of every sea, and brings home the fruits and treasures of all latitudes. Our schools and seminaries pour forth the light of knowledge upon the humblest persons, however unadorned by wealth or unknown to fame. Our churches, from the unpretending chapel made of logs to the costly sanctuary of granite or marble, stand open for all, without distinction, where they may enter to worship God according to the dictates of their own consciences. Our young artists are attracting notice, praise, and admiration in London, Paris, Florence, and even the Eternal City, Rome. I heard the celebrated Carlyle say that the eloquence of our Congress, pulpit, and press was unsurpassed by that of any nation in Europe.

Where on earth is the country that can, at this moment, be pronounced in so prosperous a condition as ours? Traverse the whole globe, and where can you find a land in possession of so many blessings, contrasted with so few disadvantages, as this in which Providence has assigned us a home? God be praised that, contrary to the predictions of its enemies, both foreign and domestic, the American republic stands forth to-day, in the sight of heaven and before an admiring world, beaming with all the freshness and bloom of a young existence; perfecting her establishments by the collected wisdom of all former ages, and the fruits of its own rich experiences; a lighthouse to the whole earth, an example to all who would be free, the common benefactress of humanity, the destined redeemer of all the enslaved, oppressed, and injured millions that tread our globe. The words RATIONAL, EQUAL, WELL-DEFINED, CONSTITUTIONAL LIBERTY for all, is the motto inscribed upon our banner, our device, our polar star, the secret of all our glory. This diffuses the lustre of heaven over every part of our land; this is the crowning beauty of our mountains, plains, valleys, rivers, lakes, seas, homes, schools, churches, tribunals of justice, and halls of legislation; this is an essential ingredient of the atmosphere we breathe, and is embedded in our soil firmly as the granite of the ever-enduring hills.

The American government rests upon the great principles that God is the Father of all; that all men are equally precious in his sight — equally important in the counsels of the Infinite One; and that we are under sacred, most imperative obligations to respect the rights, welfare, and happiness of all, whatever may be their origin or color. Instead of traducing, depreciating, and wishing to dissolve this government, those who enjoy its blessings should strive to maintain it inviolate, as a legacy of inestimable value, dearer than life itself, and be willing to pour out their hearts' blood, if necessary, to transmit it unimpaired to succeeding generations. May the universal Father, in his infinite mercy, grant that, as age after age shall pass away, adding to our population and multiplying our resources, the people of this great republic may become more and more wise, thankful, and self-governed, more devoted in their attachment to private and to public virtue, be actuated by more generous affections for each other and for mankind, and be ennobled by a profounder consciousness of their responsibility to the God of nations.

Every point relative to the perpetuity of our Union is of general, transcendent, and ineffable moment; for the experiment which we are now making is to determine the problem whether the whole human family will hereafter be free, intelligent, and happy, or ignorant, enslaved, and miserable. Were I not permitted to believe that the unfavorable predictions relative to the stability of our precious institutions, uttered by so many, were the mere effusions of disappointed, murmuring, splenetic ambition, in despair I should bid adieu even to the hopes of the universal triumph of civil and religious freedom, and the exaltation of man to millennial glory.

Once more, I thank God that my lot has been cast in an age rendered illustrious by the rapid increase and more extended diffusion of useful knowledge. When Lord Bacon wrote the Novum Organum, when Newton composed his Principia, and Locke wrote his Essays, when Milton and Shakspeare sang the never-dying strains of poetry divine, the idea of a common school education had not been seriously entertained by any of the wise men living in Great Britain. It was thought that the mass of the people were destined to grope their way forever in a thick night of ignorance and mental bondage. What a revolution has passed over that country since!

As to our own happy land, I may almost say, without qualification, that the humblest operatives understand reading, writing, and numbers. They have their newspapers, journals, books, and literary associations. After the labors of the day are over, instead of going to pass the evening in some haunt of dissipation, they repair to a lyceum or club room, where the lecturer spreads out before them the glittering phenomena of the heavens, or the recently-developed wonders of geology. In these calm, peaceful retreats, they listen to able discussions on the weightiest matters of history, law, political science, and religion. On the Sabbath, they can go to the church, and, with perfect freedom and safety, criticise the sermon they have heard. If it so please, they boldly proclaim that the preacher is in error, and that his discourse was a miserable failure. When Calvin lived, and preached in Geneva, no person could openly condemn his creed or homilies, without being exposed to imprisonment, exile, or some other form of martyrdom.

But in our day, the pulpit is less gloomy, appalling, and repulsive. It is no longer chiefly employed in sending forth what have been called the thunders, lightning, and anathemas of divine wrath, but, clothed with beauty and love, it speaks the language of a fond mother to her dear children. It has come down from the cold, misty, mountainous regions of dogma and denunciation, to describe, in terms which the dullest intellect can understand, and in tones sufficient to soften the hardest heart, the boundless wonders of a Saviour's love. Most encouraging fact, the pulpit is ceasing to philosophize, and delights rather to point the poor sinner to that cross which is the memento of infinite mercy — the memento of that light with which Heaven is pleased to irradiate this dark valley of graves, and make sorrow, bereavement, and mortality rounds in that spiritual ladder on which we may ascend to everlasting mansions in the skies.

Furthermore, I rejoice to have lived in a day when the Bible has passed through the severest ordeal to which it has ever been subjected, and has come forth from the trial, shining not only with undimmed, but with increasing brightness. Strauss and his coadjutors have employed all the resources of their learning and fascinating style to throw discredit upon the miracles of the New Testament. Let Christianity be assailed by every weapon that can be found in the armory of sound discussion and legitimate reasoning. It is ill defended by refusing audience or toleration to the objections of honest inquirers. We pay but a poor compliment to the sacred volume by supposing it liable to be injured or destroyed by the pens of philosophers. Could the ablest scholars, by putting forth their profound and charming productions, overthrow men's confidence in arithmetic, Euclid's geometry, Cicero, Virgil, Newton, or Laplace ? Could their pens demolish the loom, the plough, the press, the chronometer, the compass, the railway, the telegraph, or the steamer? No more can their words destroy Moses and the prophets, Jesus and his apostles, whose writings have withstood the assaults of infidelity for so many centuries. A book that is adapted to man's highest and eternal wants, and to his noblest aspirations, can never die. This is the secret of that indestructible life which the Holy Scriptures possess.

Mr. David Hume was at the head of a literary club in Edinburgh, composed of the greatest scholars in Scotland. These gentlemen openly avowed the opinion, that at the expiration of one hundred years, the Bible, in the minds of enlightened men, would stand upon the same level with all the uninspired poets and philosophers of superior genius that have come down to us from by-gone ages. A century has passed, and what has become of the prophecy? The Bible is more loved and rightly appreciated now than it was then. The tornado of infidelity, all these long years, has been sweeping over the sturdy trunk of revealed religion. "It has not even been bent by the fury of the storm; none of its leaves, flowers, fruits, nor branches, have been shaken down, nor so much as the dependent parasites clinging to their tops." There is hardly a family in the United States, that can read, where the Bible is not found and cherished. As the clouds which interpose between us and the rising sun often reflect the richest hues, so the works written to obscure the word of God have only served to unfold and recommend its divine, ineffaceable glories. And now an open, deep, genuine reverence for the gospel characterizes the freest, profoundest, and most successful inquiries in science, philosophy, and literature.

The divines of my native state — Massachusetts — have been foremost in their endeavors to restore the

Scriptures to their original simplicity, power, and glory. In no part of the world has the spirit of improvement achieved greater wonders, since the commencement of the present century, than in New England. All over the variegated surface of that romantic land, new villages, towns, and even large cities, have suddenly sprung into existence, as if indeed raised by the magician's wand. But more memorable than any outward creations or triumphs, that reflect so much glory on the north, are the valuable researches and discoveries which her accomplished scholars have lately made in the departments of biblical criticism and theological science. In the spirit of a humble, but thorough, fearless, and independent inquiry, the New England clergy have ventured to scrape off the moss from the rock of "eternal truth," not, as enemies insinuate, with the presumptuous, wicked intention of erasing the words engraved thereon "by the diamond pen of inspiration," but rather to ascertain whether the autographs — the original letters inscribed upon these unwasting pillars — have not been slurred, glossed, changed, or corrupted, during a long course of dark and superstitious ages, by the dexterous management of uninspired, unauthorized hands. In other words, they have simply taken the liberty to discriminate between what is human and divine in their formulas, creeds, catechisms, religious books, and sacred institutions in general.

To me it is a subject of thanksgiving, that within the last few years, a new and more efficient system of religious literature has been brought into existence. The Roman Catholics, the Episcopalians, and the various Protestant denominations, are enlightening the American people with *vade mecums*, prayer books, spiritual guides, sermons, pamphlets, reviews, newspapers, and tracts, on innumerable subjects, adapted to all classes of minds. Who can describe the extent, variety, and riches of our Sunday school and juvenile libraries? When I was a boy, there was only one book in our Union, besides the Scriptures, especially intended for the use of children — the New England Primer. Now, religious truth is served up in every shape most likely to arrest, beguile, and please the youthful mind — in a fable, a romance, a poem, a story, even in books of travels, of natural history, and natural philosophy. Some clergymen object to these modes of conveying spiritual instruction, but, as it seems to me, without good reason. The great Mr. Wesley introduced some tunes into church music, which for a long time had been appropriated exclusively to plays, theatres, and convivial entertainments. In reply to those who censured him for doing so, he said he had no idea that sin and Satan should have all the best music to themselves. So I would say of fine literature, — let it not be entirely devoted to the cause of irreligion. It is an engine of inconceivable power, and is just beginning to be wielded with effect for the promotion of Christianity. In our religious reading, there are, to be sure, for the present, some crudities and imperfections; but these will soon be removed, when a stream of pure, beautiful erudition will flow forth, spreading a divine light and life over every part of our beloved republic.

Within the last year, I have heard many worthy and enlightened persons remark, that to their eyes, Christianity has of late been rapidly declining in the United States, and that if it go on much longer to fall in the same ratio, it will soon be obliterated from the map and hearts of the American people. Now, such a gloomy prediction is alike opposite to my judgment, faith, and strongest aspirations; I cannot bear to entertain it; I cannot believe that it has the slightest foundation in truth. To me the very reverse is the case. Christianity, I think, has been more flourishing among us the last thirty years than at any former period.

The basis of this opinion is the universally acknowledged fact, that within this time there has been a great and unprecedented multiplication of churches and kindred organizations among us, and that of every name and denomination. I rejoice in the rapid increase of all those various societies called churches, as furnishing conclusive evidence of the growth of genuine Christianity; for they all recognize the Bible as their standard of faith and practice. I look with unqualified delight upon the founding and building up of a temple for the use of any sect. When I behold such a sight, I do not pause to ask what it is called, nor what its particular creed and forms are to be; nor do I cherish any other wish concerning them, than that they may be congenial to the taste and advancement of the congregation for whose benefit the new edifice is erected. Every church seems to me a most beautiful spot, like an oasis in a surrounding desert. I regard it as adding important strength to that holy bond, which I trust will cement in unbroken, everlasting union the confederated states which compose our great republic. It is like gazing upon a lovely landscape, to see a building where my fellow-beings meet to forget for an hour the vanities and vexations of earth ; to offer their united orisons to a common Father; to trust in that Redeemer who died for them, who is the connecting link between earth and heaven, the mortal and deathless, time and eternity; to obtain a partial respite from the ennui and burdens of life, by catching glimpses of that higher and better world revealed in the gospel, towering in all the glories of immortality beyond these shadowy and evanescent scenes.

There is another proof that evangelical religion is on the increase in this land. I allude to the rapid decline of the spirit of sectarianism. The fact is not denied. As explanatory of this phenomenon, I will state a curious circumstance. For hundreds of years, the different denominations of Christians were alienated and kept asunder by the sincerest conviction that erroneous opinions, honestly held, were a sufficient cause for refusing to fraternize with each other, though they might all agree in accepting the Scriptures as a divinely-inspired standard of faith and duty. In the present day, this ground is almost entirely abandoned. Now, a reception of the Bible, without any particular creed, is nearly the universal bond of Christian union. It is a memorable fact, that the only heresy condemned in the New Testament, is not an error of the understanding, honestly entertained, but a sin of the heart. St. Paul teaches that the only Antichrist is an evil intention, a bad state of the affections — " hatred, variance, emulation, wrath, strife, envyings, ill-will, and murder;" but that all who are actuated by the pure sentiments of "joy, peace, meekness, gentleness, goodness, forbearance, love, and charity, are acceptable to God, and entitled to the respect and approbation of man." Here is a broad scriptural platform, on which all the clergy and laity of Christendom may meet, to maintain a heartfelt, an harmonious, and a heavenly intercourse.

It is laid down by Washington, in his Farewell Address, that a belief in the principles of revelation is requisite to make a man a good member of political society. He expresses the opinion that, without the aid of the Bible, no form of free government can have a lengthened existence. Thank Heaven, the humble Christian pastor can now greet as his co-laborers, in commending and upholding the word of God, presidents, senators, governors, and representatives, judges, members of the bar, all the learned professions, and every one of superior grade in intellect and influence throughout the land. So long as all feel that the glorious superstructure of our freedom is based upon the sacred volume, must they not cling to it as our ark, our palladium, the sheet anchor of our nation's prosperity and glory?

It is not enough that reform, secular improvement in every department, arts, education, schools, and learning should be carried on among us with all possible skill and energy. They, indeed, are all wanted, and are divinely appointed instruments of usefulness and refinement. But something more is requisite to perpetuate our civil institutions, which is forever beyond their reach, too mighty for mere human agents and instrumentalities to accomplish. This is the sublime ideas of God, virtue, and immortality, derivable only from the sacred Scriptures. This is the subordination of the hearts of the American people, with their dark, wild, wayward, ungoverned passions, to the spirit and laws of the Christian religion. A nation may possess a boundless physical prosperity, yet, without the guiding and guardian genius of the gospel, it will be only a more shining mark for the shafts of destruction; like some gallant ship, the owner's pride and glory, richly freighted, but launched upon the boisterous main without star, rudder, or compass, to enable her to find a haven of safety. If the majority of this republic repudiate Christian principles, our existence will indeed be short and troubled, and we shall speedily go down, to be mingled with the ashes of our predecessors in the vast cemetery of departed states and empires.

In consequence of early training and associations, I left my native state (Massachusetts) carrying with me the prejudices which the people of New England are very generally accustomed to cherish towards their neighbors at the south. Among the wise men who directed my education, it was an undisputed principle, that instances of superior intellect, cultivated taste, and high moral worth, were seldom found in the slaveholding states. They seemed to be unconscious of the fact that philosophic culture, creative art, and the inspirations of immortal genius, rose the highest in the civilized nations of antiquity, when three fourths, at least, of their inhabitants were disfranchised, and doomed through life to endure the evils of a slavery vastly more aggravated than that which now exists in any part of the world.

The Bible furnishes incontrovertible evidence that slaveholders may be saints, sages, apostles, and patriots; that it is quite possible for them to exercise towards their dependants (and that in the greatest perfection) all those strong and tender sensibilities comprehended in the precept, "Thou shalt love the Lord thy God with all thy heart, and thy neighbor as thyself." For the wise and holy men whose names are mentioned in Genesis and other portions of the Old Testament, and whose characters are declared to be models of benevolence, justice, and patriotism, in accordance with the express permission of Heaven, sustained precisely the same relation to that part of their families denominated *servants* in Scripture, as southern masters, at the present day, do to their slaves. Yes, in every age and clime, as far back as history runs, the greatest, wisest, and best men on earth, both in theory and practice, have sanctioned the principle of slavery. How absurd, then, the idea that it is of necessity only corrupting and deleterious in its effects on the character of masters and the most precious interests of civilization!

For forty years past, it has been my lot to reside

south of Mason and Dixon's line. I went there fresh from the Theological Seminary at Andover, Massachusetts, a firm believer in the superiority of the north, in every respect, over all the rest of the Union. Though a youth " to fortune and to fame unknown," I was cordially welcomed, and treated with a more noble hospitality, a more marked and uniform kindness, than I had ever experienced in the land of the Puritans. I found the slaveholders in general possessed of a wider range of knowledge, much more refined, gentle, and condescending in manners, far superior in the graces and amenities of social intercourse, to those regarded as well-bred and respectable people throughout the cities, towns, and villages of New England. I was sorry that the prejudices of education and northern society had led me, even in thought, to undervalue and disparage a large class of fellow-citizens entitled to my sincerest respect and admiration. In a worldly point of view, I had nothing calculated to recommend me to their civilities and attention. Yet I was admitted into the most distinguished circles as a friend, equal, and intimate companion. Nowhere, in any part of the world, have I observed less of aristocratic pretensions, of pharisaic, cold-hearted, unsympathizing conduct towards the poor, humble, and unfortunate.

By an acclimating process suffered in Louisville, Kentucky, my life was brought near unto death. After convalescence commenced, when still in a very weak and precarious condition, an opulent planter in the neighborhood, with whom I was personally unacquainted, but who had once listened to my words from the pulpit, heard of my illness, and, unsolicited, paid me a visit. Immediately, he employed the requisite means to have me removed from the heated, enervating atmosphere of the city to his own delightful villa, which was fanned by cool, refreshing breezes, and replenished with rural charms in the greatest variety and abundance. His wife and daughters nursed me with as much assiduity and attention as the most affectionate mother could bestow on a beloved child. Such unexpected kindness from the hands of total strangers revived my sinking spirits, enlarged my views of human nature, and taught me the sublime lesson, that the noblest forms of Christian excellence are not confined to any particular class, creed, sect, or condition of humanity.

This gentleman, who under God was instrumental in preserving me from an early grave, had always lived in the State of Kentucky, and never journeyed beyond its boundaries, except in a single instance. Yet he was a person of varied and extensive information, a great reader, and a profound logician. I have met but few clergymen in any land whose conversation was more edifying, even in relation to those topics of inquiry peculiar to the clerical profession. In defiance of the narrowness of early teaching, and the prevailing forms of faith around him, he had unconsciously imbibed, from a careful and systematic perusal of the Holy Scriptures, Unitarian views of Christianity. At that time, my own creed respecting the Trinity was Calvinistic. Touching this theme, I had listened to the reasonings of the greatest theologians at Yale College and Andover, and fancied myself in possession of all that could be said on the subject.

One day, this gentleman proposed to me the following question: " Does the Bible teach that there is but one uncreated, undivided, indivisible Being in the universe, possessing the attributes of infinite, independent life, power, wisdom, truth, rectitude, and love?" This question was answered in the affirmative — "There is only *one God.*" He then added, " You cannot, therefore, with propriety, use the term *Trinity* to denote the idea that there are three separate persons or beings in the Godhead — three individuals, each of whom is absolutely infinite, in the divine nature; for you have already said that there is but *one* boundless individual, or person, in existence. What, then, do you mean, when you say that there are *three* persons in the Godhead?" I was compelled to acknowledge, after a lengthened discussion, that it was impossible to give any definite, rational, or scriptural signification of the word *Trinity*, except upon the plan of exegesis adopted by the Unitarians. From that day to the present, I have uniformly repudiated the distinguishing views of the Athanasian creed. I am under everlasting obligations to this gentleman, denounced by the fanatics as a godless slaveholder, for opening to me trains of thought, by the pursuit of which I was so happy as to obtain an answer to my doubts, and rest to my inquiries, in regard to one of the most difficult and sublime themes of Christian theology. And if I had passed my life in the Orthodox atmosphere of my native state, I should probably have died in darkness and unbelief as to the real character of my heavenly Father, and the true teachings of his Son Jesus Christ, our Lord and Saviour.

The instructive conversations which I enjoyed, when entertained by the hospitalities of this benefactor, led me to change and modify my ideas on many important topics relating to morals, society, political science, and religion. To him might be applied the following lines: —

> "Unbiased or by favor or by spite;
> Not dully prepossessed, nor blindly right;
> Though learned, well-bred; and though well-bred, sincere;
> Blessed with a taste exact, yet unconfined,
> A knowledge both of books and humankind,
> Generous converse, a soul exempt from pride,
> Who loved to praise with reason on his side."

When I became strong enough to travel, this noble-hearted man sent me off, in his own private carriage, and at his own expense, to seek the recuperation of my health at a celebrated watering place. If I had been a son, he could not have done more for me. When memory retraces the past, I cannot call to mind a more beautiful character. He was adorned with every species of 'moral excellence — wisdom, humility, unsullied honor, unswerving truth; all the gentle, soft, social, and refined virtues — mildness, compassion, generosity; and the most conscientious regard to the rights and welfare of the bondmen whom God had committed to his hands. Yet he was a self-made man. His genius had been developed entirely by private study and application, without the fostering aid of any public institution of learning.

Having been graduated at Yale College, under the presidency of Dr. Dwight, as a general student, in the regular progress of a university education, I was of course made acquainted with the outlines of the principal branches of human knowledge. Notwithstanding, during my stay with this gentleman, no topic of conversation engaged our attention which did not appear familiar to him. Indeed, the combined resources of science and literature seemed to shed their lustre over his intellect and words, with the exception of what are called the ancient classics, or a knowledge of Latin and Greek authors in their vernacular tongues. The best translations of these works he had diligently perused.

Now, although, in my forty years' sojourn at the south, I have not met numerous instances, in rural districts, of persons equally enlightened and exalted with the one just named, yet I can testify that, throughout the entire range of the slaveholding communities, the owners and cultivators of the soil are quite as intelligent as in any section of the free states. And although the children of poor parents too often grow up with little or no schooling, yet from other sources they obtain a degree of knowledge vastly superior to what they are generally reputed to possess by their northern brethren. In almost every family, however humble, the newspaper, teeming with the thoughts of the best scholars, statesmen, and thinkers of the land sheds a cheering light. Even the cabin or cottage, whose inmates are devoid of the rudiments of learning, usually has within its reach some neighbor who reads and writes for his unlettered acquaintances. There is hardly a hamlet or house in the Southern States which is not embraced in the circuit of some itinerant Methodist or Baptist clergyman. By preaching, Sunday schools, class meetings, and other instrumentalities, the noble and self-sacrificing pioneers of the gospel spread abroad much valuable information on secular matters among the ignorant, besides initiating them into the fundamental principles of the Christian faith. Moreover, the universal practice of listening to popular orations from aspirants for political offices, which prevails at the south, is a great means of diffusing knowledge and wisdom throughout all the humbler classes of society, so that most of those who have not enjoyed the advantages of even a rudimental education have the intelligence requisite to fill their stations in life with honor to themselves and usefulness to others. Often have I formed the acquaintance of persons that could not write nor read, who moved with reputation and success in the sphere of duty which had been assigned them by Providence. Among such I have seen many pure-minded, conscientious, and lovely characters.

I have been struck with the marked and peculiar character of southerners, in their hospitality to those who come to reside among them, either from the old world, or from the free states of the Union. In almost every parish of Louisiana are persons living born in New England, whom the generous encouragement of their Creole neighbors has raised from indigence and obscurity to the possession of wealth, honor, and usefulness. Among the Catholic Creoles there are persons not unfrequently to be met, whose lives reflect the highest charms of moral excellence — integrity, truth, honor, disinterestedness, and Christian worth. When I call to mind the pure, high-minded, liberal friends, who were my stay and support throughout the trying scenes which constituted my allotments in the Crescent City, I can say, in the language of Scripture, " If I forget them, let my right hand forget her cunning. If I do not remember them, let my tongue cleave to the roof of my mouth, if I prefer not them above my chief joy."

I remember that the purchase of Louisiana, during Jefferson's administration, was considered by my venerable father, and the majority of wise and good men in Massachusetts, as a measure imperilling the perpetuity of our Union, as fraught with the most destructive consequences to the peace and prosperity of the American people. The clergy condemned it in terms of coarse and bitter denunciation, pronounced from the pulpit, amid the holy services of the sanctuary. Mr. Jefferson, in a printed sermon, was called a " traitor," " infidel," " profligate," " an apostate from the political principles of Washington and his illustrious compeers." What has been the result?

Fifty years have passed since the dreadful deed was done which annexed Louisiana to these confederated states. And our population has grown from five to nearly thirty millions of inhabitants. An area larger than that of the old thirteen states has ceased to be a wilderness, and is to-day filled with plantations, towns, cities, churches, schools, manufactories, inextinguishable enterprise, learning, equitable laws, and all the unnumbered blessings of the highest civilization. No part of the country has been more benefited by this extension of our territory than the New England people themselves, who once allowed their groundless fears to cheat them into the delusive idea that it would ultimately prove the ruin of our glorious republic. Now they all exclaim, " What a wise, just, far-seeing, and provident statesman was Jefferson !" He is ranked in the same class with Washington, Franklin, Adams, Hamilton, and other American patriots of world-wide and everlasting renown. And I doubt not but after the lapse of a few years, the intelligent, patriotic men of the north will look back upon the policy and measures of our national government at the present day with approbation and joy, and pronounce them to have been, all things considered, as wise, just, and beneficent as those of any preceding administration with which it has pleased Heaven to bless and build up this confederacy of states.

Humble as I am in every particular, few persons have lived to my age who could call to mind a happier retrospect than that which memory presents to my grateful, contented, and rejoicing heart. I have always had troops of friends, who delighted to do their utmost to promote my honor and prosperity. There is not a person living whom I regard as an enemy. Even among those who reprobate my religious teachings as erroneous, and calculated to sow moral contagion, I have many warm and affectionate friends, who, if it were necessary, would be willing to lay down their lives to secure my everlasting salvation. In the allotments of a lowly life, Providence has invited me to taste freely of every kind of temporal happiness which earth can afford. For though without wealth, I have had access to all the selfish pleasures which the largest wealth is able to bestow.

To my eye the future, whether relating to myself or to the entire race of man, — the future both of time and eternity, — is inexpressibly bright and glorious. The world is just beginning to see the power and sublimities of the principle expressed in the following words of inspiration: "Love your enemies, bless them that curse you, do good to them that hate you," &c. Throughout civilized lands it is now the prevailing conviction of the wisest and best of patriots, Christians, and philanthropists, that the resources of that love of which Jesus Christ was a living, spotless embodiment, as set forth in the New Testament, may be so wielded as to overcome all the moral evil on earth.

The worst person is not totally depraved, nor wholly and forever cast off, and shut out from the vivifying beams of infinite, inexhaustible, unchanging Love. The elements of undying virtue lie dormant in the most corrupt heart, waiting for the auspicious moment, when, quickened by the Holy Spirit, they will arouse from the trance of sin to run the race of everlasting progression in refinement and glory. No sinner ever was, no sinner ever will be, no sinner ever can be, placed beyond the reach of final redemption. Let the truth that *God is love* penetrate the mists of error and ignorance which becloud the most abandoned mind; let the veriest wretch feel that the Creator has showered upon him the richest blessings, by ordaining his existence in this world of death and depravity, and that He is infinitely more devoted to the welfare of the poorest sinner than the fondest mother to that of an only and beloved infant,— then the scales would immediately fall from his eyes, allowing him to gaze with unobstructed vision upon the perfections of the Supreme Divinity, and the transporting prospects of a spiritual state rising in all the glories of immortality beyond the dark ruins of earth and time.

The Bible authorizes us to anticipate a millennial era, when every individual will enjoy the knowledge of God — the only source of man's highest good; when all the impoverished, prostrate, broken and contaminated millions of our race will rise to intellectual culture, freedom, faith, penitence, sanctity, and that everlasting life which Infinitude, Omnipotence, Boundless Mercy has provided for man's present and everlasting inheritance.

Moreover, it is an item of revealed truth that all the events, errors, and calamities of time are overruled by Infinite wisdom, so as to secure the highest happiness of each member of the human family. God cannot be disappointed. He has his own way. His whole pleasure is accomplished in defiance of the sins and follies of his children. All things are contained in the Eternal Cause, as the oak is contained in the acorn; and without the will, the appointment of that Cause could never have come into existence, whether good or bad.

> " One adequate support
> 'Midst the calamities of mortal life
> Exists, one only — an assured belief
> That the procession of our fate, however
> Sad, or disturbed, is ordered by a Being
> Of infinite benevolence and power,
> Whose everlasting purposes embrace
> Whatever happens, converting it to good."

The criminal, the drunkard, the libertine, and the gambler — the most atrocious transgressors of every grade — are unconsciously and every moment under the government of laws which cannot fail to work out, ultimately, the great and beneficent results for which they were created — the enjoyment of a perfectly holy and happy existence.

This divine faith has been my panoply against the assaults of foes without and within. It has constantly opened to my view a boundless prospect of beauty, a prospect all brightness and beatitude, undimmed by the clouds of gloom, despondency, and secret scepticism, which must, of course, darken and chill the souls of those who cannot see Infinite Love enthroned and reigning over the destinies of every human being throughout time and eternity. When I look upon the most forbidding forms of sin and suffering around me, I am encouraged by the teaching of Scripture, that they are the necessary means, to us inscrutable, of spreading before an admiring universe the sublimest dispensations and counsels of Heaven's highest wisdom and benevolence. I am happy because Jesus Christ has enabled me to see the hand of God directing all the events and ordinances, fates and fortunes, trials and vicissitudes which make up the allotments of man's mysterious life on earth, causing even disease, disappointment, error, depravity, infatuation, the excesses and frivolities of pleasure, avarice, and pride, sadness and sorrow, oppression and injustice, sickness, mortality, and the grave, to work out issues, like himself, good and glorious only, and whose consequences will be commensurate with the unfoldings of eternity.

When I commenced these sketches, it was a part of my programme to dwell with a good deal of particularity on the remarkably noble and generous deportment towards me invariably practised, not by my parishioners alone, but also by all classes of inhabitants in New Orleans, both Protestant and Catholic. In most cases the opposition which I encountered while residing there was started and kept up by strangers and non-residents. My own congregation stood firmly by me when I was maligned, denounced, and excommunicated by the general voice of ministers and churches beyond the limits of New Orleans. There, in the darkest hours, when storms of vituperation beat upon me, I always found a refuge, a complete asylum, in the smiles and encouragement, the protection and sympathy, of enlightened, disinterested, and munificent friends. I look back upon those instances of kindness as the most beautiful spots in the retrospect of the past, as the happiest scenes of my earthly allotments, and with the liveliest emotions of joy and gratitude to my heavenly Father.

Though receiving a salary of five thousand dollars a year, yet I laid up nothing, in consequence of incessant disbursements for the relief of the distress and destitution which parochial visits or direct applications brought me acquainted with, nearly every day of my life. Who can refuse to administer to the wants of the sick and dying within his reach? But though always poor, I was never embarrassed or straitened, with respect to either the necessaries or comforts of life. The bounty of my personal friends, when the church treasury happened to be empty, was a rich and inexhaustible bank, and my drafts thereon, however exorbitant, were never dishonored. My parishioners did not care to ask what my poor services were worth, upon the *quid pro quo* principle of commercial transactions, but simply what was necessary to supply my reasonable wants. No minister ever lived in the United States more blessed with the sunshine of warm, liberal, and unwavering friends, than I have been. They threw over me the ægis of their protection in the dark hour when the storm of popular prejudice and persecuting clamor was imperilling, not simply my standing in the church, my *Christian character*, but also my reputation as a man of honor and fair dealing. My congregation enriched me with unfailing stores of sympathy and love, more precious, in the estimation of a right-minded pastor, than all the gold of California. The attachment which always characterized my relation to the church in New Orleans is dimly shadowed forth in the following communication: —

To the Members of the First Congregational Unitarian Church,
New Orleans, Louisiana.

DEARLY BELOVED BRETHREN: Compelled by ill health to relinquish a pastoral connection of thirty-five years' standing, — a connection endeared to me by all that is sacred, precious, and affecting in memory, by those absorbing and unspeakable hopes, which, crossing the theatre of time and the gulf of death, open to our view the ever-expanding scenes, wonders, and glories of an immortal being, — the mournful duty devolves upon me of bidding you each and all a most affectionate farewell! Farewell! I have written the word weeping — with a heart overflowing with those deep and tender emotions which no language has power to express.

For a long time, it has been one of my strongest desires that I might be permitted to breathe my last in your presence, surrounded by those who are as dear to me as my own soul. Yes, it was ever to me a most cherished, favorite hope, that the hands of kind parishioners would at last close my eyes, and consign my frail body to its final resting place, to the long, peaceful sleep of the tomb — that gate of a nobler life, that portal through which, after the trials, distresses, and bereavements of time are over, we shall pass to enter upon joys unimaginable, unalloyed, and unceasing, in the presence of God, and Jesus, and all the loved and lost ones of our earthly pilgrimage.

But a wise and merciful Father has been pleased to disappoint me; and this disappointment is the severest trial which I have ever been called on to endure. There are hours when it comes down upon me like a crushing, insupportable burden. I solicit an interest in your daily prayers, that the grace of God may be sufficient for me. New Orleans is rendered to my soul the sweetest spot on earth, by innumerable associations of the most interesting character, by those heartfelt attachments, by those joyous and sorrowful experiences, and by those elevated, sanctifying contemplations and labors with respect to the great themes of religion, which the oblivious waters of time, change, or death itself can never erase, but will only stamp thereon the seal of an endless perpetuity.

The happiest portions of my past life were the calm, sacred hours of heavenly peace and satisfaction enjoyed when I met you from Sabbath to Sabbath, to be baptized in the life-giving truths and hopes of Jesus, the author and finisher of our faith — a peace and satisfaction never marred by a single instance of serious alienation, harshness, or discordance of feeling, during the thirty-five years' continuance of that most exalted and affecting relationship by which we were united. The spiritual peace of which I have been so long a partaker in your communion is worth more, in my most deliberate estimation, than all the perishable treasures of earth. Most tenderly, sacredly, and thankfully shall I remember it, until memory has lost its seat in my soul.

I wish it were in my power to find words to convey to you my grateful sense of your uninterrupted friendship and kindness from the beginning of our acquaintance to the present hour. More especially do I thank you for the considerate and forbearing spirit which you have invariably manifested, in throwing the mantle of charity and oblivion over the numerous peculiarities of my constitutional temperament, and the many short-comings and imperfections that marked my professional career whilst with you. I rejoice to hear of the safe arrival of my successor in New Orleans. He comes to you in all the freshness of youth, animated with the fire of a superior genius, ardent piety, noble sensibilities, a copious fund of knowledge, and powers of oratory, by which, united to habits of systematic, persevering exertion, and the blessing of Heaven, he may become a most useful, honored, and brilliant minister of the gospel, and build up a church that will be a light and ornament to the city in which it has pleased Providence to cast your lot.

And now, dear brethren, I commend you to God, and to the word of his grace, which is able to build you up, and to give you an inheritance among all them which are sanctified. However separated in space, may we be cemented by tender and hallowed memories on earth, and beyond the grave meet again, to unite in the ineffable worship of that temple not made with hands, eternal in the heavens. The grace of the Lord Jesus Christ, the love of God our Father, and the communion of their Holy Spirit, be with you all, now and forevermore. Amen.

T. CLAPP.